EMERGENCE AND INNOVATION
IN DIGITAL LEARNING

Issues in Distance Education

Series editor: Terry Anderson

Distance education is the fastest-growing mode of both formal and informal teaching, training, and learning. It is multi-faceted in nature, encompassing e-learning and mobile learning, as well as immersive learning environments. Issues in Distance Education presents recent research results and offers informative and accessible overviews, analyses, and explorations of current topics and concerns and the technologies employed in distance education. Each volume focuses on critical questions and emerging trends, while also situating these developments within the historical evolution of distance education as a specialized mode of instruction.

Series Titles

The Theory and Practice of Online Learning, Second Edition
Edited by Terry Anderson

Mobile Learning: Transforming the Delivery of Education and Training
Edited by Mohamed Ally

A Designer's Log: Case Studies in Instructional Design
Michael Power

Accessible Elements: Teaching Science Online and at a Distance
Edited by Dietmar Kennepohl and Lawton Shaw

Emerging Technologies in Distance Education
Edited by George Veletsianos

Flexible Pedagogy, Flexible Practice: Notes from the Trenches of Distance Education
Edited by Elizabeth Burge, Chère Campbell Gibson, and Terry Gibson

Teaching in Blended Learning Environments: Creating and Sustaining Communities of Inquiry
Norman D. Vaughan, Martha Cleveland-Innes, and D. Randy Garrison

Online Distance Education: Towards a Research Agenda
Edited by Olaf Zawacki-Richter and Terry Anderson

Teaching Crowds: Learning and Social Media
Jon Dron and Terry Anderson

Learning in Virtual Worlds: Research and Applications
Edited by Sue Gregory, Mark J. W. Lee, Barney Dalgarno, and Belinda Tynan

Emergence and Innovation in Digital Learning: Foundations and Applications
Edited by George Veletsianos

EMERGENCE AND INNOVATION IN DIGITAL LEARNING

foundations and applications

Edited by
George Veletsianos

AU PRESS

Copyright © 2016 George Veletsianos

Published by AU Press, Athabasca University
1200, 10011 – 109 Street, Edmonton, AB T5J 3S8

ISBN 978-1-77199-149-0 (print)   978-1-77199-150-6 (PDF)   978-1-77199-151-3 (epub)
doi: 10.15215/aupress/9781771991490.01

A volume in Issues in Distance Education series:
ISSN 1919-4382 (print) 1919-4390 (digital)

Several chapters in this volume were first published in the book referenced below.
Those chapters have been significantly updated and revised for this publication.

Veletsianos, G. ed. (2010). *Emerging Technologies in Distance Education.*
Edmonton: Athabasca University Press.

Cover and interior design by Sergiy Kozakov
Printed and bound in Canada by Friesens

Library and Archives Canada Cataloguing in Publication

Emergence and innovation in digital learning : foundations and applications /
edited by George Veletsianos.
Includes bibliographical references and index.
Issued in print and electronic formats.

1. Distance education–Technological innovations. 2. Educational technology.
I. Veletsianos, George, author, editor

LC5800.E44 2016   371.35'8   C2016-902638-8
                                                C2016-902639-6

We acknowledge the financial support of the Government of Canada through the
Canada Book Fund (CFB) for our publishing activities.

 Canadian   Patrimoine
Heritage   canadien

Assistance provided by the Government of Alberta, Alberta Media Fund.

Government

Contents

Acknowledgements

This volume would not have been possible without the work of the contributors who shared their valuable insights.

I am indebted to the Canada Research Chairs program for the support provided to my research endeavours.

I am also thankful for the support, assistance, and hard work I received from the staff at Athabasca University Press.

Throughout my academic career, I have had the good fortune to interact with a network of peers and students who have helped me become a better educator, scholar, and academic citizen.

Many of my colleagues at Royal Roads University have supported me in innumerable ways to complete this work. My thanks to Jo Axe, Doug Hamilton, Elizabeth Childs, Samantha Wood, Robynne Devine, Deborah Zornes, Mary Bernard, matt heinz, and Steve Grundy.

I am indebted to Laura Pasquini who worked with me as a post-doctoral associate and edited some segments of this volume.

My students in Canada, the UK, and the US, through their insightful questions, eagerness to learn, and inquisitive natures have helped made me a better teacher and scholar—and I appreciate them for that.

Introduction

▶ *George Veletsianos*

Educational systems worldwide are facing enormous shifts as a result of sociocultural, political, economic, demographic, and technological changes. Emerging technologies (social media, serious games, adaptive software) and emerging practices (openness, user modeling) in particular, have been heralded as providing opportunities to transform education, learning, and teaching. Such discussions often postulate that new ideas—whether technologies or practices—will address educational problems (open textbooks may perhaps make college more affordable) or provide opportunities to rethink the ways that education is organized and enacted (for example, the collection and analysis of big data may enable designers to develop algorithms that provide early and critical feedback to at-risk students). Yet, the ways that emerging innovations and practices are used in digital learning contexts are much more complex and elusive. In this book, I amalgamate work associated with emergence in online education to conceptualize, design, critique, enhance, and better understand online education. This edited volume gathers international experiences, dispersed knowledge, and multidisciplinary perspectives for use by both members of research communities and innovative digital learning practitioners.

This introduction addresses three questions:

1. What are the scholarly contributions of the book as a whole?
2. What are the themes that unify the book and why are all the chapters that follow included in this book?
3. What is the focus of each chapter?

While each chapter in this book improves our understanding of emerging technologies and practices, the book as a whole makes three significant contributions.

First, the book provides sound scholarship. Balanced scholarship on emerging technologies and emerging practices in the context of digital education is crucial. Most often, researchers, designers, and educators present hopeful descriptions of the potential of emerging approaches to education, but ignore or resist the complex conditions under which learning occurs. In this book, contributors discuss emerging technologies and practices in digital learning, without losing sight of the fact that what designates technologies and practices as *emerging* is the context under which they operate. They recognize that technologies and practices shape and are shaped by sociocultural environments.

Second, the book brings together scholars and practitioners. Digital education researchers and practitioners rarely interact, rendering the sharing, dissemination, and improvement of their work a formidable task. This problem has recently been brought to the forefront because educational technology has received considerable attention from stakeholders that were not previously associated with the use of technology in education (such as investors, independent developers, and artificial intelligence labs). By way of this book, I hope to provide more opportunities for interaction between researchers, educators, designers, and developers, seasoned and newcomers alike.

Third, this book brings new voices to digital education, voices that are significant to its improvement, refinement, and understanding. This contribution is particularly significant because of the burgeoning interest that the field is experiencing. In reviewing a recently-published book on online education, Tony Bates (2014) asks, "Where are the young researchers here, and especially the researchers in open educational resources, MOOCs, social media applications in online learning, and above all researchers from the many campus-based universities now mainstreaming online learning?" This book includes several chapters from emerging leaders situated in campus-based organizations that are pushing the boundaries of digital learning. These individuals are shaping the future of digital learning and in this volume they address issues pertaining to openness, analytics, MOOCs, and social media.

Four themes unify all of the chapters in this volume. Firstly, all chapters examine concepts associated with emerging technologies or emerging practices in digital education. Whether examining the theoretical foundations of learning (chapter 3), the messiness of learning in emerging learning contexts (chapter 2), the use of learning analytics to understand emerging learning environments (chapter 8), or individuals' perspectives on emerging approaches to education (chapters 7, 10), these authors contribute to a greater understanding of what exactly constitutes emergence in education.

Secondly, all chapters in this book resist simplistic notions of technological determinism and show how technology's lack of neutrality is negotiated on the ground. The contributors describe how particular features of the technology shape practice and how practice shapes the ways that technology is used (chapters 1, 2, 4, 7, 9). By resisting techno-deterministic narratives, this book aims to inform readers of the negotiated relationships between technology and practice and the complex realities that arise when theory meets practice.

Another core theme that runs throughout the book is the tension that exists between calls for efficiency vis-à-vis calls for humanized learning. On the one hand, educational institutions and stakeholders are facing increasing calls for accountability and efficiency, often resulting from the economic realities of our times. On the other, there is an increasing need to "humanize the online experience with greater compassion, empathy and open-mindedness" (Herrington, Oliver, & Reeves, 2003). The tension between these two issues is evident in the conversations surrounding digital learning and in the scholarship that is presented in this book.

Finally, all the chapters are implicitly concerned with how emerging technologies and associated phenomena reconfigure the role of learners and instructors and how learners and instructors reconfigure the roles that technologies play in digital education. While this issue is explicitly explored in chapter 5, chapters 8 and 9 investigate learners' roles in self-directed learning environments and chapter 4 examines how emerging approaches to data collection and analysis shift instructional roles to technological artifacts?

The book is divided into two sections: foundations and applications. In the "Foundations" section, authors examine conceptual and theoretical aspects of emerging technologies and emerging practices in online education.

In chapter 1, I examine the meaning of the terms "emerging technologies" and "emerging practices" and note that these two terms are often used haphazardly without a clear understanding of what they really mean. I propose that emerging technologies and emerging practices are defined by the context in which they are situated, and suggest that they share four characteristics: not-newness, coming into being, not-yetness, and unfulfilled but promising potential. The conceptualization of the terms proposed in chapter 1 situates the chapters that follow and establishes a common ground upon which one can examine emergence and innovation in digital education. This definition has been updated from the definition proposed in *Emerging Technologies in Distance Education* (the precursor to this book) to reflect a more refined understanding of the characteristics of emergence.

Ross and Collier (chapter 2) identify the need for evaluation of learning design and teaching practices for digital education, specifically with regard to measurement, and the challenges emerging technologies pose for postsecondary institutions. This chapter provides insights and discussion into not-yetness, the messiness of learning, and the complexity of learning design.

Anderson (chapter 3) presents the theoretical foundations of learning in emergent contexts by reviewing established and contemporary perspectives intended to answer the question of how people learn in digital contexts. The work presented in every chapter of this volume can be traced back to the theoretical foundations discussed by Anderson.

In chapter 4, Kimmons and Hall provide a set of standardized criteria for comparing technology integration models in a meaningful way. Technology integration models are frameworks used by organizations to guide thinking concerning the use of emerging technologies in education, and Kimmons and Hall provide the means for stakeholders to make informed decisions when choosing appropriate integration models to guide technology use, adoption, and integration.

Wellburn and Eib (chapter 5) investigate how emerging technologies could affect and transform the role of educators and learners, and how emerging online practices could influence the ways that education is organized. They outline how relevant online experiences can be brought into our teaching and learning practices.

In the "Applications" section, authors examine applications of emerging technologies and emerging practices in online learning, and investigate the complex social, organizational, and contextual landscape of emergence in online learning.

An emerging practice in the field is that of learning analytics, specifically the collection and analysis of data that participants leave behind in the online environments that they frequent. In chapter 6, Baker and Inventado discuss the use of data mining and learning analytics for online education and examine how educational institutions can use such emerging practices. In the interest of provoking discussion, the authors focus on a few key examples of the potential of learning analytics, rather than exhaustively reviewing the ever-increasing literature on the topic.

In chapter 7, Whitworth and Benson illustrate how *practices*, as well as technologies, can be studied as "emerging." In particular, the authors present two case studies that describe the perspectives of both educational researchers and practitioners as they adopt Moodle, an open-source learning management system. The authors found that Moodle came to be used with divergent aims, communities, and practices. The evidence presented in this chapter is a powerful demonstration of the negotiated relationship that exists between technology and practice. The authors demonstrate how technology influences digital education practice and how educational practice influences the use, implementation, and adoption of technology.

The emerging practice of using social media and open technologies for learner-learner and learner-instructor interactions is discussed in chapter 8, under the concept of Personal Learning Environments (PLEs). PLEs represent tools and processes that enable individuals to monitor and regulate their learning inputs and experiences, and have developed as a result of the growth and recognition of the importance of informal learning. Martindale and Dowdy outline the history of the PLE, identify why it is useful, provide examples of PLEs, and discuss challenges that institutions face when considering adopting PLEs in contrast to other online learning environments.

In chapter 9, Couros and Hildebrandt describe an innovative online course inspired by philosophies of the open source movement, trends in social media, and pedagogies around networked learning. This case study provides insights into the use of online networks and social media for learning, and shares lessons learned throughout the development, facilitation, and evolution of the course since its initial offering.

Moe (chapter 10) explores the emergence of the Massive Open Online Course (MOOC) movement and examines how experts perceive it and how the movement itself affects the manner in which educators and researchers practice and examine online education.

Finally, Perry and Edwards (chapter 11) argue that online communities are founded on artistic elements. They outline how to apply instructional strategies that use artistic pedagogical practices. Central to the arguments and examples presented in this chapter is the idea that emerging technologies provide opportunities for enhancing presence, interaction, and participation.

The precursor to this book *Emerging Technologies in Distance Education* was published in 2010. Numerous reasons, including evolutions in technology, pedagogical practices, and research on digital learning, necessitate the development of an update. Most significant perhaps is the fact that since 2010, there has been a growing realization that the higher education sector is in a state of transformation and as a result educational technology in general, and digital learning in particular, have been thrust to the forefront of debates on the future of education. The rise of the MOOC phenomenon has "prompted popular mass media interest at levels not seen with previous educational innovations" (Bulfin, Pangrazio, & Selwyn, 2014) and narratives of the potential impact of technology on education are pervasive. Within this environment, this book provides nuance, insights, and research to make the practice of digital education more effective and meaningful. In the furtherance of this endeavor, some chapters first published in *Emerging Technologies in Distance Education* have been reprinted here as a part of this volume. However, these chapters have been updated to reflect current realities and debates and have incorporated new research findings where necessary. The chapters that are new provide much-needed insights on topics that are at the core of higher education practice at a time when the field needs it the most. The work presented here continues the ever-expansive conversation about emerging practices and technologies for digital learning that was started in 2010 with *Emerging Technologies in Distance Education*. I would like to see these conversations extend into conferences, journal articles, blog posts, and online social networks so as to further refine the ideas presented here and make a significant contribution to enhancing research and practice and improve educational and scholarly practices. This book, offered by Athabasca University Press freely and openly to anyone interested, aims to do just that.

REFERENCES

Bates, T., (2014). Review of "Online Distance Education: Towards a Research Agenda." Blog post. Retrieved from http://www.tonybates.ca/2014/10/18/review-of-online-distance-education-towards-a-research-agenda/

Bulfin, S., Pangrazio, L., & Selwyn, N. (2014). Making "MOOCs": The construction of a new digital higher education within news media discourse. *International Review of Research in Open and Distance Learning, 15*(5).

Herrington, J., Oliver, R. and Reeves, T. C. (2003). Patterns of engagement in authentic online learning environments. *Australian Journal of Educational Technology, 19*(1), 59–71.

PART I

FOUNDATIONS

1 The Defining Characteristics of Emerging Technologies and Emerging Practices in Digital Education

▶ *George Veletsianos*

The growing need for an educated workforce, changing student demographics, opportunities presented by new technologies, and increases in the cost of accessing higher education have led many educators, researchers, policymakers, and business people to engage with a variety of emerging approaches to education, including competency-based assessment, open educational resources, flipped classrooms, micro credentials, and private-public partnerships in degree offerings. Concomitantly, many scholars have been engaging in an ever-expanding array of emerging practices, including blogging, networking on social media, and sharing their scholarship in different forms (such as via videos and open courses).

Many of these approaches to education and scholarship can be categorized as either emerging technologies (such as automated grading applications within MOOCs) or emerging practices (such as sharing instructional materials online under licences that allow recipients to reuse them freely). The terms "emerging technologies" and "emerging practices," however, are catch-all phrases that are often misused and haphazardly defined. As Siemens (2008, para.1) argues, "terms like 'emergence,' 'adaptive systems,' 'self-organizing systems,' and others are often tossed about with such casualness and authority as to suggest the speaker(s) fully understand what they mean." A clearer and more uniform understanding of emergence and of the characteristics of emerging technologies and practices will enable researchers to examine these topics under a common framework and allow practitioners to better anticipate potential challenges and impacts that may arise from their integration into learning environments.

In *Emerging Technologies in Distance Education*, I described emerging technologies as "tools, concepts, innovations, and advancements," intentionally defining "technologies" broadly to include not just tools and software but also concepts, such as pedagogies (Veletsianos, 2010). A number of researchers and students have found this definition helpful in framing the contested and complex nature of technologies and online learning environments. Returning to this work six years later, however, it is clear to me that the term "emerging technologies" does not fully capture what is emerging in digital education. At the time, I argued that contextual factors determine whether a technology is emerging or not; I now also believe that the notion of emerging phenomena in education can be better captured by differentiating between "emerging technologies" and "emerging practices." This differentiation, I believe, will help practitioners and researchers make better sense of the innovations and advances currently occurring in educational technology worldwide. This change emphasizes the social, political, cultural, and economic contexts that surround emerging technologies and provides a timeliness that transcends particular advances and innovations.

Both in 2009 and 2015, my review of the literature did not provide adequate definitions or descriptions of what individuals mean when they refer to emerging technologies and emerging practices. The literature is littered with casual uses of the term and spans content areas and disciplines. The view espoused in this chapter and in this book is that the terms "emerging technologies" and "emerging practices" transcend academic disciplines. New technologies and practices have emerged in diverse disciplines, even if some technologies might be more appropriate for specific content areas (e.g., Geometer's Sketchpad for mathematics-related disciplines), some practices may be more pronounced in some disciplines that others (e.g., open scholarship in the sciences), and some technological affordances may render some tools more appropriate for certain purposes than others (e.g., wikis and blogs for community-focused and writing-intensive approaches). An October 2014 search on the PsychInfo database, for example, revealed that emerging technologies were being examined in a number of disciplines across the social sciences, humanities, formal sciences, and professional fields. Within education, emerging technologies were being used in teacher training, instructional design, language learning, distance education, higher education, adult education, and medical education. The term "emerging practices" was used less often, but again in numerous disciplines. The lack of a clear framework with which to consider emerging technologies and emerging practices calls for an education-specific definition that can guide our thinking, research, and practice. Establishing a common understanding of these widely used terms will provide a significant step toward meaningful conversations and inquiry.

HOW HAVE EMERGING TECHNOLOGIES BEEN DEFINED IN THE PAST?

When composing the introduction to *Emerging Technologies in Distance Education* in 2010, I began with what seemed a logical starting point, attempting to define the term "emerging technologies." To this end, I scanned my personal bibliography, typed the term in my favorite search engine, searched the academic literature, and to my amazement (and increasing angst), discovered that a definition for the omnipresent term was nowhere to be found. Searching magazines, periodicals, and industry reports, I discovered a few descriptions but no formal, commonly accepted definition.

Could it be that a definition existed and I had simply been unable to locate it? I emailed colleagues, posted requests on social media, and contacted all the authors whose papers were going to appear in the book, asking for possible definitions. The answers I received were informative and helped shape my thinking, but a clear definition was still elusive. It appeared that the term central to the book I was editing had never been defined, or, if it had been defined, neither my colleagues nor I had been able to locate that definition. This experience provided the impetus for converting what I had envisioned as a short introduction into a chapter.

In my searches, I was able to locate four significant publications that focused on the terms "emerging technology" and "emerging practice." These are described and summarized below.

In a report for the Australian Capital Territory Department of Education and Training, Green and Putland (2005) stated that a technology is still emerging if it is not yet a "must-have." Email, for instance, moved from what was once an optional communication technology to a must-have, must-use technology for most people in most organizations. This definition helped me understand that "new" may not be a necessary descriptor for emerging technologies and practices, and that all technologies not currently used in educational institutions can be considered emerging. Educators explore and adopt technologies even before they become "must-haves," and some technologies that may become must-haves for other industries and venues will not necessarily become must-haves for educational providers.

The second publication is a series entitled *The Horizon Reports*, which the New Media Consortium (NMC) has released every year since 2004 to lay out adoption horizons for key technologies. The descriptions of emerging technologies given in these reports suggest that emerging technologies are those that (a) have not yet been widely adopted, and (b) are expected to influence a variety of educational organizations. The descriptions of emerging technologies in each report vary slightly, indicating that uncertainty exists with respect to the definition of the term "emerging technology" and the expected magnitude of its impact.

The third publication is a series of reports entitled *Emerging Technologies for Learning*, published by the British Educational Communications and Technology Agency (Bryant et al., 2007; Oblinger et al., 2008; Stead et al., 2006). As with the *Horizon Reports*, these emphasized the possibility of a near-future impact.

The fourth publication is *Emerging Practice in a Digital Age*, published by the Joint Information Systems Committee or JISC (Knight, 2011). In this report emerging practice was described as involving "experimentation and openness—the ability to respond to changing circumstances and to embrace unforeseen benefits" as institutions move "to changes of approach, and to more collaborative ways of working" (p. 5)

THE CHARACTERISTICS OF EMERGING TECHNOLOGIES AND EMERGING PRACTICES

As noted earlier, this chapter argues that what makes technologies and practices emerging are *not* specific technologies or practices, but the environments in which particular technologies or practices operate. This definition recognizes that learning, teaching, and scholarship are sociocultural phenomena situated in specific contexts and influenced by the cultures in which they take place (Brown, Collins, & Duguid, 1989; Vygotsky, 1978). This perspective is particularly appropriate for digital learning situated on the contemporary Web which has social and co-producing capabilities and practices. According to this view, technology is itself socially shaped. It embeds its developers' worldviews, values, beliefs, and assumptions into its design and the activities it encourages (Oliver, 2013). Learners and instructors can accept or reject particular technologies or practices. They are also capable of finding alternative uses for them that will better meet their needs and values. Thus, sociocultural factors make technologies and practices emergent.

To provide an example of why it makes sense to consider technologies *and* practices as emerging, consider online journals and social media such as Facebook, Twitter, and YouTube. These technologies have become an integral part of open scholarship, which is often seen as a major breakthrough in radically rethinking the ways in which knowledge is created and shared (Nielsen, 2012; Weller, 2011). Much of the existing literature argues that scholars can amplify and transform their scholarly endeavors by adopting open practices supported by technology, and a multitude of ways to do so have been developed (Veletsianos, 2013). For instance, a cultural anthropologist might share draft versions of her research on her blog, a geographer might post his syllabus on a document-sharing website, a World War II historian might enlist the help of online crowds to obtain digital copies of letters to examine personal communication during the era, and a political scientist might use social media data to investigate political campaigns during elections. These are examples of the emerging practice of Networked Participatory Scholarship (Veletsianos & Kimmons, 2012; Veletsianos, 2016), which refers to the use of participatory technologies, online social networks, and other emerging technologies to share, reflect upon, improve, validate, and further scholarship. Scholarly blogging, for instance, is an emerging practice within an increasingly digital scholarly life (Kirkup, 2010; Martindale & Wiley, 2005; Nardi, Schiano, & Gumbrecht, 2004; Walker, 2006).

Emerging technologies and emerging practices, therefore, may be adopted in a variety of educational settings to serve various purposes (such as instructional, social, and organizational goals). After an extensive examination of these emerging educational phenomena and the literature about them, all appear to share these four characteristics: not defined by newness; coming into being; not-yetness; and, unfulfilled but promising potential.

Emerging technologies and emerging practices are not defined by newness

Although the words *emerging* and *new* are often treated as being synonymous, emerging technologies and practices may or may not be new. Emerging technologies and practices may be recent developments (such as using 3D printers, publishing open data) or older ones (using open-source learning management systems). Even though it may be true that most emerging technologies are newer technologies, the mere fact that they are new does not necessarily categorize them as emerging. For example, synthetic (or virtual) worlds were described as an emerging technology in the mid-1990s (Dede, 1996), and research on Multi-User Dungeons dates back to the 1980s (Mazar & Nolan, 2008). Yet virtual worlds are still widely referred to as emerging technologies (Warburton, 2009; Dawley & Dede, 2014), particularly in some fields, such as healthcare (Boulos, Hetherington & Wheeler, 2009; Rogers, 2011) and hospitality (Huang, Backman, Chang, Backman, & McGuire, 2013), where their appropriateness shines. Newness by itself, then, is a problematic indicator of emergence.

Emerging technologies and emerging practices are evolving organisms that exist in a state of "coming into being"

The word "evolving" refers to a dynamic state of change in which technologies and practices are continuously refined and developed. To illustrate this, consider the chalkboard and dry-erase board, the use of which is generally established within the educational community and thus, while still in use, is no longer evolving. Contrast this to Twitter, the currently popular social networking and micro-blogging platform. Although various practices and activities on the Twitter platform can be said to be established (e.g., the ReTweet (RT) activity (boyd, Golder, & Lotan, 2010)), numerous aspects of the technology, as well as practices associated with it, are emerging as platform refinements change the way the technology is used and users engage in practices that may depart from those originally anticipated.

For example, Twitter's early success and popularity caused frequent outages, which were most noticeable during popular technology events such as the 2008 MacWorld keynote address. Early attempts to satisfy sudden surges in demand included using more servers and on/off switches on various Twitter features, while later efforts included re-designing the application's architecture and withdrawing services such as free SMS and instant-messaging support. Existing in an evolutionary state, Twitter is continuously being developed and refined. At the time of writing, for example, Twitter engineers are considering introducing filtering algorithms aimed at refining and curating user timelines. Twitter practices are also in a continuing state of evolution. For instance, it has been used for scholarly purposes (Veletsianos, 2012) and as a tool to engage learners (Dabbagh & Kitsantas, 2012; Junco, 2012), establish instructors' social presence (So & Brush, 2008; Pollard, Minor, & Swanson, 2014), and conduct research (Chong, 2010; Darling, Shiffman, Côté, & Drew, 2013). Researchers have argued that tweeting has emerged as a new literacy practice, a practice that consists of both traditional and new literacies (Greenhow & Gleason, 2012).

As emerging technologies and practices evolve, some will be integrated into the day-to-day operations of educational organizations, while others will fade into the background. The context surrounding emerging technologies and practices also shifts and changes over time, creating a negotiated relationship between the maturation of a technology/practice and the environment that surrounds it.

Not-yetness: Emerging technologies and emerging practices are not yet fully understood or researched

One distinguishing characteristic of emerging technologies and practices is that we are not yet able to understand their implications for education, teaching, and learning or for learners, instructors, and institutions. We also lack an understanding of the contextual, negotiated, and symbiotic relationship between practices and technologies. For example, what effect might the opportunity to socialize with classmates via social networking sites have for online learners? How do automated grading practices reconfigure the role of instructors? Could social networking sites or MOOCs break down digital divides between haves and have-nots? Or are social networking sites simply another medium through which societal inequalities are perpetuated? What are the pedagogical affordances of social networking sites? How may learning analytics support online instructors? How may we design supportive and engaging self-paced learning environments? Can location-aware devices enhance communal learning experiences?

Emerging technologies and practices are not fully understood largely because they have not yet been thoroughly researched. Initial investigations of emerging technologies are often evangelical, overly optimistic, or dystopian in their conclusions and describe benefits and drawbacks without empirically examining the role, impact, and implications for online education. Because of the evolutionary nature of emerging technologies and practices, most of the research conducted about them takes a case study or formative evaluation approach (Dede, 1996), reflecting the early stage of our attempts to understand them. Because emerging technologies/practices have not yet been fully studied, initial deployments of emerging technology applications tend to replicate familiar processes. For example, linear PowerPoint slides replace slideshow projectors and blogs replace personal reflection diaries, despite the opportunities they offer for rethinking practice. Ross and Collier (chapter 2) delve into a more detailed examination of not-yetness and its implications.

Emerging technologies and emerging practices have promising but as yet unfulfilled potential

The final characteristic of an emerging technology or practice is its promise of significant impact, which is as yet mostly unfulfilled. Individuals and organizations may recognize that particular technologies and practices offer significant potential for enacting change (e.g., improving learner-learner interaction, reducing student cost, supporting classroom equity), but such potential has not yet been realized. The fields most associated with the use of technology in education, including online and distance learning, often exhibit techno-utopian and techno-deterministic thinking. In particular, technology and certain practices associated with it are often expected to revolutionize the way individuals learn and teach. Yet scholars and practitioners alike are wise to maintain some skepticism about promises of transformation that ignore the environmental factors that surround innovations. Even though technology has had a significant impact on how education is delivered, managed, negotiated, and practiced, this book, and past research, remind us that the environment in which such impacts occur is influenced by a variety of factors, including politics and economics.

The reasons can be found in the characteristics already discussed. For instance, educational institutions are relatively slow to change for a variety of organizational, cultural, and historical reasons (Cuban, 1993; Lortie, 1975); emerging technologies and practices exist in the context of sociocultural systems; and mature research on their impacts and uses has not yet been conducted. Additionally, the potential to transform practices, processes, and institutions is often simultaneously welcomed and opposed by various stakeholders. The openness movement is an illustration of this fact. Supporters of openness have claimed that free and open access has the potential to transform the ways research and knowledge are disseminated and evaluated, but for a number of reasons, open practices and scholarly uptake of social media for professional purposes are still at a nascent stage (Jordan, 2014; Veletsianos, 2013).

THE COMPLEXITIES OF INCORPORATING TECHNOLOGIES INTO EDUCATION

The four defining characteristics identified and discussed in this chapter provide a glimpse into the complexities that arise when emerging technologies and practices are integrated into educational contexts. Although practitioners and researchers anticipate and hope that emerging technologies and practices will prove to be powerful instruments in our quest to enhance teaching, learning, research, and educational institutions, we are still exploring the possibilities and implications of these technologies. The absence of a large empirical or practitioner knowledge base to guide the use of emerging technologies and practices should be seen as an opportunity to conduct research into educational practice. We should remain open to the idea that the existing ways of teaching, learning, and designing learning environments may not adequately serve contemporary or future educational purposes. Expanding and applying what we know about learning, teaching, and education from such diverse fields as educational psychology, instructional design, sociology, and the learning sciences will be important to understanding and applying emerging approaches in education.

At the same time, technology is changing the way we live and act in the world (for instance, digital overlays allow us to experience the world differently); therefore employing emerging approaches to education may necessitate the development of new theories, pedagogies, and roles. If we employ emerging technologies in our work, we should also be prepared to be open to new ways of viewing the world and ways of exploring knowledge, scholarship, collaboration, and even education itself. While doing so, we should remain cognizant that resistance and failure are possible, but also, if documented in the literature, helpful. Numerous advances on this front are described in this book, including net-aware theories of learning (chapter 3), open and social learning (chapter 9), personal learning environments (chapter 8), and data mining and learning analytics (chapter 6).

The proposed characteristics of emerging technologies and practices also imply that technologies and practices cannot be seen as being "emerging" out of context (chapter 7). More specifically, technologies may be emerging in one area while already established in another area. For example, the sharing of open data may be an acceptable and established practice in some fields (say, bioinformatics), but not in others (education). A practice or technology may also be established and emerging at the same time. For example, competency-based assessment and credentialing is an established practice among a number of online education providers in the United States (Klein-Collins, 2012; Alssid, 2014), but it has just begun to emerge in the broader higher education landscape (Feldstein, 2014; Haynie, 2014; Fain, 2014). In the context of alternative credentialing models, therefore, competency-based assessment is both emerging and established at the same time. Another example is the practice of online and distance education, which, while an established model of education in several institutions worldwide (such as The Open University in the UK), has more recently become an emerging activity in numerous campus-focused colleges and universities that once considered themselves residential and wanted little to do with online learning. The contextual nature of emerging technologies also holds true for differences across nations, regions, and even organizations. Examples include countries that have bypassed landline infrastructure and leapfrogged to mobile phones when others, such as Canada, are finding it difficult to support innovations in mobile technologies due to heavy regulation and geography—within a single province or state some cities have fibre-optic Internet access while others do not. Technology may be used to support problem-based teaching techniques in one classroom in a K–12 school, and for drill-and-practice exercises in a different classroom within the same school.

The sociological theory of emergence also suggests implications that emerging technologies and practices may have for education (Clayton, 2006). Emergence theory posits that events and phenomena do not happen in a formal or predetermined way, but rather occur spontaneously and unexpectedly in dynamic environments that both influence activities and are influenced by those activities (Cole & Engestrom, 1993; Moje & Lewis, 2007). The implications are two-fold: technologies and practices developed for purposes other than education find their way into educational institutions and processes (e.g., wikis, openness); and once such technologies and practices are integrated into education, they both mould and are moulded by micro-educational practices, such as teaching and learning activities and communities (chapter 7).

DEFINING CHARACTERISTICS MATTER

In 2007, the Association of Educational Communications and Technology returned to the use of the term "educational technology" to define a field that, over the years, has been referred to by numerous names, including "instructional design," "instructional systems," and "instructional systems technology" (Reiser, 2006). In response to the name change, Lowenthal and Wilson (2009) argued that definitions and labels are critical because they establish a common ground upon which we can have conversations. An agreed-upon definition can enable practitioners and researchers to examine concepts with a shared understanding, enabling the field to move forward. Without an agreed-upon definition, the very foundations of our work are precarious. In the same way, the characteristics of emerging technologies and emerging practices for educational purposes provided in this chapter are intended to provide a foundation upon which to position our work. In addition to highlighting important issues for future research and practice, this chapter also refines the meaning of the terms *emerging technologies* and *emerging practices* and provides further scaffolding upon which our work can be conceptualized, refined, and evaluated.

REFERENCES

Alssid, J. L. (2014, August 26). What is competency-based education, and why does it matter? *Huffington Post*. Retrieved from http://www.huffingtonpost.com/julian-l-alssid/what-is-competencybased-e_b_5716779.html

BECTA. (2006). The BECTA review 2006: Evidence on the progress of ICT in education. British Educational Communications and Technology Agency, Coventry. Retrieved from http://dera.ioe.ac.uk/1427/.

Boulos, M. N. K., Hetherington, L., & Wheeler, S. (2007). Second Life: An overview of the potential of 3-D virtual worlds in medical and health education. *Health Information and Libraries Journal, 24*(4), 233–45.

boyd, d., Golder, S., & Lotan, G. (2010). Tweet tweet retweet: Conversational aspects of retweeting on Twitter. Proceedings of HICSS-43. Kauai, *HI: IEEE Computer Society*. 5–8 January 2010. Retrieved from http://www.danah.org/TweetTweetRetweet.pdf

Brown, S. (2003). Interactive whiteboards in education. TechLearn for Joint Information Systems Committee. Retrieved from http://www.jisc.ac.uk/uploaded_documents/Interactivewhiteboards.pdf

Bryant, L., Downes, S., Twist, J., Prensky, M., Facer, K.,Dumbleton, T., & Ley, D. (2007). Emerging technologies for learning. British Educational Communications and Technology Agency (BECTA). Retrieved from http://dera.ioe.ac.uk/1502/

Chong, E. K. (2010). Using blogging to enhance the initiation of students into academic research. *Computers and Education, 55*(2), 798–807.

Clayton, P. (2006). Conceptual foundations of emergence theory. In P. Clayton & P. Davies (eds.), *The re-emergence of emergence: The emergentist hypothesis from science to religion* (pp. 1–31). Oxford: Oxford University Press.

Cole, M., & Engestrom, Y. (1993). A cultural-historical approach to distributed cognition. In G. Salomon (ed.), *Distributed cognitions: Psychological and educational considerations* (pp. 1–46). New York: Cambridge University Press.

Cuban, L. (1993). *How teachers taught: Constancy and change in American classrooms, 1880–1990.* (2nd ed.). New York: Teachers College Press.

———. (2001). *Oversold and underused: Reforming schools through technology 1980–2000*. Cambridge, MA: Harvard University Press.

Dabbagh, N., & Kitsantas, A. (2012). Personal Learning Environments, social media, and self-regulated learning: A natural formula for connecting formal and informal learning. *The Internet and Higher Education, 15*(1), 3–8.

Darling, E. S., Shiffman, D., Côté, I. M., & Drew, J. A. (2013). The role of Twitter in the life cycle of a scientific publication. *PeerJ PrePrints 1:16*(1) http://dx.doi.org/10.7287/peerj.preprints.16v1

Dawley, L., & Dede, C. (2014). Situated learning in virtual worlds and immersive simulations. In *Handbook of Research on Educational Communications and Technology* (pp. 723–34). New York: Springer.

de Freitas, S. (2008). Serious virtual worlds: A scoping study. Joint Information Systems Committee. JISC report. Retrieved from http://www.jisc.ac.uk/publications/publications/seriousvirtualworldsreport.aspx

Dede, C. (1996). Emerging technologies and distributed learning. *American Journal of Distance Education, 10*(2), 4–36.

Fain, P. (2014, October 28). Big Ten and the next big thing. *Inside Higher Ed*. Retrieved from https://www.insidehighered.com/news/2014/10/28/competency-based-education-arrives-three-major-public-institutions

Feldstein, M. (2014, October 23). What faculty should know about competency-based education. *e-Literate*. [Blog post]. Retrieved from http://mfeldstein.com/faculty-know-competency-based-education/

Fenn, J., & Raskino, M. (2008). *Mastering the hype cycle: How to choose the right innovation at the right time*. Cambridge, MA: Harvard Business School Press.

Gartner Inc. (2006). Hype Cycle for Higher E-Learning, 2006. Retrieved from https://www.gartner.com/doc/493556

———. (2008a). Hype Cycle for Emerging Technologies, 2008. Retrieved from https://www.gartner.com/doc/717415

———. (2008b). Hype Cycle for Higher Education, 2008. Retrieved from https://www.gartner.com/doc/709014

Hall, I., & Higgins, S. (2005). Primary school students' perception of interactive whiteboards, *Journal of Computer Assisted Learning, 21*(2), 102–17.

Haynie, D. (2014, July 11). Competency-Based learning provides perks for online students. *U.S. News*. Retrieved from http://www.usnews.com/education/online-education/articles/2014/07/11/competency-based-learning-provides-perks-for-online-students

Huang, Y. C., Backman, S. J., Chang, L. L., Backman, K. F., & McGuire, F. A. (2013). Experiencing student learning and tourism training in a 3D virtual world: An exploratory study. *Journal of Hospitality, Leisure, Sport and Tourism Education, 13,* 190–201.

Junco, R. (2012). The relationship between frequency of Facebook use, participation in Facebook activities, and student engagement. *Computers and Education, 58*(1), 162–71.

Kennewell, S., & Higgins, S. (2007). Introduction. Special issue, *Learning, Media and Technology, 32*(3), 207–12.

Klein-Collins, R. (2012). Competency-Based degree programs in the U.S.: Postsecondary credentials for measurable student learning and performance. Council for Adult and Experiential Learning. Retrieved from http://www.cael.org/pdfs/2012_competencybasedprograms

Lakhana, A. (2014). What is educational technology? An inquiry into the meaning, use, and reciprocity of technology. *Canadian Journal Of Learning And Technology, 40*(3). Retrieved from http://www.cjlt.ca/index.php/cjlt/article/view/823/399

Lortie, D. (1975). *Schoolteacher: A sociological study.* Chicago: University of Chicago Press.

Lowenthal, P., & Wilson, B. G. (2009). Labels DO Matter! A Critique of AECT's Redefinition of the Field. *TechTrends, 54*(1), 38–46.

Mazar, R., & Nolan, J. (2008). Hacking say and reviving ELIZA: Lessons from virtual environments. *Innovate, 5*(2). Retrieved from http://eric.ed.gov/?id=EJ840520

Miller, J., Green, I., & Putland, G. (2005). *Emerging technologies: A framework for thinking.* Australian Capital Territory Department of Education and Training. Retrieved from http://trove.nla.gov.au/version/41286248

Moje, E. B. & Lewis, C. (2007). Examining opportunities to learn literacy: The role of critical sociocultural research. In C. Lewis, P. Enciso, & E. B. Moje (eds.), *Reframing sociocultural research on literacy: Identity, agency, and power.* Mahwah, NJ: Lawrence Erlbaum Associates.

Oblinger, D., Van't Hooft, M.,Greenfield, A.,De Freitas, S.,Tonkin, E.,& Haller, M. (2008). Emerging technologies for learning. British Educational Communications and Technology Agency (BECTA). Retrieved from http://dera.ioe.ac.uk/1503/

Pollard, H., Minor, M., & Swanson, A. (2014). Instructor social presence within the community of inquiry framework and its impact on the classroom community and the learning environment. *Online Journal of Distance Learning Administration, 17*(2). Retrieved from http://www.westga.edu/~distance/ojdla/summer172/Pollard_Minor_Swanson172

Reiser, R. A. (2006). What field did you say you were in? Defining and naming our field. In Reiser, R. A., & Dempsey, J. V. (eds.), *Trends and issues in instructional design and technology* (pp. 2–9). Upper Saddle River, NJ: Merrill/Prentice Hall.

Rogers, L. (2011). Developing simulations in multi-user virtual environments to enhance healthcare education. *British Journal of Educational Technology, 42*(4), 608–15.

Siemens, G. (2005). Connectivism: A learning theory for the digital age. *International Journal of Instructional Technology and Distance Learning, 2*(1). Retrieved from http://www.itdl.org/Journal/Jan_05/article01.htm

———. (2009, October 19). Complexity, chaos, and emergence. [Website]. Retrieved from https://docs.google.com/document/pub?id=1SbKRX97g1tVgxE3gVWIvA8injDYe_9JVwGjYCLzXe3k

So, H. J., & Brush, T. A. (2008). Student perceptions of collaborative learning, social presence and satisfaction in a blended learning environment: Relationships and critical factors. *Computers and Education, 51*(1), 318–36.

Stead, G., Sharpe, B., Anderson, P. Cych, L. & Philpott, M. (2006). Emerging technologies for learning. British Educational Communications and Technology Agency (BECTA). Retrieved from http://dera.ioe.ac.uk/1501/

Veletsianos, G. (2012). Higher education scholars' participation and practices on Twitter. *Journal of Computer Assisted Learning, 28*(4), 336–49

———. (2013). Open practices and identity: Evidence from researchers and educators' social media participation. *British Journal of Educational Technology, 44*(3), 639–51.

———. (2016). *Social Media in Academia: Networked Scholars.* New York, NY: Routledge.

Veletsianos G., & Kimmons, R. (2012). Networked Participatory Scholarship: Emergent Techno-Cultural Pressures Toward Open and Digital Scholarship in Online Networks. *Computers and Education, 58*(2), 766–774.

Warburton, S. (2009). Second Life in higher education: Assessing the potential for and the barriers to deploying virtual worlds in learning and teaching. *British Journal of Educational Technology, 40*(3), 414–26.

2 Complexity, Mess, and Not-Yetness

Teaching Online with Emerging Technologies

▶ *Jen Ross and Amy Collier*

This chapter argues for the place and value of mess and complexity in digital education, in particular with regard to emerging technologies. Such an argument is both necessary and relevant at the present moment, when so many of the visions of education being put forward gravitate toward extreme utopian or dystopian positions. As Hand (2008, p. 15–16) describes it best, "digital technologies are now *the* engines of promise and threat in a global information culture" seen as either "indicative of a break with particular modernities, in terms of socioeconomic structures and/or cultural objects and practices" or "augmenting the continuously dominant structures of capitalism." Digital education is not sheltered from these tensions, and it is frequently looked at as either the cause of or a solution to multiple "problems" in education. Utopian and dystopian narratives of technology are widespread in discussions of online education, often manifested in a technologically determinist position, and in a rhetoric that invokes the "technological imperative": "because a particular technology means that we *can* do something (it is technically possible) then this action either *ought* to (as a moral imperative), *must* (as an operational requirement) or inevitably *will* (in time) be taken" (Chandler, 2002).

Recent headlines about the Massive Open Online Course (MOOC) phenomenon are indicative of how some perceive opportunities while others fear the influence of new educational delivery modes. As exampled in these excepts from a variety of recently published articles, some journalists have asked if MOOCs will:

- revolutionize corporate learning and development (Meister, 2013);
- create divisions in society (Montague, 2014);
- kill university degrees (Stokey, 2013);
- de-professionalize higher education (Carter, 2014);
- help democratize higher education (MacGregor, 2013); and
- massively disrupt higher education (Booker, 2013).

Where utopian dreams of technology meet commercial interests, educators and researchers see commonalities in the nature of these fantasies. Advertising for educational technology is saturated with promises of speed, simplicity, and efficiency. Educational technology and software companies have evidently found that these promises will sell their products to institutions and teachers: this is what educators indicate they want and need. For example, the following claims, presented anonymously here to avoid critiquing any particular platform or service, are indicative of how such products are marketed:

"The design of our platform is based on sound pedagogical foundations that aim to help students learn the material quickly and effectively."

"The student knowledge profile clearly and quickly shows students (and their teachers) where the knowledge gaps are, and how to fill them."

"Easy drag-and-drop editing marks, voice comments and rubrics make grading faster."

"Grade any open-response assessment. Fast."

"Offload content delivery to jump-start the learning process."

The desire for these types of products is shaped and spread by what Gough (2012) refers to as the "politics of complexity reduction" (p. 47) in education and educational research. Gough's criticisms of such politics echo earlier calls from scholars focusing on complexity and supercomplexity in higher education, which requires "a view of learning construed as, at least in part, the acquisition of those human capabilities appropriate for adaptation to conditions of radical and enduring uncertainty, unpredictability, challengeability and contestability" (Barnett & Hallam, 1999, p.142). McArthur (2012) claims that complexity reduction has led to "bad" rather than "virtuous" mess: "Seeking to force the inherently messy into a respectable tidy form can result in something that distorts, hides or falsifies the actual social world" (p. 421).

Educators, students, researchers and instructional designers who value critical perspectives on digital education and emerging technologies often are caught in an unproductive cycle of critiquing overly optimistic *and* overly pessimistic narratives. One way to break out of these unhelpful extremes is to attend to the complexity and messiness of education itself. Focusing on teaching, we argue that emerging digital practices that contribute to the fruitful mess that characterizes education cast a new light on issues of power, responsibility, sustainability, reach, and contact. We discuss approaches that may help us steer away from indulging in overly simplistic utopian or dystopian explanations that unhelpfully limit "possible fields of thought and action" (Hand, 2008, p.40).

Those of us interested in emerging technologies and emerging practices would do well to resist constraints on thought and action wherever possible, because a key element of emerging technologies and emerging practices is their *not-yet-ness*. In chapter 1 Veletsianos argues that there is much educators and researches are not aware of while engaging with emerging technologies and practices. We must therefore choose to dwell as teachers in the state of radical and enduring uncertainty that Barnett and Hallam (1999) describe. We need practices that acknowledge and work with complexity to help us stay open to what may be genuinely surprising about online learning and teaching intersecting with emerging technologies. In this sense, our focus as educators should be on *emergent* situations, where complexity gives rise to "new properties and behaviours . . . that are not contained in the essence of the constituent elements, or able to be predicted from a knowledge of initial conditions" (Mason, 2008, p.2).

Online teaching can be theorized to counter utopian and dystopian accounts of digital education. As is claimed in the *Manifesto for Teaching Online* (Ross, Bayne, Macleod, & O'Shea, 2011), we aim to persuade you that "'best practice' is a totalising term blind to context—there are many ways to get it right." To do so, we explore three key dimensions of emerging technologies, emerging practices, and digital education: design, embodiment, and the wider sociopolitical context of accountability. In each section we argue for messier forms of thinking and practicing, and suggest possible approaches to work with complexity and not-yetness in productive ways.

TEACHING BORN DIGITAL: DESIGNING FOR NOT-YETNESS

The *Manifesto for Teaching Online* (Ross et al., 2011), a useful touchstone for not-yetness, stated that "the best online courses are born digital." The "online version"—the object that emerges when someone begins their course design process with the question "Can I put this offline course online?"—is well known to learning technologists and educational developers (Sinclair, 2009). It often involves the use of virtual classroom software, uploaded lecture slides, and other attempts at structures to mimic the campus-based course (sometimes replicating its constraints while missing its advantages). Indeed, most educational digital products and services, such as the virtual learning environment, are based on metaphors and structures drawn directly from the face-to-face classroom (Bayne, 2008; Cousin, 2005).

Often this digital version emerges from a wish to render digital environments unthreatening and to protect instructors, or learners, or the institution (or all three) from having to grapple with the possible difference of the digital. There seems to be a belief that online instruction can offer what the *Manifesto* (Ross et al., 2011) described as "networks and flows" in place of "boundaries" that need policing online. Such policing, however, often silences rather than avoids the disorientation that instructors and learners experience in these digital spaces. In the gaps between the original and the digital version, we might accidentally leave students to fend for themselves, where they could instead benefit from a critical engagement with webness (Ross, 2012a).

How should online instructors take account of not-yetness, and what does it really mean for a course to be born digital? Few educational technologies embrace messiness or not-yetness as a value. For many online instructors, designing courses presents tensions between the complexities of online teaching and learning and the rigidity of the technologies and environments they must use to teach. How might instructors design for complexity in learning in spite of these rigidities?

Asynchronicity; new forms of academic writing that include multimodal and collaborative writing; and also working with speed, brevity and serendipity are a few of the pedagogical possibilities that work best in the online environment. That prominent but under-theorized claim that "the pedagogy must lead the technology" (Cousin, 2005, p. 117) can be creatively undermined in favour of giving technologies (including those not yet fully understood) their due. We are often shaped by and with the technologies we use, and teaching is no exception. The biggest difference between the "version" and the "born digital" is whether we take technologies of the web into account when we design, or whether they assert themselves in largely unintentional ways.

Some instructors embrace the open web as a vehicle for complexity and emerging practice. Initiatives such as the University of Mary Washington's *Domain of One's Own* (Division of Teaching and Learning Technologies, 2014) encourage faculty to leave behind learning management systems that constrain where, how, and for how long learners participate in learning experiences, and instead "educat[e] students and faculty about the essential building blocks of the web and encourag[e] them to take an active role in the construction of their own digital identity" (Morgen & Rorabaugh, 2014). The use of the open web for learning encourages learners to develop what Stewart (2013) calls the "new literacies of participation," illuminating a complex view of learning-focused process and dialogue, rather than transmission of information toward the development of specific outcomes.

Cormier (2014a) wrestled with complexity as he designed *Rhizomatic Learning: The Community as the Curriculum* (Rhizo14), a course offered at the University of Prince Edward Island. The intention of Rhizo14 was to create a community around the topic of rhizomatic learning, which is defined as a form of learning in which the community is the curriculum (Cormier, 2014a). Hence, the community of learning was both the object of study and the process of learning. Cormier (2014b) did not set narrow learning outcomes for the participants; as he expected learners to create their own maps for what and how they would learn. He provided structure to the course by posing challenging questions related to the topics, such as "Cheating as Learning" (Cormier, 2014b). We have foregrounded design here because it is such an important aspect of the instructor's role in online education. However, a second dimension of teaching with not-yetness is that, having been so thoughtful about course design and choices of environments and how to foreground the digital, instructors have to hold that lightly. The multiple factors involved in any class are bound to produce a certain amount of the unexpected. Adding emerging technologies and emerging practices to the mix inevitably brings the outside in. By definition, what is emerging will not yet be fully understood, and its uses will not yet be set in stone (chapter 1). Often technologies are reflected outside formal education, and that reflection can be disorienting. Blogging is a key example of this: Wider cultural practices and perspectives create significant tensions and complexity for its use in educational settings (Ross, 2012b). Emerging digital environments open the teacher to experiences which can be unfamiliar and sometimes uncomfortable, and which require new strategies (Macleod & Ross, 2011). Turning to the notion of the "body" of the online teacher, we explore the impacts of complexity on the practice of digital education.

COMPLEXITY AND THE INSTRUCTOR'S (ONLINE) BODY

My body teaches so much (Radtke & Skouge, 2012, p. 98).

From early and influential constructivist accounts that privilege "facilitation" in the online domain (Palloff & Pratt, 1999), to the highly authoritative and trans-mission-based approach of some MOOC designs, the instructor's role in online learning is contested and varied. The instructor's body, far from being erased or inconsequential in online contexts, is in fact underdetermined (Poster, 2001). It is made up of many sometimes contradictory practices, including digital environments, course design, learner assumptions and expectations, the teacher's educational philosophies, habits, and communication styles, and institutional politics, while still being open enough to "solicit social construction and cultural creation" (Poster, 2001, p. 17). It is, in a word, messy. For example, Ross, Sinclair, Knox, Bayne, and Macleod (2014) drew on the literature of academic identity to explore the many ways that teaching can be understood, and argued that the prominent MOOC conceptualisations, of teacher as rock star, automaton, or "co-learner," are inadequate to the complexity of the role.

The importance of the body of the instructor in face-to-face classroom contexts has been investigated and theorized in a number of ways, notably from critical perspectives that explore issues of power, asking how gender, race, sexual orientation, and disability inscribe the instructor's body, shape their identity, and influence relationships in the classroom (Erlandson, 2005; Freedman & Holmes, 2003; Kelan, 2010; Latta & Buck, 2008). The instructor's body has a symbolic and a sensual role in the classroom that goes well beyond the view of the instructor as a transmitter of knowledge (Smith, 2012; McWilliam, 1996). It might seem as though this role disappears in the digital teaching space—and indeed an "incorporeal fallacy" (Land, 2004, p. 532) has permeated notions of cyberspace since its inception, fostering beliefs that the body is left behind when we go online. However, in both literal and metaphorical ways, digital embodiment transforms rather than erases (Bell, 2002).

Research into online teaching indicates that instructors perceive their cognitive, affective, and managerial roles to be more complex in online environments and often struggle to adjust to those roles (Coppola, Hiltz, & Rotter, 2001; Lin, Dyer, & Guo, 2012). Attention to embodiment plays an important part in understanding and handling this complexity (Bayne, 2005; 2010; Dall'Alba & Barnacle, 2005; Land, 2004; McWilliam & Taylor, 1996). Educational technologies, however, have largely overlooked the embodiment of instructors (and learners), and have claimed that identity can be dissociated from what people do online.

The instructor's body and presence is deployed in a range of ways in online courses—from singular and stable (as in the lecture-based MOOC) to distributed and mutable (for example, in courses where textual communication is central; Bayne, 2010). Studies of online instructional videos sparked debates on the effects of specific media on learners (Clark & Mayer, 2011; Kozma, 1994), but the complexities of embodiment and physical representation in videos for learning are less understood. For example, eye-tracking and surveys of learners in one study showed that MOOC learners preferred videos that included the instructor's face, indicating that the face increased the perceived value of the videos; however, videos did not improve learners' performance on subsequent knowledge tests (Kizilcec, Papadopoulos, & Sritanyaratana, 2014).

Even the singular and stable may be less of either than we imagine. A study by Adams, Yin, Vargas Madriz, and Mullen (2014) on the experiences of MOOC completers suggests that the video lecture can create a "powerful sphere of intimacy" for its recipients, as the video only requires the teacher to *perform* a personal address (by looking directly at the camera lens, for instance). The extent to which co-presence matters in learning is brought into question by the fact that such intimacy is less about contact (whether mediated or not) than about perception. The MOOC instructor can have a powerful impact on learners even when not really there.

Emerging technologies, which support immersive virtual environments, are another area of complexity. Immersive virtual environments may involve visual, auditory, olfactory, and/or haptic stimulation to create the sensation of an embodied physical experience. Collaborative virtual environments allow multiple users to interact in immersive simulations using avatars, or digital representations (Bailenson, Yee, Blascovich, Beall, Lundblad, & Jin, 2008). Instructors' avatar bodies create learning effects of which their "controller" may be unaware. For example, Bailenson et al. (2008) found that student avatars seated centrally to the gaze of a teacher avatar in an immersive learning environment performed better than those seated in the periphery of that perceived gaze. Yet in immersive environments, it is possible to reconfigure the geometry of a space so that all learners are "seated" directly ahead of a teacher's gaze or to program avatars of teachers to be rendered individually to each learner based on what she wants or needs to see (for example, one student may prefer to learn from a teacher who smiles often; Bailenson et al., 2008).

Sociomaterial perspectives on education (Fenwick & Edwards, 2010) offer theoretical support for the exploration of the online instructor's body. As the human body becomes increasingly inextricable from the technology that surrounds, monitors, and interacts with it (such as quantified self / biometrics, smart prostheses, and haptic devices), we must consider the ways technology becomes part of the human assemblage, or "complex and dynamic configurations of flesh, others' bodies, discourses, practices, ideas and material objects" (Lupton, 2013, p.6).

As Watters (2014) notes, "bodies matter when we learn; communities and affinity and situatedness matter; digital learning, even though some of it is 'virtual,' does not—or should not—change that." However, our understanding of embodiment in emerging online learning environments merits additional scrutiny and inquiry. Theories of online embodiment should acknowledge the complex interplay between physical bodies, the digital objects that are constructed or perceived as the instructor's online body, and the online learners and their physical and digital bodies. In the next section, we highlight a further element in this interplay: the current historical moment of accountability in education, and its impact on teaching with emerging technologies.

MESS IN AN AGE OF ACCOUNTABILITY

As discussed in chapter 1, educational technologies emerge within social, cultural, and ideological frameworks that shape their design and use. A scan of educational technologies arriving to market point to what Denzin and Lincoln (2013) have called a "backlash associated with the evidence-based social movement" (p. 5). An age of evidence and accountability, made salient by global financial crises (Burke, 2003), carries narrow views of how products and services (including education) can demonstrate value to consumers. Denzin and Lincoln (2013) refer specifically to research, but educational institutions are affected in all areas, and especially teaching, by calls for narrowly defined evidence of learning, or "outcomes-based learning."

It can be difficult to resist a focus on evidence and accountability in teaching as the terms of the debate invoke the rational and scientific, and often imply disorder and irresponsibility as their inevitable opposite. Accountability and evidence offer simplicity and tidiness, and the notion that instruction can be made better by assembling and deploying content, techniques, and approaches is endorsed by unproblematic evidence. Arguing in favour of accountability, Popham (2009) notes that accountability simplifies teaching since "once teachers have a fix on what their students are supposed to learn, almost all subsequent decision will revolve around how those students ought to learn it" (p. 6). The focus on accountability and evidence condenses instruction to a series of decisions—the determining of what students will learn, think, and do, and the measurement of outcomes thought to be based on the effects of these determinations.

Values of accountability and evidence-based learning are seen in a range of emerging practices associated with online learning. Specifically, digital environments are seen as sites of great promise because of the opportunities they can provide for collecting data about learners as such environments interact with them (chapter 6). Despite increasing concerns over learners' privacy, many researchers and educators see these data as precipitating a "new data science of learning" (Collier, 2014). This new data science is largely predicated on the evolving computational methods offered by data mining and learning analytics of digital environments. Learning analytics focus on learners' data trails in digital environments, and researchers leverage the scale and breadth of accessible data to provide power to computational methods. At the same time, online learning environments are increasingly designed and deployed with the production of such data in mind. Analytics are premised on the assumption that what *can be tracked* in relation to educational activity is also *valuable* in terms of understanding learning—at least, at scale. Tracking and interpreting digital traces of behaviours in the search for stable and predictable measures of learning is fully compatible with the accountability and evidence-based paradigm. In a sense, learning analytics is the methodology required by the age of accountability.

Problems arise, however, when we behave as if we believe that everything worth knowing about learning and learners can be revealed through these methods via learning analytics (Veletsianos, Collier, & Schneider, 2015) and the "all-representing database" (Law, 2003, p. 7). Biesta (2007) identified problems for both research and practice which emerge from an unquestioning reliance on evidence: "the focus on 'what works' makes it difficult if not impossible to ask the questions of what it should work *for* and who should have a say in determining the latter" (p. 5). As Campbell (2014) argues, the push toward evidence does not necessarily result in responsible action or marked improvements in learning. It may, instead, reward narrow conceptions of what it means to be a good student and "marching toward compliance and away from more elusive and disruptive concepts like curiosity or wonder." Then, instruction risks been seen as a matter of implementing routines, with "shared values, discourse, inquiry, and personal growth and labour," as well as serendipity, play and exploration, de-emphasized in favour of "accountability mechanisms that delimit human interactions to quantifiable behaviours reinforced by external rewards and punishments" (Leahy, 2013, p.10).

Furthermore, data science approaches are shaping and informing research, development, and practice in online teaching and learning, while often failing to acknowledge what is privileged and what cannot be explained through analyses. For example, MOOC-related research has granted great power to large-scale computational analyses of learner behaviours, as evidenced by statements such as the following: "What 6.9 million clicks tell us about how to fix online education" (Conner-Simons, 2014). In terms of future development, these approaches can become self-fulfilling prophecies, closing off some avenues of investigation and research while pouring resources into forms of analysis that promise nothing more (and nothing less) than the tracking and replication of practices deemed successful.

This view, and the research and instructional practices that emerge around it, runs counter to the perspective that teaching and learning are messy activities. Research should attempt to explore, not simplify, these complexities. Working with mess in an age of accountability means acknowledging that learners, too, have complex identities and are embodied in various ways. Learners are connected to families and communities, and located within economic, cultural, and political systems (Morrison, 2008). Ignoring mess limits the extensibility of what is taught in a virtual (or face-to-face) classroom and the usefulness of research conducted in those environments. As McArthur (2012) notes, a lack of complexity or mess signals that important individual and social experiences of learners are being missed, as attempts to define narrow outcomes tidy away lived experience. Measurement alone tells us very little about learning (Morrison, 2008); we need to look at learning in a holistic, contextually sensitive way. This requires pushing back on outcomes-focused practices in teaching and learning, the technologies that simplify complexities in learning, and research that purports to explain more about learning that it can legitimately claim to explain.

Digital education, and educational research on emerging technologies and practices, should not concern itself only with how well learners perform on tasks and assessments, but also on their ecologies and lifeworlds, and the complexities of how these things interact, because "to atomize phenomena into measurable variables and then to focus only on certain of these is to miss synergies and the significance of the whole" (Morrison, 2008, p. 25). Instructors are well placed to contribute to such research, and to participate in revisiting a range of social science methodologies. Qualitative approaches, in particular, can contribute to a richer picture than that provided by accountability-based analytics alone (Veletsianos, Collier, & Schneider, 2015). Paradigm proliferation, as Patti Lather (2006) describes it, can act as a much-needed corrective to an over-focus on, and currently exaggerated claims for, data science.

CONCLUSION

This chapter offered perspectives on three aspects of emerging technologies and emerging practices in relation to online education. The first proposed that instructors focus on designing for not-yetness, finding ways to engage with the digital on its own terms, rather than attempting to mask it with versions of more established practices that mimic the constraints of the classroom. The second perspective drew attention to the complexity of instructor identity and embodiment, and the fruitful learning which might come from thinking of the body as a relevant site of exploration of the online instructor's role. The third perspective put the previous two in the context of the "age of accountability" in which digital education is currently operating, and probed what we see as a growing and problematic reliance on emerging technologies and practices with data science and analytics at their core.

In each of these sections we have aimed to persuade you that what we need in the practice, conceptualisation, and investigation of digital education is *more* rather than *less* complexity and mess. This claim flies in the face of pressures to simplify, to speed up, to expand, to focus on the measurable and replicable; it pushes back against the demands for efficiency that often accompany institutional interest in online provision. This claim also acknowledges how much we do not yet know about our emerging technologies and practices, and so invites "responsible experimentation to establish matters of concern" (Edwards, 2010, p. 13).

In calling for paradigm proliferation and diversity in our teaching and research practices, it is evident that

> events and processes are not simply complex in the sense that they are technically difficult to grasp . . . they are also complex because they *necessarily exceed our capacity to know them*. . . . The world in general defies any attempt at overall orderly accounting. (Law, 2004, p. 6; italics in original)

The correct response to the world's refusal to be orderly or knowable is not to narrow our vision to see only what we *can* account for. Nor is it to conclude that education, that unfailingly complex set of ideas, practices, relationships, and materialities, is broken and that "fixing" it (in both senses of the word) is the next great computer science challenge. It is to keep looking for ways to broaden our view. Here we can get help from emerging technologies and emerging practices, which are not only "not yet" but also in a sense "never there"—underdetermined and still open to many understandings and methods. Indeed, learning analytics and the data sciences can and do contribute tremendously to a search for these broader perspectives, when we find ways to uncouple them from prevailing discourses of accountability and limited conceptions of education, and bring them to bear on messier questions.

REFERENCES

Adams, C., Yin, Y., Vargas Madriz, L. F., & Mullen, C. S. (2014). A phenomenology of learning large: The tutorial sphere of xMOOC video lectures. *Distance Education, 35*(2), 202–16.

Bailenson, J., Yee, N., Blascovich, J., Beall, A. C., Lundblad, N., & Jin, M. (2008). The use of immersive virtual reality in the learning sciences: Digital transformations of teachers, students, and social context. *The Journal of the Learning Sciences, 17*, 102–41.

Barnett, R., & Hallam, S. (1999). Teaching for supercomplexity: A pedagogy for higher education. In P. Mortimer (ed.), *Understanding Pedagogy and Its Impact on Learning* (pp. 137–54). London: SAGE.

Bayne, S. (2005). Deceit, desire and control: The identities of learners and teachers in cyberspace, in R. Land and S. Bayne (eds.), *Education in Cyberspace*. London: RoutledgeFalmer.

———. (2008). Higher education as a visual practice: Seeing through the virtual learning environment. *Teaching in Higher Education, 13*(4), 395–410.

———. (2010). Academetron, automaton, phantom: Uncanny digital pedagogies. *London Review of Education, 8*(1), 5–13.

Bell, D. (2002). *An introduction to cybercultures.* London: Routledge.

Biesta, G. (2012). Giving teaching back to education: Responding to the disappearance of the teacher. *Phenomenology and Practice, 6*(2), 35–49.

———. (2007). Why "what works" won't work: Evidence-based practice and the democratic deficit in educational research. *Educational Theory, 57*(1), 1–22.

Booker, E. (2013, August 30). Will MOOCs massively disrupt higher education? *Information Week.* Retrieved from http://www.informationweek.com/software/will-moocs-massively-disrupt-higher-education/d/d-id/1111357

Burke, J. C. (2003). The new accountability for public higher education: From regulation to results. *Research in University Evaluation, 3,* 67–87. Retrieved from http://www.rockinst.org/pdf/education/2003-08-the_new_accountability_for_public_higher_education_from_regulation_to_results_research_in_university_evaluation.pdf

Campbell, G. (2014). Understanding and learning outcomes. *Gardner Writes.* [Blog post]. Retrieved from http://www.gardnercampbell.net/blog1/?p=2239

Carter, D. (2014, January 10). Will MOOCs "de-professionalize" higher education? *eCampus News.* Retrieved from http://www.ecampusnews.com/top-news/moocs-higher-education-921/

Chandler, D. (2002). Technological or media determinism. *Media and Communications Studies,* University of Aberystwyth. Retrieved from http://www.aber.ac.uk/media/Documents/tecdet/tecdet.html

Clark, R., & Mayer, R. (2011). *e-Learning and the science of instruction.* San Francisco: John Wiley and Sons.

Collier, A. (2014). Building the "new data science of learning" — #eli2014 reflections. *Red Pincushion.* [Blog post]. Retrieved from http://redpincushion.me/2014/02/10/building-the-new-data-science-of-learning-eli2014-reflections/

Coppola, N. W., Hiltz, S. R., & Rotter, N. (2001, January). Becoming a virtual professor: Pedagogical roles and ALN. *Proceedings of the Hawai`i International Conference on System Sciences.* Wailea, Maui, HI: *IEEE Computer Society*

Conner-Simons, A. (2014). What 6.9 million clicks tell us about how to fix online education. *MIT News.* Retrieved from http://newsoffice.mit.edu/2014/what-69-million-clicks-tell-us-about-how-fix-online-education

Cormier, D. (2014a). *Making the community the curriculum: Rhizomatic learning in action.* PressBooks. [Blog post]. Retrieved from http://davecormier.pressbooks.com/

———. (2014b). Your unguided tour of Rhizo14. *Dave's Educational Blog*. [Blog post]. Retrieved from http://davecormier.com/edblog/2014/01/12/your-unguided-tour-of-rhizo14/

Cousin, G. (2005). Learning from cyberspace. In R. Land & S. Bayne (eds.) *Education in cyberspace* (pp. 117-129). London, UK: Routledge.

Crocco, M. S., & Costigan, A. T. (2007). The narrowing of curriculum and pedagogy in the age of accountability: Urban educators speak out. *Urban Education, 42*, 512–35.

Dall'Alba, G., & Barnacle, R. (2005). Embodied knowing in online environments. *Educational Philosophy and Theory, 37*(5), 719–44.

Denzin, N., & Lincoln, Y. (2013). Introduction: The discipline and practice of qualitative research. In N. Denzin & Y. Lincoln (eds.), *The landscape of qualitative research*, 4th ed. (pp. 1–19). Thousand Oaks, CA: SAGE.

Division of Teaching and Learning Technologies (2014, July 26). A domain of one's own. About. *University of Mary Washington*. Retrieved from https://umwdomains.com/details/

Edwards, R. (2010). The end of lifelong learning: A post-human condition? *Studies in the Education of Adults, 42*(1), 5–17.

Erlandson, P. (2005). The body disciplined: Rewriting teaching competence and the doctrine of reflection. *Journal of Philosophy of Education, 39*(4), 661–70.

Fenwick, T., & Edwards, R. (2010). *Actor-network theory in education*. Abingdon: Routledge.

Freedman, D. P., & Holmes, M. S. (2003). Introduction. In D. Freedman & M Stoddard Holmes (eds.), *The teacher's body: Embodiment, authority, and identity in the academy* (pp. 1–14). New York: SUNY Press.

Gough, N. (2012). Complexity, complexity reduction, and "methodological borrowing" in educational inquiry. *Complicity: An International Journal of Complexity and Education, 9*(1). Retrieved from http://ejournals.library.ualberta.ca/index.php/complicity/article/view/16532

Hand, M. (2008). *Making digital cultures: Access, interactivity, and authenticity*. Hampshire, UK: Ashgate Publishing Limited.

Kelan, E. (2010). Moving bodies and minds—the quest for embodiment in teaching and learning. *Higher Education Research Network Journal, 3*, 39–46.

Kizilcec, R. F., Papadopoulos, K., & Sritanyaratana, L. (2014). Showing face in video instruction: Effects on information retention, visual attention, and affect. *CHI '14 Proceedings of the SIGCHI Conference on Human Factors in Computing Systems* (pp. 2095–102). Toronto, Canada. Retrieved from http://dl.acm.org/citation.cfm?doid=2556288.2557207

Kozma, R. (1994). Will media influence learning? Reframing the debate. *Educational Technology Research and Development, 42*(2), 7–19.

Land, R. (2004). Issues of embodiment and risk in online learning. *Proceedings of the 21st ASCILITE Conference*, (pp. 530–38). Perth, Australia. Retrieved from http://www.ascilite.org.au/conferences/perth04/procs/land.html

Lather, P. (2006). Paradigm proliferation as a good thing to think with: Teaching research in education as a wild profusion. *International Journal of Qualitative Studies in Education, 19*(1), 35–57.

Latta, M. M., & Buck, G. (2008). Enfleshing embodiment: 'Falling into trust' with the body's role in teaching and learning. *Educational Philosophy and Theory, 40*, 315–29.

Law, J. (2003). *Making a mess with method.* Centre for Science Studies, Lancaster University. Retrieved from http://www.lancaster.ac.uk/fass/sociology/research/publications/papers/law-making-a-mess-with-method.pdf

——. (2004). *After method: Mess in social science research.* Abingdon, UK: Routledge.

Leahy, C. (2013). Catch-22 and the paradox of teaching in the age of accountability. *Critical Education, 4*(6), 1–19.

Lin, H., Dyer, K., & Guo, Y. (2012). Exploring online teaching: A three-year composite journal of concerns and strategies from online instructors. *Online Journal of Distance Learning Administration, 11*(3). Retrieved from http://www.westga.edu/~distance/ojdla/fall153/lin_dyer_guo153.html

Lupton, D. (2013). The digital cyborg assemblage: Haraway's cyborg theory and the new digital health technologies. In F. Collyer (ed.), *The handbook of social theory for the sociology of health and medicine.* Houndmills, UK: Palgrave Macmillan.

McArthur, J. (2012). Virtuous mess and wicked clarity: struggle in higher education research. *Higher Education Research and Development, 31*(3), 419–30. doi:10.1080/07294360.2011.634380

McWilliam, E. (1996). Corpor/realities in the classroom. *English Education, 28*(4), 340–48.

McWilliam, E., & Taylor, P. (1998). Teacher im/material: Challenging the new pedagogies of instructional design. *Educational Researcher, 27*(8), 29–35.

MacGregor, K. (2013, June 23). Will MOOCs help to democratise higher education? *University World News.* Retrieved from http://www.universityworldnews.com/article.php?story=20130622164019140

Macleod, H., & Ross, J. (2011). Structure, authority and other noncepts: Teaching in fool-ish spaces. In R. Land & S. Bayne (eds.), *Digital difference: Perspectives on online learning* (pp. 15–28). Rotterdam, Netherlands: Sense.

Mason, M. (2008). Complexity theory and the philosophy of education. In M. Mason (ed.), *Complexity theory and the philosophy of education* (pp. 1–15). West Sussex, UK: John Wiley and Sons.

Meister, J. (2013, August 13). How MOOCs will revolutionize corporate learning and development. *Forbes*. Retrieved from http://www.forbes.com/sites/jeannemeister/2013/08/13/how-moocs-will-revolutionize-corporate-learning-development/

Montague, S. (2014, March 4). Online MOOC courses 'could create divisions in society.' *BBC News*. Retrieved from http://www.bbc.com/news/education-26431790

Morgen, D., & Rorabaugh, P. (2014). Building community and critical literacies with the Domain of One's Own incubator. *Hybrid Pedagogy*. Retrieved from: http://www.hybridpedagogy.com/journal/building-community-critical-literacies-domain-ones-incubator/

Morrison, K. (2008). Educational philosophy and the challenge of complexity theory. In M. Mason (ed.), *Complexity theory and the philosophy of education* (pp. 1–15). West Sussex, UK: John Wiley and Sons.

Palloff, R., & Pratt, K. (1999). *Building learning communities in cyberspace: Effective strategies for the online classroom*. San Francisco, CA: Jossey Bass.

Popham, J. (2009). *Instruction that measures up: Successful teaching in the age of accountability*. Alexandria, VA: Association for Supervision and Curriculum Development.

Poster, M. (2001). *What's the matter with the Internet?* Minneapolis, MN: University of Minnesota Press.

Radtke, R., & Skouge, J. (2012). My body, myself: A quadriplegic's perception of and approach to teaching. In D. Freedman and M. Stoddard Holmes (eds.), *The teacher's body: Embodiment, authority, and identity in the academy* (pp. 83–92). New York: SUNY Press.

Ross, J. (2012a). The spectacle and the placeholder: Digital futures for reflective practices in higher education. In V. Hodgson, C. Jones, M. de Laat, D. McConnell, T. Ryberg, & P. Sloep (eds.), *Proceedings of the 8th International Conference on Networked Learning 2012* (pp. 260–65). Retrieved from http://www.lancaster.ac.uk/fss/organisations/netlc/past/nlc2012/abstracts/pdf/ross.pdf

———. (2012b). Just what is being reflected in online reflection? New literacies for new media learning practices. In L. Dirckinck-Holmfeld, V. Hodgson, & D. McConnell (eds.), *Exploring the theory, pedagogy and practice of networked learning* (pp. 191–207). New York: Springer. Retrieved from http://www.springerlink.com/content/q13101092v13125j/

Ross, J., Bayne, S., Macleod, H., & O'Shea, C. (2011). The text. *Manifesto for Teaching Online. Part of the MSc in Digital Education at the University of Edinburgh.* [Blog post]. Retrieved from http://onlineteachingmanifesto. wordpress.com/the-text/

Ross, J., Sinclair, C., Knox, J., Bayne, S., & Macleod, H. (2014). Teacher experiences and academic identity: The missing components of MOOC pedagogy. *Journal of Online Learning and Teaching, 10*(1). Retrieved from http://jolt.merlot.org/vol10no1/ross_0314.pdf

Sinclair, C. (2009, December). "Can you do an online version?" Challenges in, from and about elearning. Presented at the *Society for Research into Higher Education, SRHE,* Newport, UK. Retrieved from http://www.srhe.ac.uk/ conference2009/abstracts/0182.pdf

Smith, S. (2012). Caring caresses and the embodiment of good teaching. *Phenomenology and Practice, 6*(2), 65–83.

Stewart, B. (2013). Massiveness + openness = new literacies of participation? *Journal of Online Learning and Teaching, 9*(2). Retrieved from http://jolt. merlot.org/vol9no2/stewart_bonnie_0613.htm

Stokey, N. L. (2013, October 1). Will MOOCs kill university degrees? *The Economist.* Retrieved from http://www.economist.com/blogs/economist-explains/2013/10/economist-explains

Veletsianos, G., Collier, A., & Schneider, E. (2015). Digging deeper into learners' experiences in MOOCs: Participation in social networks outside of MOOCs, Notetaking, and contexts surrounding content consumption. *British Journal of Educational Technology, 46*(3), 570–587.

Watters, A. (2014, July, 31). Student data, privacy, ideology, and context-less-ness. *Hack Education.* [Blog post]. Retrieved from http://www. hackeducation.com/2014/07/31/privacy-data-ideology-identity-context/

③ Theories for Learning with Emerging Technologies

▶ *Terry Anderson*

While educational theory is often construed by graduate students as a necessary evil of little practical use, and frequently required by professors and research committees, the value of theory in education development and design (Anderson, 2004b) is summed up by Kurt Lewin's (1952) famous quote, "there is nothing so practical as a good theory" (p. 169).

I begin this chapter with a short personal anecdote. During the summer of 2003, I saw a flood of new web-based information and communication technologies providing opportunities to create learning activities in formal education. I became obsessed with the notion that there must be some sort of rational law that would help educators and instructional designers decide when to use which particular technology. Moreover, the mere fact that a technology is popular for personal or business use provides little evidence that it will be useful in educational contexts—a notion instantiated by the phenomenal growth of Facebook! In addition, I was worried (and still am) that the adoption of any new technology is hard work and will likely have unanticipated consequences. It is imperative, therefore, to identify theoretical constructs to guide technology-enhanced interventions.

I was drawn to thinking about technologies in the context of Moore's (1989) description of educational communications as being made up of student-student, student-content, and student-teacher interactions. We had already written (Anderson & Garrison, 1998) about three other possible interactions

— teacher-content, teacher-teacher, and content-content — but continued to focus on the ones most relevant to a learning-centric view, those that involved students. Figure 3.1 demonstrated how these three student interactions were more or less equivalent. Through the creation of very high-quality levels of any one type of interaction, it would be sufficient to produce a high-quality learning experience. If this was the case, the other two interactions could be reduced or even eliminated, with very little impact on learning outcomes or learner attitudes. If true, this "learning equivalency theory" could be used to rationalize expenditures in one area, yet allow for time and money savings in the other two. I further speculated that "more than one of these three modes will likely provide a more satisfying educational experience, though these experiences may not be as cost- or time-effective as less interactive learning sequences" (Anderson, 2003).

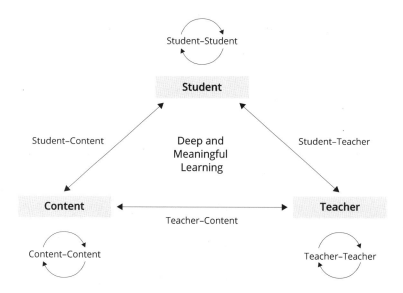

Figure 3.1 Learning interactions

The problem with this "theory" rests on Popper's (1968) claim that a good theory is one that can never be proved true, but should be capable of being proved false. To disprove this theory would deny its contribution to the education field as only an interesting hypothesis and rubric for course designers. Bernard et al. (2009) established a set of protocols to conduct a meta-analysis of distance education studies designed to validate these contentions and concluded that, "when the actual categories of strength were investigated through ANOVA, we found strong support for Anderson's hypothesis about achievement and less support for his hypothesis concerning attitudes" (p. 1265). Thus, Anderson's (2003) "equivalency theory" gained some empirical support, and has helped researchers to research, and practitioners to design and deliver, effective and efficient interventions, demonstrating that large *and* small theories associated with learning and teaching can serve to explain and to inspire. In the rest of this chapter, I review older and newer theories of learning that I find of most interest and value in my own thinking and practice, and I hope this overview helps the reader to understand and act effectively in the complex online learning environments that we are creating.

HISTORICAL THEORIES OF EDUCATIONAL TECHNOLOGY

Good theories stand the test of time and continue to be of use because they help individuals understand education and act appropriately. These theories are useful today because emerging technologies and practices are often applied to the same challenges and problems that inspired educators and researchers working with older technologies, technologies that, while now established, were once emerging (chapter 1).

As stated by Larreamendy-Joerns and Leinhardt (2006, p. 568), "the visionary promises and concerns that many current educators claim as novel actually have a past, one whose themes signal both continuities and ruptures." In their review of educational technology research and its application to online learning, these authors defined three views or visions that propel educational technology use and development. These are: the presentational view, the performance-tutoring view, and the epistemic-engagement view.

The *presentational view* focuses on theory and practice to make discourse and visualizations clearly accessible to learners. Theories of multimedia use focus on the cognitive effects of selecting and transmitting relevant images and words, organizing these transmissions effectively, and ensuring that the messages delivered through multiple channels do not interfere with each other or with the cognitive processing of the learners (Mayer, 2001). Much of this work benefited from studies of brain activity, and an increased understanding of the complex ways in which individuals process presentations to create learning expositions in most effective ways. A current example of this is view can be found in the study of short video segments frequently used in massive open online courses (MOOCs) and the Khan Academy video episodes (Giannakos, Chorianopoulos,

Ronchetti, Szegedi & Teasley, 2013). The *performance tutoring* view derives its roots from the feedback, reinforcement, and theory of behavioural psychology.

SOCIAL CONSTRUCTIVISM

The *epistemic engagement* view of learning identified by Larreamendy-Joerns and Leinhardt (2006) has been the most recent educational vision driving educational technology. This vision focuses on the evolutionary propensity for curiosity, discovery, sharing, and understanding for the skillful use of tools, and it is most closely associated with social constructivist learning theories. Constructivism has long philosophical and pedagogical roots associated with the works of Dewey, Mead, and Piaget. Like many popular theories, constructivism has been defined and characterized in various ways. However, all forms of this theory share the understanding that individuals' construction of knowledge is dependent upon individual and collective understandings, backgrounds, and proclivities. Debate arises, however, over the degree to which individuals hold common understandings, and if these understandings are rooted in any single form of externally defined and objective reality (Kanuka & Anderson, 1999). As much as constructivism is present in the current educational discussion, it should be noted that it is a philosophy of learning and not one of teaching. Despite this incongruence, many authors have extracted tenets of constructivist learning and from them developed principles or guidelines for learning design contexts and activities. Among these are the following: that active engagement by the learners is critically important, and that multiple perspectives and sustained dialogue lead to effective learning. Social constructivist theories have focused on the role of scaffolds provided by both human and nonhuman agents that assist more able or knowledgeable learners or teachers to prompt and support learners in acquiring their own competence (Vygotsky & Luria, 1981).

Constructivists also stress the contextual nature of learning, and argue that learning happens most effectively when the task and context are authentic and hold meaning for the learners. Constructivist learning activities often focus on problems and require active inquiry techniques. These problems often work best when they are ill-structured, open-ended, and are deemed "messy." Such problems force learners to go beyond formulaic solutions to develop capacity for effective problem-solving behaviours across multiple contexts.

COMPLEXITY THEORY

Complexity theory, or more recently, the "science of complexity," arose from the study of living systems, and it has been attracting interest among a variety of disciplines. Perhaps the most familiar examples of complexity theory are those drawn from evolutionary study, where organisms adapt to and even modify complex environments, creating unusually stable, yet complex systems. In such systems one component of an ecosystem cannot be understood in isolation from the context or total environment in which it lives (for further discussion of this, see chapter 2). Complexity theory teaches educators and researchers to look for emergent behaviours that arise while autonomous yet interdependent organisms interact. In particular, educational theorists examine and attempt to predict "transformations or phase transitions that provide the markers for growth, change, or learning" (Horn, 2008, p. 126). Complexity theorists are often at odds with positivist researchers and educators, who attempt to eliminate or control all the variables that influence learning. Rather, complexity seeks to create learning activities to allow effective behaviour to emerge and evolve, and ineffective ideas to be extinguished. Conversely, complexity theorists seek to understand features of the environment; especially the social or structural norms or organizations created that resist overt or covert attempts at self-organization. McElroy (2000) noted that "the point at which emergent behaviours inexplicably arise, lies somewhere between order and chaos" (p. 196). This sweet spot is known as the "edge of chaos," where systems "exhibit wild bursts of creativity and produce new and novel behaviours at the level of the whole system . . . complex systems innovate by producing spontaneous, systemic bouts of novelty out of which new patterns of behavior emerge" (McElroy, 2000, p. 196).

Implications of complexity theory for learning and for education operate on at least two levels. At the level of the individual learner, complexity theory, like constructivist theory, supports the learner's acquisition of skills and power such that he or she can articulate and achieve personal learning goals (chapters 8 and 9). By noting the presence of agents and structures to support and impede the emergence of effective adaptive behaviour, individual learners are better able to survive in occasionally threatening and very complex learning environments, and even to influence them.

At the organizational level, complexity theory highlights the social structures created to manage learning. When these management functions begin to inhibit the emergence of positive adaptive behaviour, or give birth to behaviours that are not conducive to deep learning, educators can expect negative results.

Organizational structures are intended to enable learners to surf at the "edge of chaos," and not to eliminate or constrain the creative potential of actors engaged at this juncture. Further, this understanding can guide creation and management of these complex environments, not with the goal of controlling or understanding learning, but intending to create systems in which learning emerges rapidly and profoundly. Complexity theory also encourages educators and researchers to think of learning contexts (classrooms, online learning cohorts, and more) as entities themselves. Such entities can be healthy, sick, emerging, growing, or dying, and these characterizations can help researchers and educators improve them. By thinking at the systems level, reformers search for interventions, tools, and languages that promote healthy adaptation and produce healthy human beings.

Finally, complexity theory helps us to understand and work with the inevitable unanticipated events that emerge when disruptive technologies are used in once stable systems (Christensen, 1997). Learning to surf this wave of equal opportunity and danger (and do it masterfully) becomes the goal of educational change agents.

The teaching and learning theories derived from pre-Internet visions for technology-enhanced learning and related theories of learning still resonate with and add value to educators and researchers today. However, it is important to examine theories that have been developed since the rise of the web and which have deliberately exploited the affordances of this new context for teaching and learning.

NET-AWARE THEORIES OF LEARNING

The Internet (or net) context created an environment that is radically different from pre-net contexts, but carries with it evolutionary genes from previous cultures and technologies. There are three affordances of the web that define its value for teaching and learning (Anderson & Whitelock, 2004).

First, the net offers the capacity for powerful, yet very low-cost, communications. This capacity forms the platform upon which epistemic-engagement visions of learning are instantiated. Communication may occur in synchronous, asynchronous, or near-synchronous (e.g., text messaging) modes and may be expressed through text, voice, video, and immersive interaction modes (i.e., any combination of the media). Communication artifacts can be stored, indexed, tagged, harvested, searched, and sorted. All of this capacity is available at low or affordable cost. Net communications can be one-to-one, one-to-many, or involve many, with very little cost differentiation among the three modes. Communication has also ceased to be expensive, geographically restricted, or privileged (i.e., it is available to those individuals with hearing, movement, or visual disabilities, and it is not limited to those with expensive production facilities). Finally, communications affordances can be used in a multitude of ways. The emergence of social networking tools, for example, affords learners the opportunity to self-organize, to seek and share questions, understandings, and resources outside of the formal virtual or campus classroom, thus creating learner-organized tutoring and support opportunities (see chapters 8 and 9). This capacity creates opportunities for many forms of collaborative informal and lifelong learning (Koper & Tattersall, 2004; Wenger, Trayner & de Latt, 2011).

Second, the net created a context of information abundance. From You-Tube videos to wide-scale distribution and production of Open Educational Resources (OER), the net provides learning content with many different display and presentation attributes. Such content exists in many formats, and often uses multimedia to enhance presentational value. Most exciting is the capacity for learners and teachers to add user-created content and to edit and enhance the work of others using produsage production modes (Bruns, 2008). "Produsage" is a combination of the words "production" and "usage," and it refers to user-led content creation, consumption, and active production online. As important as scaling content is the power of effective search and retrieval methods. Current online search engines make this task surprisingly fast and accurate. The transition from scarcity to abundance introduces massive amounts of information and choice, challenging students and instructors to develop their judgment, comparison, and evaluation skills.

The third affordance is the development of active and autonomous agents, which are free to gather, aggregate, synthesize, and filter the net for content and communications relevant to individuals and groups of learners and teachers. In Dron and Anderson (2014) we discussed this capacity for knowledge generation through distributed machine cognition as "collective" affordances to enhance formal and informal learning. The educational semantic web is rapidly emerging, with serious methodological (Doctorow, 2001) and epistemological (Kalfoglou, Schorlemmer, & Walton, 2004) challenges to its emergence. An increasing number of applications utilize autonomous agents (Liemhetcharat &Veloso, 2012; Sato, Azevedo, & Barthès, 2012) to induce and support learning. The most visible of these applications are the search-engine algorithms used to find and retrieve online content, products, and services. Most search engines, for example, work through active monitoring on online traffic patterns, with regard to the links and collective actions of users, and their algorithms produce an intelligent guess as to the searcher's desired result. Agents monitoring these searches extract additional information used by marketers and social researchers to further understand our collective ideas, choices, and interests (Tancer, 2008). Researchers and educators studying interventions in online learning environments are increasingly making use of such algorithms for learning analytics (chapter 6).

While net-based agents will continue to add value to visions for educational technology practice and research, being in awe of stunning technical affordances does little to direct teaching and learning. For this reason, I discuss two recent theories that may help explain the practice of networked learning online.

HEUTAGOGY

Hase and Kenyon (2000) developed the heutagogical theory of learning, named after the Greek word for self. This theory has roots in self-directed learning, and specifically renounces the teacher dependency associated with both pedagogy (the study of teaching) and andragogy (the study of teaching adults). Heutagogy extends control to the learner and sees the learner as the major development and control agent in his or her learning (Hase & Kenyon, 2007; Blaschke, 2012). The self-determinism that defines heutagogical approaches to teaching and learning is seen as critical to life in the rapidly changing economy and cultures that characterize postmodern times. As Hase and Kenyon ("Heutagogy," 2000, para. 6) note, "heutagogy looks to the future in which knowing how to learn will be a fundamental skill given the pace of innovation and the changing structure of communities and workplaces." This future demands that education move beyond instructing and testing for learner competencies, and toward supporting learners in a journey to capacity rather than competency. Capacity includes being able to learn in new and unfamiliar contexts. Older models of competence test only the time-dependent achievement of the past. Instructional design for heutagogical learning veers away from prescriptive content to an exploration of problems that are relevant to the learner (chapter 8 and 9). The instructor becomes a facilitator and a guide in learners' interactions with varied resources to resolve problems and to gain personal understanding. Heutagogy thus emphasizes self-direction and focuses on the development of efficacy in utilizing the online tools and information available.

CONNECTIVISM

The second recent network-centric theory was first developed by George Siemens, who coined the term "connectivism" (2005) and laid out principles to define connected learning. Specifically, Siemens argued that "competence [is gained] from forming connections" and the "capacity to know more is more critical than what is currently known" (Siemens, "Connectivism," 2005). The metaphor of the network, whose nodes consist of learning resources, machines to store and generate information, and people, is one that dominates connectivist learning. Learning occurs as individuals discover and build connections between these nodes. Learning environments are created and used by learners to access, process, filter, recommend, and apply information with the aid of machines, peers, and experts within the learning network. In the process, learning expands based on the power of the network to create and personalize knowledge, connections, and artifacts of those within it. Being able to see, navigate, and develop connections between nodes is the goal of connectivist learning. Rather than learning facts and concepts, connectivism stresses learning how to create paths to knowledge when it is needed. Siemens also argues that knowledge, and indeed learning itself, can exist outside the human being — in the databases, devices, tools, and communities within which a learner acts. A goal of connectivist learning is to create new connections, regardless of formal education systems, to expand upon and build learning networks. Connectivist theorists are primarily interested in allowing and stimulating learners to create new learning connections. In the process, learners are expected to increase the pool of expertise and resources that they can draw from, to increase social capital, and to curate valued resources.

Connectivism also sees the need for formal education to expand beyond classrooms and bounded systems that manage learning:

> Learning . . . occurs in communities, where the practice of learning is the participation in the community. A learning activity is, in essence, a conversation undertaken between the learner and other members of the community. This conversation, in the Web 2.0 era, consists not only of words but of images, video, multimedia and more. (Downes, "A Network Pedagogy," 2006, para. 4)

Though connectivism has yet to become widely accepted as the learning theory for the digital era as envisioned by Siemens (2005) and Downes (2006), there is an increasing engagement in the field with ideas associated with connectivism. Verhagen (2006) argued that connectivism is a theory of curriculum, specifying the ultimate goal of education and the methods learners use to interact with learning materials, rather than a theory of learning. Kerr (2007) criticized this theory by stating it offered nothing new in learning theory that is not accounted for in earlier works, such as complexity theory and constructivism. Kop and Hill (2008) identified two problems with the theory: the lack of a substantive role for the instructor and the extensive requirements placed on the learner who would need to be capable of and motivated sufficiently to engage in self-directed learning. Finally, Clara and Barbera (2014) noted that the theory is unable to explain a range of significant learning phenomena.

GROUPS, NETS, AND SETS

Dron and Anderson (2014) expanded the discussion of social networks and inter-actions within formalized education; specifically to differentiate three important but substantively different contexts in which connectivist learning is employed.

The first of these learning contexts is the familiar *group*. Groups, typically referred to as "classes" in formal education systems, are secure places where students aggregate (face-to-face or online) and proceed through a series of inde-pendent and/or collaborative learning activities. Groups tend to be housed in closed environments with strong leadership from an instructor or group owner, and, in formal education, might be temporally bounded by an academic term. These synchronized activities result in learners supporting each other, and levels of trust can be built such that learners collaboratively engage, support, and cri-tique each other. In well-organized groups, considerable social, cognitive, and teaching presence is developed to create a community of inquiry (Garrison & Anderson, 2003). However, groups are also noted for the development of hidden curricula, constrictive and occasionally coercive acts, groupthink, and teacher dependency (Downes, 2006).

A second form of aggregation is called the *network*. Networked learning activities expand connectivity beyond the learning management system (LMS) to allow learners, alumni, and the general public to engage in formulating networked learning opportunities (see chapter 9). Network membership is much more fluid than that of groups, where leadership is emergent rather than imposed and networks easily expand or contract as learners use the network to solve problems. Networks are less temporally bonded and may continue to exist long after formal study terminates.

The third aggregation we call the *set*. Sets are created by a shared interest or characteristic, and can be of enormous value in education. For example, when an instructor polls a classroom (using a show of hands or clickers), this method helps determine the set of students who correctly understand a concept. More recently wikis have had the ability to aggregate and extract knowledge from the set of individuals with interest/expertise in any topic. Learning in sets involves aggregating and synthesizing the myriad activities that occur in online environments. The application of knowledge gained by these aggregations can cause particular challenges for learning. For example, searching very large aggregations of resources online (such as with Google, YouTube, or Flickr), and filtering these resources for perceived value or use permits learners to selectively mine the activities of thousands of individuals. These types of filtering can be socially magnified through collaborative resource tagging services, such as citeulike.org and diig.com, or through systematic curation websites, such as Pinterest or Learnist. Sets face challenges as well: contagion, crowd stupidity, filter bubbles, and privacy invasion are possible tribulations. However, sets also allow learners to benefit from traces, recommendations, and activities of others. It is through the digital traces of others that learners may formulate connected pathways to accessible online learning resources. This discussion of groups, nets, and sets continues to expand for educational purposes as learning activities capitalize on the use of collective intelligence and teaching the crowd (Dron & Anderson, 2014).

THRESHOLD CONCEPTS

Throughout my career, I have been working and struggling with teachers as they learn to integrate emerging technologies and pedagogies into their practice. It always seems to be hard work and results are not always either as I had hoped or planned. Thus, I end this chapter with a brief overview of theories designed to help both adopters and change agents working with emerging technologies in education.

The growing literature on "disruptive" technologies introduced by Christensen (1997) continues to be discussed in education. Although the notion that everything new is disruptive has resulted in overuse of the term, and the value of the theory for predictive use has been questioned (Lepore, 2014), there is little doubt that many of Christensen's descriptions resonate with the educational sector. In fact, Christensen has written two books directly applying his disruptive technology theories to education (Christensen, 1997; Christensen, Horn, & Johnson, 2008). Readers may, however, be less familiar with the notion of 'threshold concepts."

The theory of threshold concepts identifies attributes that impact teaching and learning issues: "Threshold concepts are 'conceptual gateways' or 'portals' that lead to a previously inaccessible, and initially perhaps 'troublesome', way of thinking about something" (Meyer & Land, 2005, p. 373–74).

Of particular interest is the notion that changing one's approach and behaviour, and thus one's design, through the application of emerging technology involves instructors wrestling with very significant "threshold concepts"—what Ross and Collier call "messiness" in chapter 2. McGowen (2012) identified two such thresholds that instructors must experience:

> First they may have a preconception that technology is merely an add-on, not an integral part, of teaching; and, second, they believe that they should know exactly what they are doing before using new technology in the classroom, resisting a period of experimentation, or even play, that others find helpful when teaching with technology. (p. 25)

Meyer and Land (2005) identified four characteristics of threshold concepts:

Transformational. The ideas of learner centeredness, produsage of content, extensive sharing with peers and other features of the current generation of emerging technologies force a transformation of teachers from source of information to facilitator of learning (chapters 5, 11). The technologies also spill out beyond professional practice to both support and challenge activities in many other social, political and commercial activities.

Integrative. Following from complexity theory, new adopters find that the use of emerging technologies tends to open new possibilities while making others redundant. Only through deeper understanding can educators learn to change parts of their environment to integrate with the changes induced by the use of emerging technologies and practices.

Irreversible. Learning to teach (as we were taught to teach or observed other teachers) forced us across threshold concepts. Teaching effectively with emerging technologies, likewise, forces educators to relearn, to reconceptualize, and to abandon obsolete practices.

Troublesome. Emerging technologies and practices, like any substantive change, challenge older ways of doing things, which are often defended by the vested interests of learners, instructors, and institutions.

Thus educators as both adopters and change agents need to overcome challenges to disruption and be ready to cross over their own "threshold concepts" as well as those of their colleagues and students, "resisting constraints of thought and action" (chapter 2).

CONCLUSION

This brief overview is intended to illustrate how learning and learning designs that use emerging technologies can be enhanced via the lens of theory. A historical theoretical lens allows us to conceptualize how learning and teaching interactions affect outcomes. Much of our understanding of how and why learning happens and the best ways to design effective learning activities is enhanced when we work from theoretical models. The net, with its affordances, seems to speed up and accentuate many of the ideas found in online learning theories.

However, as much as theories add value, these same pedagogical foundations also need to evolve to account for networked affordances, digital disruptions (Christensen et al., 2008), and unanticipated consequences (Taleb, 2007). We are witnessing the birth and refinement of learning theories that work under the assumption of the ubiquitous net. Like online and networked cultures, these learning theories borrow from and expand pre-net ideas to consider how our teaching and learning practices support new ways in which knowledge is created, shared, and refined.

REFERENCES

Anderson, T. (2003). Getting the mix right: An updated and theoretical rationale for interaction. *International Review of Research in Open and Distance Learning*, 4(2). Retrieved from http://www.irrodl.org/index. php/irrodl/article/view/149/708

——. (2004a). The educational semantic web: A vision for the next phase of educational computing. *Educational Technology*, 44(5), 5–9.

——. (2004b). Towards a theory of online learning. In T. Anderson & F. Elloumni (eds.), *Theory and practice of online learning* (pp. 271–94). Athabasca, AB: Athabasca University.

———. (2005). Distance learning: Social software's killer app? Paper presented at the ODLAA Conference, Adelaide. Retrieved from http://auspace. athabascau.ca/bitstream/2149/2328/1/distance_learning.pdf

Anderson, T., & Garrison, D.R. (1998). Learning in a networked world: New roles and responsibilities. In C. Gibson (ed.), *Distance learners in higher education* (pp. 97–112). Madison, WI: Atwood Publishing.

Anderson, T., & Whitelock, D. (2004). The educational semantic web: Visioning and practicing the future of education. *Journal of Interactive Media in Education, 1*. Retrieved from http://www-jime.open.ac.uk/2004/1

Bernard, R. M., Abrami, P. C., Borokhovski, E., Wade, C. A., Tamim, R. M., Surkes, M. A., & Bethel, E. C. (2009). A meta-analysis of three types of interaction treatments in distance education. *Review of Educational Research, 79*(3), 1243–89.

Blaschke, L. M. (2012). Heutagogy and lifelong learning: A review of heutagogical practice and self-determined learning. *International Review of Research in Open and Distance Learning, 13*(1), 56–71.

Bruns, A. (2008). *Blogs, Wikipedia, Second Life, and beyond: From production to produsage.* New York: Lang.

Christensen, C. (1997). *The innovator's dilemma: When new technologies cause great firms to fail.* Cambridge, MA: Harvard University Press.

Christensen, C., Horn, M., & Johnson, C. (2008). *Disrupting class: How disruptive innovation will change the way the world learns.* New York: McGraw Hill.

Doctorow, C. (2001). Metacrap: Putting the torch to seven straw-men of the meta-utopia. Retrieved from http://www.well.com/~doctorow/metacrap. htm#0

Downes, S. (2006, October 16). Learning networks and connective knowledge. Posted on IT Forum (paper 92). Retrieved from http://itforum.coe.uga.edu/paper92/paper92.html

Dron, J., & Anderson, T. (2014). *Teaching crowds: Learning and social media.* Edmonton, AB: Athabasca University Press.

Garrison, D. R., & Anderson, T. (2003). *E-Learning in the 21st century.* London: Routledge.

Giannakos, M. N., Chorianopoulos, K., Ronchetti, M., Szegedi, P., & Teasley, S. D. (2013). Analytics on video-based learning. Paper presented at the Proceedings of the Third International Conference on Learning Analytics and Knowledge, Leuven, Belgium.

Hase, S., & Kenyon, C. (2000). From andragogy to heutagogy. *UltiBase.* Retrieved from http://www.psy.gla.ac.uk/~steve/pr/Heutagogy.html

———. (2007). Heutagogy: A child of complexity theory. *Complicity: An International Journal of Complexity and Education, 4*(1), 111–18. Retrieved www.complexityandeducation.ualberta.ca/ COMPLICITY4/documents/ Complicity_41k_HaseKenyon.pdf

Horn, J. (2008). Human research and complexity theory. *Educational Philosophy and Theory, 40*(1).

Kalfoglou, Y., Alani, H., Schorlemmer, M., & Walton, C. (2004). On the emergent semantic web and overlooked issues. In S. McIlraith, D. Plexousakis, & F. van Harmelen (Eds.), *The Semantic Web –ISWC 2004* (pp. 576–90). Berlin: Springer.

Kanuka, H., & Anderson, T. (1999). Using constructivism in technology-mediated learning: Constructing order out of the chaos in the literature. *Radical Pedagogy, 2*(1). Retrieved from http://www.radicalpedagogy.org/ radicalpedagogy.org/Using_Constructivism_in_Technology-Mediated_ Learning__Constructing_Order_out_of_the_Chaos_in_the_Literature.html

Kerr, B. (2007). A challenge to connectivism. Transcript of Keynote Speech. Paper presented at the Online Connectivism Conference. Retrieved from http://ltc.umanitoba.ca/wiki/index.php?title=Kerr_Presentation

Kop, R., & Hill, A. (2008). Connectivism: Learning theory of the future or vestige of the past? *International Review of Research in Open and Distance Learning, 9*(3). Retrieved from http://www.irrodl.org/index.php/irrodl/ article/view/523/1103

Koper, R., & Tattersall, C. (2004). New directions for lifelong learning using network technologies. *British Journal of Educational Technology, 35*(6), 689–700.

Larreamendy-Joerns, J., & Leinhardt, G. (2006). Going the distance with online education. *Review of Educational Research, 76*(4), 567–605.

Lewin, K. (1952). *Field theory in social science: Selected theoretical papers.* London: Tavistock.

Liemhetcharat, S., & Veloso, M. (2012). Modeling and learning synergy for team formation with heterogeneous agents. Paper presented at the Proceedings of the 11th International Conference on Autonomous Agents and Multiagent Systems, Volume 1, Valencia, Spain. Retrieved from http:// dl.acm.org/citation.cfm?id=2343628

Mayer, R. (2001). Multimedia Learning. Cambridge: Cambridge University Press.

McElroy, M. (2000). Integrating complexity theory, knowledge management and organizational learning. *Journal of Knowledge Management, 4*(3),195–203. Retrieved from 10.1108/13673270010377652

Meyer, J. F., & Land, R. (2005). Threshold concepts and troublesome knowledge (2): Epistemological considerations and a conceptual framework for teaching and learning. *Higher Education, 49*(3), 373–88. http://dx.doi.org/10.1007/s10734-004-6779-5.

Moore, M. (1989). Three types of interaction. *American Journal of Distance Education, 3*(2), 1–6.

Popper, K.R. (1968). *The logic of scientific discovery*. New York: Harper and Row.

Sato, G. Y., Azevedo, H. J., & Barthès, J.-P. A. (2012). Agent and multi-agent applications to support distributed communities of practice: A short review. *Autonomous Agents and Multi-Agent Systems, 25*(1), 87–129

Siemens, G. (2005). A learning theory for the digital age. *Instructional Technology and Distance Education, 2*(1), 3–10. Retrieved from http: www.elearnspace.org/Articles/connectivism.htm

———. (2005, April 5). Connectivism: A learning theory for the digital age. *Elearnspace*. Retrieved from http://www.elearnspace.org/Articles/connectivism.htm

Sloep, P., van Rosmalen, P., Brouns, F., van Bruggen, J., de Croock, M., Kester, L., & de Vries, F. (2004). Agent support for online learning. Open Universiteit Nederland Educational Technology Expertise Centre. Retrieved from http://dspace.learningnetworks.org/retrieve/498/Agent_support_for_online_learning.pdf

Taleb, N. (2007). *The black swan: The impact of the highly improbable*. New York: Random House.

Tancer, B. (2008). *Click: Unexpected insights for business and life*. New York: Hyperion.

Verhagen, P. (2006). Connectivism: A new learning theory? *SurfSpace*. Retrieved from http://www.connectivism.ca/?p=75

Vygotsky, L., & Luria, A. (1981). The genesis of higher mental functions. In J. V. Wertsch (ed.), *The concept of activity in Soviet psychology* (pp. 144–88). Armonk, NY: Sharpe.

Wenger, E., Trayner, B., & de Latt, M. (2011). Promoting and assessing value creation in communities and networks: A conceptual framework. Ruud de Moor Centru, Open Universiat, Netherlands, 18. http://www.open.ou.nl/rslmlt/Wenger_Trayner_DeLaat_Value_creation.pdf.

4   Emerging Technology Integration Models

▶ *Royce Kimmons and Cassidy Hall*

This chapter explores theoretical models of technology integration, which have emerged in response to new technologies, and the criteria we should use to evaluate them. In chapter 3, Anderson describes how theories "force us to look deeply at big picture issues and grapple with the reasons why our technology use is likely to enhance teaching and learning." Focusing on what he terms "net-centric theories of learning," he explains how emerging approaches to education, such as connectivism, have evolved in connection with the web and empowered educators and learners to exploit its new affordances. Just as theory is essential for understanding the interface between emerging technologies and learning, theoretical models are essential for guiding thoughtful technology integration practices in existing educational contexts. In recent years we have seen the birth of a number of models and frameworks intent upon guiding meaningful technology adoption in both K-12 and higher education settings. Yet, as a field, we have not maturely explored how to reconcile competing or conflicting models and frameworks with one another nor even considered the possibility of evaluating theoretical models on the basis of their utility in practice.

Practitioners and researchers commonly use technology integration models to guide their educational technology initiatives in face-to-face and online settings. Such models may be seen as lenses through which we interpret the role that technology plays in the learning process and the effects that it has upon learning experiences and outcomes.

As stated by Veletsianos in chapter 1, emerging technologies and emerging practices may not be strictly defined by newness, are evolving, are not yet fully understood, and are potentially disruptive but mostly unfulfilled. Technology integration models are frameworks that one can use to guide thinking around the use of emerging technologies in education and as such provide a way to examine the myriad ways stakeholders make decisions pertaining to technology use, adoption, and integration.

As theoretical constructs, technology integration models empower researchers and practitioners to ask certain questions and to understand technology integration in key ways. Much like the lens of a telescope, these models have great practical value for improving perceptions and guiding inquiry, and it is for this reason that various technology integration models have been posited in recent years as means for understanding technology integration phenomena. Some prominent examples include the Technological Pedagogical and Content Knowledge (TPACK) model, Substitution Augmentation Modification Redefinition (SAMR) model, Replacement Amplification Transformation (RAT) model, Technology Integration Matrix (TIM), Technology Acceptance Model (TAM), and Technology Integration Planning (TIP) model. Each provides different opportunities for understanding and interpreting technology integration efforts.

Within the educational literature, different models exhibit different levels of adoption. Some are widely adopted across geographic regions and content areas, while others have more isolated adoption. It is unclear from the literature why some groups adopt certain models over others, and throughout the literature there is typically little discussion about competing models and reasons for choosing one over another. Rather, it seems that technology integration models are adopted based on convenience and comfort on the part of adoptees without any clear explanation as to why. Furthermore, because the education field is permeated with a general sense of theoretical pluralism, which allows for competing and contradictory theoretical constructs to coexist and enjoy pragmatic use among practitioners and researchers, there does not seem to be a call for adoptees of different models to seek consensus or to reconcile models with one another. As a result, the educational literature does not contain a robust discussion of theory development in this regard, and it seems to be the norm that alternative theories need not compete with one another. Instead, they may be adopted and discarded based upon the current attitudes of the individual and trends in the field.

Researchers suggest that such theoretical concepts would benefit from ongoing development and critical discussion (Graham, 2011; Kimmons, 2015). The method by which discussion should occur is not clear, however, because theorists must reconcile the perceived value of theoretical pluralism with the clear need to create standardized conceptual understandings. Furthermore, there does not seem to be a general sense of urgency in this regard, because adoptees may view particular models as superior to alternatives without requiring clear and explicit criteria for doing so.

"GOOD" THEORETICAL CONSTRUCTS

Though we often quote Lewin's (1951) famous statement that "there is nothing so practical as a good theory" (p. 169), we have not taken the step together as a field of considering what constitutes good theory nor considered the tautological implications of Lewin's statement that the quality of theoretical concepts should be evaluated based upon their practicality. Rather, it seems that we have heretofore been content with assuming that the value of a theoretical concept, like beauty, lies in the eye of the beholder.

This general lack of theoretical discussion may have serious implications for the credibility and validity of the educational technology field as a site of serious academic endeavor (Selwyn, 2011) and has left us in a strange predicament: though we may believe that theoretical models are good insofar as they are practical, we have not as a field established methods for determining model practicality (and therefore value). Likewise, we have not maturely considered the possibility that some theoretical models may be more appropriate in certain contexts than others. Rather, the flavor of the educational literature in this regard seems to be highly subjective and uncritical, wherein a theoretical model may be adopted for a particular research study, but no justification is provided as to why the model was chosen over alternatives; models themselves are not critically evaluated based upon empirical outcomes. We seem to subjectively choose models and allow those models to dictate how we interpret our findings, rather than using our findings to drive theoretical model development and adoption.

In previous work, we and other authors have explored the affordances and limitations of specific models along with recognized needs for ongoing theory development (Brantley-Dias & Ertmer, 2014; Graham, 2011; Kimmons, 2015), but this has been done without standardized expectations of the function that theoretical models should fulfill, and we have typically done so with a single, monolithic perspective of educational context dictating how we interpret a given model's value. Yet it seems obvious that if theoretical models represent ways of perceiving technology integration, then the value of a model will be established upon the expectations and assumptions of those who wield it.

In our outreach and teaching efforts, we find the use of technology integration models to be extremely helpful for teaching various stakeholders about technology integration, but we also find that certain models are more appropriate for some situations than others. For this reason we do not believe that there is a single total package of theoretical concepts that serves all the needs represented by stakeholder groups, but we do believe that existing models may be effectively applied to address education needs as educators come to understand the value of each model and the criteria that make each model a good fit for some contexts and a poor fit for others.

As practitioners and researchers who have explored technology integration across a number of contexts, we believe that technology integration is a highly complex process that needs to include multiple considerations in order to be successful. For this reason, we embrace theoretical pluralism in the field and contend that various models are appropriate and valuable in different contexts. Technology integration models are very diverse and, like tools in the hands of a carpenter, should be applied in a manner that is contextually appropriate and that properly meshes the model with intended goals. We also believe that technology integration models should serve to guide and simplify, rather than confuse and obfuscate, the process of technology integration. We are therefore frustrated with a lack of clarity regarding model selection.

In this chapter, we propose a set of criteria that we believe to be important when weighing the value of any given model. Any model that would truly encompass all pieces and roles of technology integration would be far too complex to apply and remain valuable. Though we believe that no single theoretical model should reasonably be expected to be all things to all people, we also believe that there should be some general framework for model selection that allows us to match a model's strengths to the value systems of potential adoptees.

SIX CRITERIA

Throughout this discussion, we hold that technology integration is a complex process that is influenced by nuances of context (chapters 1, 2, 7). For this reason, we anticipate that some models will be more valuable to some groups than others but also anticipate that these determinations of value are not purely arbitrary but are rather based in structured value systems representing the beliefs, needs, desires, and intents of adoptees. As such, this chapter aims to provide a set of standardized criteria for establishing the value of one model over another. We propose that the following six criteria may be used to help individuals meaningfully match models to the needs and interests of diverse stakeholders: compatibility, scope, fruitfulness, role of technology, student outcomes, and, clarity.

We will now proceed by describing each criterion and discussing how each connects to technology integration models and adoption.

Compatibility

The notion of compatibility is derived from Rogers' (2003) work on the diffusion of innovations and refers to the alignment between a technology integration model's design and existing educational and pedagogical practices. Some models are created with practitioners in mind and seek to be easily applied, while others threaten to disrupt or alter practice or have no clear bearing on the day-to-day work of educators. This means that models exhibiting high compatibility will likely be welcomed by practitioners for their directedness and ease of implementation, while models with low compatibility would be rejected due to burden of implementation and lack of connection to existing goals and practices.

For example, the SAMR model (Puentedura, 2006) is widely used by practitioners, and this is likely due to the fact that the model is generally compatible with existing practices and guides educators through four phases or hierarchical stages of technology adoption. The SAMR model conceives of technology integration as a progression of four levels of impact (Substitution, Augmentation, Modification, and Redefinition), which are organized into two categories (Enhancement and Transformation). The first two levels (substitution and augmentation) fall under the enhancement category. Substitution applies to technology use as a direct tool substitute with no functional change, while augmentation refers to technology as a direct tool substitute with functional improvements. An example of this distinction would include utilizing a printed copy of a test (substitution) versus an electronic copy of a test (augmentation). Both examples utilize technology as a direct substitute for previous practice (typewritten tests), but the functional difference would be that the electronic copy could provide an improvement by cutting down on paper and providing immediate feedback to students. These two enhancement levels are transitional, with the goal to move to higher levels. The third and fourth levels (modification and redefinition), on the other hand, fall under the transformation category, which means that technology is being used to change practice. In the modification level, the technology allows for significant task redesign, while in the redefinition stage, the technology allows for the creation of new tasks that were previously inconceivable. At both of these levels, technology transforms what is happening in the classroom, but modification emphasizes practices with technology (such as podcasts), while the redefinition stage treats technology as a catalyst for enacting new patterns in student learning (such as project creation through technology).

The author of the SAMR model maintains an active blog and encourages others to share and adapt the model. The blog promotes flexible adaptation of the model to a variety of educational contexts. This alignment makes the model valuable to those who are entrenched in educational systems and are looking for a way to guide phased approaches to technology integration. SAMR likely appeals to teachers because they can easily identify a method for progression within the model and gradually move toward integrating technology within their existing learning environments.

Such compatibility would not be important to innovators, however, who may view existing educational practices as being in need of reform; leaders who are removed from day-to-day processes of teaching and learning may also not find it useful. For those who seek to use technology as a catalyst for promoting change in the status quo, models that are compatible with existing systems may be viewed as ways to reinforce the status quo and to undermine technology's potential as a social catalyst. For this reason, we anticipate that compatibility, as a valuable criterion for model selection, would be determined by stakeholders' attitudes toward and perceptions of existing educational systems. As such, the model will likely be favored by educators, designers, and local administrators but be viewed less favorably by those who are situated further from practice.

Scope

The concept of scope emerges from the works of Kuhn (2013) and Papert (1987) and deals with the depth of questioning inherent in a model and the intended purposes for integration. Some models are developed to interrogate fundamental problems of teaching, learning, and educational practice, dealing with the "why" of integration and a global scope, while others take a more technocratic approach, dealing with the "how" of integration and a local scope. Models that exhibit a more global scope may seek to catalyze social reform through effective integration, while those that exhibit a more local scope may focus on improving a single lesson plan. Papert (1987) argues that technology can serve to accentuate existing rifts in educational theory and to encourage us to push forward theory and philosophy. However, he also explains that we can mistakenly view the field in a technocentric manner, wherein we ascribe causation to technology and focus only on application. Models that provide global scope lead us to reconsider and explore assumptions about teaching, learning, and social structures, while technocentric or local models lead us to think about how we can layer technology within existing practice.

For example, connectivism (Siemens, 2005) may be framed as a technology integration model that exhibits global scope and avoids technocentrism insofar as it seeks to propose an entirely new learning theory for the digital age. According to Siemens (2005), accepted learning theories such as behaviorism, cognitivism, and constructivism were developed before learning was affected by digital technologies, and the emerging digital world requires us to rethink the relationship between learners and knowledge and the contexts in which learning takes place. As argued in chapter 2, "born digital" versions of online education may need to be theorized under alternative perspectives. Within a connectivist framework, for example, knowledge is distributed between learners and nonhuman appliances (such as databases or websites), and the purpose of learning has shifted toward improving access between the learner and information sources. Unlike other models of technology integration that treat technology as an external component that must be merged into pre-existing practices of teaching and learning, connectivism holds that learning itself is fundamentally changing as a result of technology, and integration for educational institutions means to alter institutional processes and policies to align with these new and emerging standards of learning and knowing. As such, meaningful technology integration from a connectivist perspective considers issues of information flow and ownership, cycles of knowledge creation, and the development of literacies among learners for navigating and effectively utilizing information networks.

Based on this characterization, scope and compatibility may seem at odds with one another: models that excel in compatibility may be perceived as supporting the status quo, while models with global scope may be perceived as supporting sweeping change. It may be, though, that a model can exhibit both compatibility and global scope if we consider that compatibility may extend to beliefs and attitudes in addition to practice. For instance, teachers may find themselves operating in educational institutions that do not align with their beliefs about what constitutes effective practice. High-stakes testing and standardized curricula are examples of situations in which teachers may espouse one way of thinking but operate in a system that espouses another. In each case, certain technology integration models might be applied that are compatible with teacher beliefs but that seek to undermine artifacts of the institution (thereby exhibiting both compatibility and global scope).

Global scope may not be meaningful to stakeholders whose aim is to merely incorporate technology into existing systems, however. If the system is acceptable in its present state, the technology is not recognized as a potential catalyst for change, or the adopter has no interest in enacting sweeping reform, then global scope may not be valued. For instance, a teacher merely seeking to enhance a lesson through the introduction of a new technology may find little value in a model that encourages her to completely rethink the aims of educational institutions generally. Thus, models that exhibit global scope, like connectivism, may be more useful for those seeking to rethink educational institutions, while models with local scope, like TIP or TPACK, would be more valuable for those dealing with more focused or discrete problems of technology integration.

Fruitfulness

The concept of fruitfulness is derived from Kuhn (2013), who explains that a good theoretical model should "be fruitful of new research findings . . . [and] disclose new phenomena or previously unnoted relationships among those already known" (p. 75). In this sense, a fruitful technology integration model would be adopted by a diversity of users for diverse purposes and yield valuable results crossing disciplines and traditional silos of practice. In contrast, an unfruitful model would be generally ignored or only be adopted in a manner that promotes siloing and dissuades interdisciplinary practice.

TPACK is an example of a fruitful technology integration model. Proposed by Mishra and Koehler (2006, 2007), the TPACK model of technology integration asserts that teaching with technology is difficult to do well and requires a complex set of skills incorporating three domains of knowledge: technology, pedagogy, and content. Often using a Venn diagram to illustrate relationships between these three domains, TPACK holds that knowledge domains interact with one another to create additional domains (e.g., Shulman's (1986) PCK or pedagogical content knowledge). These new domains are more than the sum of their parts, and TPACK represents the complex knowledge needed for a teacher to apply technology in educationally beneficial ways. Just as someone who understands pedagogical theory and understands mathematical content might not be able to connect the two in a way that is educationally valuable for teaching elementary mathematics, for teachers to effectively integrate technology into teaching and learning, they must not only have necessary pedagogical, content, and technical knowledge but must also understand how these three constituent components interact with one another and can be applied effectively in a given situation to support deep, meaningful learning with technology.

TPACK exhibits fruitfulness in that it has been adopted by various researchers and practitioners spanning disciplines. Because TPACK recognizes the importance of content knowledge in technology integration, specialists in different fields may feel comfortable using it as a model, because it validates the importance of their areas of expertise. Numerous research studies have been conducted that connect the TPACK model to teacher beliefs and attitudes, and a wide array of professional organizations and journal special issues suggest that the model has been fruitful in creating and sustaining meaningful conversations about technology integration.

Adopters of technology integration models might find value in fruitful models for their potential to span disciplines and generate meaningful conversation in a common language. If a model represents a commonly accepted way of thinking about a phenomenon that spans disciplines, then researchers focused on improving practice will be drawn to that model. All else being equal, however, fruitfulness may have little value to practitioners and researchers that do not mind operating within the silo of a single discipline or institution or to those who are not seeking to contribute to larger conversations of effective technology integration.

Role of technology

Technology plays different roles in different models. As alluded to in the discussion of *scope* above, technology can be seen as a means to an end or as an end itself. Some models view technology as a means for achieving socially valuable ends or for improving learning, while other models may treat technology integration itself as the goal. Because technology integration occurs within social contexts wherein attempts at integration may be mandated or expected, some may feel compelled to integrate technology without having a firm understanding of how such integration will meaningfully influence the learning environment. This may compel such adopters to view technology integration as the goal, thereby adopting models that treat technology as an end.

CAST's (2011) Universal Design for Learning (UDL) is an approach to technology integration that emphasizes the importance of addressing learners' uniqueness, strengths, and needs in curricular decision-making, thereby formulating the role of technology as a means to support access and learning. UDL is comprised of three principles. Each principle contains three guidelines and each guideline contains several checkpoints. The three principles of UDL suggest that technology should be used to:

1. Provide multiple means of representation;
2. Provide multiple means of action and expression;
3. Provide multiple means for engagement.

Every guideline in UDL can be achieved via technology, and part of the strength of UDL as a model for technology integration lies in thinking about technology as a means for minimizing barriers to students while maximizing learning outcomes. In this way, technology integration is only valuable if it helps to achieve the three principles of UDL, and integration that does not achieve these principles is not seen as valuable.

Some groups view technology integration as an end, while others view integration as a means to some other end (such as, say, universal access). Because models are created with a specific role for technology in mind, technology integration models will treat technology as either a means or an end, and potential adopters will be drawn to those models that align with their views. For example, a practitioner who has been mandated to integrate technology in some manner into her curriculum would likely be drawn to models that treat technology as an end, because if technology adoption alone is the goal, then treating technology as an end seems to be the simplest way of achieving it. In contrast, a researcher that seeks to improve learning in a specific subject area would likely be drawn to models that treat technology as a means to another end (in this case, improving learning). In both cases, model selection would be driven by the vision of the adopter and how seamlessly potential models align with that vision.

Student outcomes

In our current culture of high-stakes testing and mandatory improvement, discernible student outcomes are of great interest (chapter 10), and much of the rhetoric surrounding technology integration focuses on improving student achievement. Yet not every technology integration model includes the incorporation of student outcomes or the expectation that integration will produce a discernible impact. Similarly, though some models may allude to student outcomes, they may not give these outcomes a primary role in the technology integration process. On the other hand, some models incorporate student outcomes into their core formulations and encourage adopters to consider these outcomes prior to commencing technology integration.

The Technology Integration Planning (TIP) model is grounded on instructional design theory and consists of seven phases, which comprise three clusters of activity, to guide technology integration (Roblyer & Doering, 2013). The first cluster represents an analysis of learning and teaching needs and includes two phases: first, determine the relative advantage of the integration, and second, assess TPACK. This first cluster is the only cluster in the model that is not revisited later in the process, while all other clusters are recursive. The second cluster, planning for integration, consists of three phases: decide on objectives and assessments, design integration strategies, and prepare the instructional environment. And the third cluster, post-instruction analysis and revisions, includes the final phases: analyze results and make revisions. After determining outcomes, the third cluster cycles back to the second cluster, revisiting the planning stages in hopes of improving learning and allowing the adopter to solve problems and improve efficiencies.

A great strength of TIP is that it presents a need to plan prior to choosing a technology, thereby forcing adopters to clearly state intended student outcomes at the outset. These expectations are then revisited and evaluated, and the integration pattern is adjusted to address discrepancies between intended outcomes and actual results. It is expected that this type of approach would lead to thoughtful and impactful technology integration efforts that give primacy to student outcomes.

Models that meaningfully incorporate student outcomes would be of great value to those charged with improving achievement in a measurable manner. It may be, however, that not all benefits of technology integration are measurable or readily discernible (e.g., soft skills) and that not all technology integration efforts should be focused on students (e.g., improving institutional efficiencies). As a result, those who seek to achieve these types of results may find models that focus heavily on student outcomes to be burdensome or inappropriate.

Clarity

Finally, technology integration models vary in their clarity, in terms of both their formulation and their ongoing refinement. Clear models are simple and easy to understand conceptually and in practice, while unclear models are confusing and may be misinterpreted. Reasons for variations in clarity may vary, but some models are clearer because they are simply stated and have limited scope. Others are unclear, because much has been written to refine and extend them. In general, clear models benefit from being easier to explain and utilize, while fuzzier or more confusing models are difficult to explain, or introduce uncertainty.

For example, the RAT (Replacement, Amplification, and Transformation) model of technology integration (Hughes, 2005) exhibits a high level of clarity when compared to some of its counterparts. This model proposes that technology integration in educational settings may be interpreted by considering the impact that the introduction of technology has upon educational activities and desired outcomes, and these impacts may be categorized in one of three (mutually exclusive) categories: replacement, amplification, or transformation. Instances of *replacement* would include situations wherein introduction of technology does not change the activity being performed but rather moves it into a new medium; *amplification* would include instances of technology integration wherein its introduction improved efficiencies of an existing practice; and *transformation* would include applications of technology that fundamentally change previous practices or empower participants to do things that they could not have done without technology. In its current form, the model does not suggest that the three classifications are hierarchical or that instances of technology integration should seek to be of a certain type, though replacement may likely be interpreted as inferior to the other two.

A major affordance of this model is that it empowers researchers and practitioners to ask concrete questions about technology integration, critically evaluating their reasons for incorporating technology. An example question might be: Does the use of social media in our online course merely replace an existing practice or is it empowering us to do something new? Because RAT treats all instances of technology integration as being amenable to classification in one of the three categories, it is fairly simple for educators to comprehend and use the model to analyze a particular case of technology integration. Also, since these classifications appeal to common sense and utilize definitions that may be applied with some level of certainty across contexts, the RAT model removes many difficulties of contextual interpretation and creates a generalizable standard.

Models that exhibit a high level of clarity would be valuable in helping to remove the interpretive guesswork that goes along with less clear models. Practitioners need clear models to recognize how they should implement technologies across contexts, and researchers similarly need them for evaluation purposes. However, the use and integration of technology is a complex and nuanced process (chapter 1, 2), and clearer models may problematically lead to reductionist thinking by being overly simplistic. Thus, those focused on theory development or integration across diverse contexts may find less value in clear models due to their simplicity.

CONCLUSION

In this chapter, we argued that the field needs mechanisms to evaluate "good" theory when it comes to technology integration and we outlined six criteria for comparing theoretical models in a meaningful way. These criteria should not be used to universally evaluate models hierarchically. We believe, however, that they may be useful for aligning the strengths of particular models with the prioritized needs of potential adopters. For instance, an instructor who is being asked to teach online for the first time will likely need clear guidance on how to foster student outcomes, and would be drawn to a model that exhibits high marks in clarity and student outcomes, while a political leader intent on enacting large-scale social change using online education as a catalyst would be drawn to models that exhibit high marks in scope and role of technology.

To advance the use of technology integration models in online education, we must first create and validate mechanisms for evaluating models in accordance with adoptees' prioritized needs. For this reason, future work should empirically *identify* the prioritized needs of various groups and *evaluate* emerging models in accordance with these criteria. This chapter has served as a first step in considering what some of these criteria may be, and we encourage practitioners and researchers alike to continue the conversation around technology integration so that we can collaboratively improve theory and practice. By initiating this conversation, we hope to elicit responses from the scholarly community to refine and adjust the proposed criteria to meaningfully account for the perspectives of all groups who may benefit from technology integration model adoption. Through this process, we hope to fulfill and actualize the promise of emerging technologies and emerging practices in education.

REFERENCES

Brantley-Dias, L., & Ertmer, P. (2014). Goldilocks and TPACK: Is the construct "just right?" *Journal of Research on Technology in Education, 46*(2), 103–28.

CAST (2011). Universal design for learning guidelines (Version 2.0). *National Center on Universal Design for Learning*. Retrieved from http://www.udlcenter.org/aboutudl/udlguidelines.

Graham, C. (2011). Theoretical considerations for understanding technological pedagogical content knowledge (TPACK). *Computers and Education, 57*(3), 1953–1960.

Hughes, J. (2005). The role of teacher knowledge and learning experiences in forming technology-integrated pedagogy. *Journal of Technology and Teacher Education, 13*(2), 277–302.

Kimmons, R. (2015). Examining TPACK's theoretical future. *Journal of Technology and Teacher Education, 23*(1), 53–77.

Kuhn, T. (2013). Objectivity, value judgment, and theory choice. In A. Bird and J. Ladyman (eds.), *Arguing About Science* (pp. 74–86). New York: Routledge.

Lewin, K. (1951). *Field theory in social science.* Chicago: University of Chicago Press.

Mishra, P., & Koehler, M. J. (2006). Technological pedagogical content knowledge: A framework for teacher knowledge. *Teachers College Record, 108*(6), 1017–54.

——. (2007). Technological pedagogical content knowledge (TPCK): Confronting the wicked problems of teaching with technology. In R. Carlsen et al. (eds.), *Proceedings of Society for Information Technology and Teacher Education International Conference 2007* (pp. 2214–26). Chesapeake, VA: AACE.

Papert, S. (1987). Computer criticism vs. technocentric thinking. *Educational Researcher, 16*(1), 22–30.

Puentedura, R. (2006). Transformation, technology, and education. Presentation given August 18, 2006 as part of the Strengthening Your District Through Technology workshops, Maine, US. Retrieved from http://hippasus.com/resources/tte/part1.html.

Roblyer, M. D., & Doering, A. H. (2013). *Integrating educational technology into teaching* (6th ed.). Boston, MA: Pearson.

Rogers, E. (2003). *Diffusion of innovations* (5th ed.). New York: Free Press.

Selwyn, N. (2011). Editorial: In praise of pessimism—the need for negativity in educational technology. *British Journal of Educational Technology, 42*(5), 713–18.

Shulman, L. S. (1986). Those who understand: Knowledge growth in teaching. *Educational Researcher, 15*(2), 4–14.

Siemens, G. (2005). Connectivism: A learning theory for the digital age. Elearnspace. Retrieved from http://www.elearnspace.org/Articles/connectivism.htm.

(5) # Multiple Learning Roles in a Connected Age
When Distance Means Less Than Ever

▶ *Elizabeth Wellburn and B. J. Eib*

An ever-growing selection of emerging technologies and practices is having a profound impact on learning. Social technologies and online environments that reconfigure education challenge traditional education structures. In online social environments, individuals can switch seamlessly between the roles of expert, amateur, audience, author, learner, and educator. As we examine our learners' world outside of their formal learning environments, we see that Web 2.0 has redefined how information is created and shared, potentially enabling broad societal transformations. We must question whether informal learning has changed things so profoundly that traditional approaches to education are becoming irrelevant. Can educators embrace a multiplicity of roles and, with our learners and the general public, recognize and participate in dynamically and collaboratively constructed formal and informal personalized learning environments?

IMAGINE THE EXPERT AND THE AMATEUR

In the not-too-distant past, if we needed to learn something, we would almost certainly interact with an expert, either directly with an instructor or indirectly through some form of media (such as text documents, documentaries, photos, museum exhibits). In any of those scenarios, the source of information was filtered before it reached the learners (our teachers had to have received a set of credentials, the newspaper or book would have been edited by someone with recognized expertise). Shirky (2008) refers to this idea as the "filter then publish" model. If we eventually acquired enough information and received the appropriate degrees, we were then deemed as recognized experts ourselves, ready to be sought out by others.

This traditional role of expertise is being challenged today, with a broad range of individuals immersed as contributors and consumers of collaborative sources of information: blogs, wikis, social networks, video sharing sites, and citizen journalism websites. In this context, is it possible to ever acquire "enough" information? Which sources are to be trusted?

Unlike traditional information sources, the supply of contemporary online information has not been vetted in any conventional sense of the word. Perhaps because of this, the extent of new information constantly becoming available is unprecedented. As Johnson, Adams, Becker, Estrada, and Freeman (2014, p. 8), note: "Today's web users are prolific creators of content, and they upload photographs, audio, and video to the cloud by the billions. Producing, commenting, and classifying these media have become just as important as the more passive tasks of searching, reading, watching, and listening." For example, during a random five-day period in July 2014, Wikipedia added almost 5,000 articles, 34,000 pages, and 700,000 edits ("Wikipedia: About," 2014) and in January 2014, Facebook reported over 1 billion active users per month and most of them mobile users. As of July 2014, Twitter sees 58 million tweets a day (Statistic Brain, 2014) and YouTube reports that 100 hours of video are uploaded to the site every minute (YouTube, n.d.).

Given this influx of information created and disseminated by non-experts, is the concept of expertise changing, or vanishing entirely? Lin and Ranjit (2012) believe, "Knowledge creation and scholarly communication are moving away from the situation in which a few experts generate content to transmit to a set of users. Now there are various routes via a wide range of collaborative tools for research and content dissemination" (Lin & Ranjit, 2012, p. 2). Individuals without formal qualifications can contribute to the online information environment as easily as those who are recognized as experts. There is no guarantee, however, that when searching the Web we will find information that has authoritative weight. Is this a problem for us as educators or for education in general? If so, when is it a problem and when does it become a problem? What, if anything, should be done to address it?

In part, the changing role of expertise reflects the departure from another feature of the not-too-distant past: that it was often difficult to acquire proficiency in areas outside of one's own field, because the information was not available. Hobbies were possible, but in-depth niche learning was only for the individual who had enough time and/or money to fully pursue an area of interest. Additionally, geographic, occupational, and socioeconomic boundaries meant that a person might be isolated from any community that could support his or her growth. Today, a "passionate amateur" (Leadbeater, 2005) can easily engage with hobbies, interests, and academic and leisure pursuits in a way that is far beyond "dabbling," because information is widely and cheaply accessible, and the participatory nature of the web means that a two-way information flow is available to all. Both amateurs and experts, and all those in between, can access information, collaborate, and network online with others who share similar interests/passions. Learning can be reciprocal, with experts learning from and building upon the ideas generated by non-experts. Examples are plentiful, from the parent who put his child's medical records online to connect with researchers who might be able to work with him to help solve the puzzle of brain injury (Celizic, 2008), to stories of citizen journalism exposing events that would have been otherwise hidden, to the point where law enforcers, politicians, and others can never assume that anything is "off the record" (Slocum, 2008). Amateurs are contributing in ways that were impossible a few years ago. Shirky (2008) uses Linux—an open-source software based on suggestions solicited through an early bulletin-board style discussion forum demonstrating the potential for enormous success through the "global talent pool." If participation is cheap, even for amateurs, then it is easy to experiment with a multitude of ideas. A small but dedicated group of people can easily find each other and cooperate on projects of common interest. From profound projects, such as the work done through MIT's Center for Collective Intelligence (http://cci.mit.edu) to the more homespun and personal, such as the over 4 million knitters who connect via Ravelry (the fiber arts online community), ideas and information are being shared online like never before.

Even when experts collaborate they can now post their thinking and invite comments and contributions (Veletsianos, 2013). In particular, "social media has changed the nature of these important conversations so that they are not always behind doors, but instead viewed as an opportunity for substantial collective thinking and action" (Johnson, Adams Becker, Estrada, & Freeman, 2014, p. 9). For example, a University of Hawaii initiative aimed at encouraging faculty to re-envision the future of the higher education teaching profession (with social media as a major component) involved the broadcast of face-to-face sessions on YouTube so that anyone could participate in real-time discussions, which were encouraged and tracked with a unique hashtag on Twitter.

IMAGINE THE AUDIENCE AND THE AUTHORS

Prior to the participatory web, there was a clear distinction between an audience and a recognized author. The author was the rare individual who had enough information or talent to make it worthwhile financially to create an expensive publication; the audience was the rest of us who received that publication (or film, play, etc.). Authors who were rejected by traditional publishing houses could self-publish but this was an expensive proposition. Today, a writer can self-publish an e-book or buy specific services from companies who assist self-publishers. There are even companies that "print on demand" where printing occurs at the time of purchase (Finder, 2012) and self-publishing has been experiencing astronomical growth (see Flood, 2014).

This development is reflected by the characterization of Web 2.0 as the "read-write web" (O'Hear, 2006), as the participatory capabilities of the most recent Internet tools such as wikis or blogs allow content to be contributed and viewed by anyone who has web access. This means that small bits of information, generated by huge numbers of individuals, can be published to form vast information sources (e.g., Wikipedia). Shirky (2008) poses the vision of a world where large numbers of people contribute massive amounts of knowledge to online collaborative projects (such as Wikimedia projects), even when their contribution takes up only small portions of their time, drawn from what he calls the cognitive surplus (for instance, time that may have previously been spent watching television commercials). Large amounts of information are already abundant and freely accessible. If we are not able to find information we are searching for, we can request it (e.g., in a blog or micro-blogging platform) and it will be generated by our network. We can share our interpretations, comment, question, and critique information in a public sphere to generate further conversations. Wikipedia is a clear example of how the author and the audience are one and the same, since everyone who reads Wikipedia articles is also provided with the ability to edit and write them, as well as make comments and engage in discussion with other participants.

The ability to both generate and access information is facilitated by certain features of new, widely used technologies. Our mobile phones are Internet browsers, our computers are telephones, our tablets are both; we can send pictures and video clips instantaneously with the prospect of being viewed by millions, and we are easily able to listen to more voices than we've ever heard before. At our fingertips, at all times, the potential exists to be audience and author. It is therefore easy to become enthused if we know that it is simple to contribute, and that our small contributions can potentially be valuable. There is an increasing recognition of this and even in a formal educational context, "institutional leaders are increasingly seeing their students as creators rather than consumers" (Johnson et al., 2014, p. 7).

IMAGINE THE LEARNER AND THE EDUCATOR

Like expert/amateur and audience/author, the roles of learner and educator are increasingly becoming intermingled in the participatory web. Teachers have typically felt the pressure to keep up-to-date in their field, but it is a profound change that both the learner and the teacher have identical access to the same vast set of resources. Students are spending more time on the Internet than in the classroom as they increasingly look to it for information and news (Johnson et al., 2014, p. 32). Even more of a dilemma is the possibility that the learner may have a potential advantage by being more familiar with digital skills acquired through online participation (such as image manipulation, keyword refinement, etc.).

Such digital literacy can also lead learners to engage with information in new ways. Downes (2008) discusses how web technologies have fostered a more informal type of learning "based on a student's individual needs, rather than as predefined in a formal class, and based on a student's schedule, rather than that set by the institution." He goes on to describe how such informal learning involves "no boundaries; people drift into and out of the conversation as their knowledge and interests change" (Downes, 2008), and this concept has been integrated into the learning design he favours for massive open online courses (MOOCs), wherein learners participate in connectivist-oriented MOOCs (see chapters 2 and 9) in a similar fashion, drifting in and out as needed.

The counterpoint, showing learners' views of the traditional four-walled classroom, appears in a much-circulated YouTube video, "A Vision of Students Today" (Wesch, 2008b). Specifically the video explored how the structured environment does not connect with the learners' desire for informal learning and how the concept of categorized information does not fit with students' ways of freely accessing what they need to know. These learners explicitly state that they hate school but love learning. These learners want their education to be more relevant to life, just as they would access social networking sites in class rather than read textbooks or assigned readings. These learners do not see how multiple-choice questions will help them solve complex societal problems or allow them to succeed in a job that doesn't even exist yet; in the words of Perelman (1993), "school plods where human imagination naturally leaps" (p. 142).

Emerging approaches to education that are sometimes informed by such attitudes, such as MOOCs and competency-based models, are attracting a lot of attention—both positive and negative. What are the roles of teacher and student in a course with 30,000 students enrolled? What are the roles in self-paced courses with no instructor? Can MOOCs offer an effective way to move from formal education to personal learning (chapters 8 and 9)? Alternative assessment methods are being explored in an effort to recognize informal learning through badges and other micro-credentials.

Outside the realm of MOOCs, as today's methods of learning frequently use technology in either distance learning approaches or blended learning, educators are increasingly part of digital learning environments. Like almost all contemporary educators, we have arrived here through a system that embraced neither the notions of informal learning nor of the expert, amateur, audience, and author in the relationships described above. For instance, Liston, Whitcomb, and Borko (2009), among others, note that there is still a reliance on the transmission model of instruction wherever standardized testing is emphasized and this is detrimental to the personal development of students. We have, however, likely used some technology, and perhaps even created online resources through a learning management system (LMS). Are we confident that we are on the right path, or are we apprehensive?

One of the forms this apprehensiveness might take relates to concerns that the breadth and immediacy of informational access that new technologies facilitate could replace depth and analysis. A new responsibility seems to be upon us: to ensure that our learners have the opportunity to develop skills and literacies that are appropriate for deep learning from (or in spite of) the published but unfiltered information they are currently encountering.

THE PARTICIPATORY WEB AND OUR ROLES IN IT

From its early beginnings, the participatory web elicited diverse views with respect to education and learning. In this section we review the intriguing viewpoints of some authors that are relevant to learner and instructor roles.

Some critics:

Keen's (2007) *The Cult of the Amateur: How Today's Internet Is Killing Our Culture* expressed his concern regarding the watering-down of the concept of expertise and what he saw as the flood of misinformation. His more recent book, *Digital Vertigo* (2010), focuses on his view of social media as a threat to individual liberty; he speaks of collective self-destruction if we don't make the right choices.

Carr (2008) asked: "Is Google making us stupid?" He argued that hyperlinked reading on the Web was making us unable to focus on lengthier ideas, such as those in books. He now writes in terms of a larger "intellectual ethic" where technology is discouraging depth and encouraging skimming, thus optimizing us with respect to production and consumption but depriving us of the ability to reflect, concentrate, and contemplate.

Rosen (2013) asks "Are smartphones turning us into bad Samaritans?" and cites examples of tragedies (such as a subway shooting death) that many believe could have been averted if onlookers hadn't been engaged in cell phone use. In her 2008 book she described her concerns regarding multitasking causing neurological changes and loss of productivity.

Some enthusiasts include:

Clay Shirky, whose 2008 book *Here Comes Everybody* discussed how Web 2.0 allowed us to contribute collectively for the improvement of all by better using our cognitive surplus, published *Cognitive Surplus: Creativity and Generosity in a Connected Age* in 2010 which expanded on the idea of encouraging group work and experimentation in the various types of new social networks. In a recent blog post Shirky (2014) addressed the end of education's "golden era" not because of emerging technologies but because the post-secondary system is "trying to preserve a set of practices that have outlived the economics that made them possible." Shirky bets on emerging practices such as "the spread of large-scale, low-cost education" delivered via technology to meet "the massive demand for education, which our existing institutions are increasingly unable to handle."

John Seely Brown and Richard Adler, whose 2008 article "Minds on fire: Open education, the long tail, and learning 2.0" argued that understanding is socially constructed and that meaning is created through remixing and building on the work of others, both of which are supported by participatory emerging technologies.

Adler (2013) stated that 80 percent of learning takes place outside of school and that dynamic learning happens when the core (institutional content) meets the edge (informal content).

In looking at more recent work, we see that many of the same issues are still raised. Perhaps the critics have become more reconciled to the persistence of new networks and perhaps the proponents speak more about the potential for misuse. If we accept that there is some validity in parts of all the points of view, we should continue to explore the ways in which educators can work with (rather than fight against) what learners bring to educational pursuits so that their formal learning experiences afford them with an improved ability to evaluate and contribute at a more meaningful level. The challenges were and perhaps still are:

How to find ways to embed or scaffold critical thinking through the use of technology in general, and emerging technologies in particular;

How to respond to the changing higher education landscape created by emerging technologies and practices;

How to best assist learners to be effective participants in the participatory society and to add value to the world they are living in; and

How to advance distance education (while recognizing that distance is less and less a barrier with respect to learning) and enhance practice.

To successfully meet these challenges requires an understanding of the changing dynamics of learning. Shirky (2008b) stated "the physics of participation is more like weather than gravity. All the forces combine." This evokes images of chaos: powerful but complicated patterns with unpredictable global consequences, compared to what he seems to see as our previous, oversimplified "what goes up must come down" way of looking at the world. Five years later, Shirky (2014) viewed the chaos that led to the initial failure of the U.S. government's healthcare website in 2013 and expressed his view that to create any large-scale environment requires that developers learn from their users and learn from experience. The "waterfall" model (having an unchangeable plan in place at the onset of a project) does not work in this world of online complexity. Applied to digital education, if even a small part of what Shirky (2014) interprets about change is true then it seems clear that teaching and learning must also be in transition. Wesch (2008b) goes as far as to say that his every assumption about information and learning was shattered because of 2.0. *Shattered* is a very strong word, but, as distance educators, can *we* see any shattered pieces and find delight that some of our constraints have been lifted so we can refocus, rebuild, and reinvent?

An excellent place from which to start thinking about reinventing ourselves within the distance education context is the Wesch (2008b) lecture at the University of Manitoba, "A Portal to Media Literacy." Wesch speaks in a lecture hall and bases his discussion of traditional education on that physical environment. He describes the hall as a place designed to fit a model of learning that incorporates the following beliefs:

To learn is to acquire information.

Information is scarce (so a place must be created where an expert can convey information to a large group).

The authority of the expert must be followed (that is why the expert is at the front of the room with everyone else facing him/her).

Authorized information is beyond discussion (so the chairs are in fixed positions and learners don't turn to talk to each other).

Wesch then describes his findings that learners no longer believe in the above assumptions. He concludes that there is a serious crisis of significance. His answer is to encourage learners to work on collaborative projects, and to use media tools for the making of meaningful connections with personal relevance. Wesch has gone further with this idea, referring to learning as "soul-making" and speaking of the need for "genuine connections" to "restore the sense of joy and curiosity that we hope to instill in our students" (Wesch, 2014a). It seems inevitable from this perspective that assessment should be based on a view of whether and how learners have made those personally relevant connections rather than on the recitation of factual information (Wesch, 2014b).

The question then becomes, are we fully exploring the affordances of the web with appropriate pedagogies and ways of thinking about education and learning in investigating and embracing emerging models of distance education? Media literacy is an important key to effective education in a participatory learning environment. Wesch states, "There are no natives" (2008a). Given that the online environment is largely new to both educators and learners (and that it is changing constantly), we must not assume students are media literate (Wesch, 2008a). As an example, Wesch mentions that a large proportion of his students did not know that Wikipedia was editable and many had never edited a wiki of any sort. And since new tools are appearing nearly every day, media literacy strategies are more important than specific details about specific platforms.

Other authors agree: Alexander (2008) argues that those involved in higher education must rethink the definition of literacy: "if we want our students to engage the world as critical, informed people, then we need to reshape our plans as that world changes" (p. 200). Wesch (2009) speaks of critical analysis and metacognition and of ways in which he engages students to create notes collaboratively, all related to his view that it is important to prepare students to create content in and for a world that is both "download and upload." Based on what his students are telling him, he believes that discussion (in our view, *critical* discussion or *true dialogue*) rather than information transmission, is a key factor for engagement, and states that "the focus is not on providing answers to be memorized, but on creating a learning environment more conducive to producing the types of questions that ask students to challenge their taken-for-granted assumptions and see their own underlying biases" (Wesch, 2009).

How does critical discussion of engaged learning affect ideas and questions about distance education? The early history of distance education was often a story of isolation (Sherry, 1996). Many who lived in areas too remote for schools to be accessible, were too ill, or could not afford to attend regular classes could learn alone, with workbooks and assignments exchanged through postal mail. An occasional telephone conversation with an instructor might have been included, but solitary learning was a fundamental and central feature of the early "correspondence" model. It seemed that the correspondence model was accepted as satisfactory and generally seen as second best when compared to face-to-face learning. For instance, Garrison (1990) asserted that without connectivity, distance learning "degenerates" into the correspondence-course model of independent study. The earliest distance education technologies were unidirectional and asynchronous (e.g., radio and broadcast television) and did not incorporate interaction. When technologies able to diminish isolation and provide interaction opportunities became available, distance education entered an era of transformation.

Distance education may be well positioned to be at the forefront of innovative ways to rethink education, simply because there is little nostalgia for the early ways of teaching, studying, and learning in isolation. Having few compelling reasons to hold on to old methods means that an opportunity exists to envision new solutions for current and future challenges. With respect to education, distance and non-distance learning lines are blurring. The traditional brick and mortar classroom now incorporates digital resources and people who are not physically present. Distance learners now find it easy to have a range of people around them virtually. The distinctions between physical and virtual are likely to become blurrier as wearable technologies and augmented reality applications become increasingly common.

In this exciting online environment, there are numerous ways to achieve a learning outcome. Those distance educators familiar with a learning management system (LMS) such as Moodle or Blackboard have incorporated discussion forums and collaborative assignments into their courses and many believe that such environments are better than correspondence courses, and not as limiting as a lecture hall. Many of us are looking for ways to capitalize on this, to exploit the potential of the LMS technology even further, hoping to transcend the structure of a platform. Learning could take place through more open social media while retaining the administrative benefits of a learning platform. Key questions we should continue to ask about these learning environments include:

Does our curriculum allow for using emerging technologies to engage learners? Are we engaging learners by ensuring their learning is personally relevant? If not, could experiences like blogging or building a wiki for a real audience help?

Do we assess on the basis of meaningful connections?

By the end of their distance education experience, will learners internalize and exhibit an enhanced ability to contribute to what John Seely Brown (2008) would call an "open-source culture," and create more of what Putnam (2000) would refer to as "social capital?" Are we introducing our students to emerging practices?

WHAT ABOUT THE RISKS SUGGESTED BY THE CRITICS?

Shirky (2008c) counters Carr's (2008) argument that we are not reading as deeply in the era of abundance by declaring, "every past technology I know of that has increased the number of producers and consumers of written material, from the alphabet and papyrus to the telegraph and the paperback, has been good for humanity." Although emerging technologies provide increased opportunities to solve problems, Keen (2007) worries we will falter by having too much freedom and too much access to information not created by recognized experts. Shirky agrees that Keen (2007) poses a hard question that must be answered and Carvin (2008) asks educators to avoid the "wide-eyed cheerleader" point of view and recognize the challenges.

Part of the solution may come from the emerging technologies themselves, and the emerging practices that they make available. In the near future, there may well be technologies that evolve to provide authority to certain information. For example, Internet founding father Tim Berners-Lee (2008, interviewed by Ghosh) is working on a project to provide scientific websites with reliability ratings, something he sees as being crucial for particular types of content (e.g., medical information/ advice). But in general, as Keohane (2008) notes about Wikipedia, and by association Web 2.0, user-generated content is largely self-correcting.

What is required are ways to ensure that user self-correction is ongoing and that users keep track of where any particular piece of information might be in that self-correction process (the first iteration of a Wikipedia article may be suspect; after a thousand edits, it may well be a highly reliable source). In many ways this reflects what critics have always been calling for: critical thinking and a type of virtual "street smartness." Without that awareness, the perils are indeed real. With awareness, the potential, in the view of all but the harshest critics, is truly amazing. Can we move forward, with a spirit of adventure, applying our imagination and inventiveness to authentic questions?

The importance of authenticity in learning has long been discussed in K–12 education (e.g., Brown, Collins, & Duguid, 1989). Instead of merely studying history, learners should become historians, emulating the research techniques used by experts and even examining original sources that would not have been available before but are now online. Learners should learn science by doing science, and so on. We believe that authentic learning is increasingly made possible by the participatory nature of emerging technologies. If, as critics suggest, the inability to filter is one of the greatest arguments against a participatory web (thus staying with the model of "experts only" as content providers), then authentic learning provides a strong counterargument. When a consumer knows what's involved in creation, and is, in fact, a creator able to use the same techniques that experts use, there is a much smaller possibility that he or she will be misled. Authentic learning requires critical thinking based on experience.

CONCLUSION

As distance educators we can take on multiple roles through the participatory web. Our learners, and the general public, can also take on multiple roles. At their best, emerging technologies and associated practices serve to easily and democratically connect people who may have previously had little or no opportunity to connect with each other. Such connections can foster new roles for learning, teaching, knowledge creation, and knowledge consumption. Perhaps emerging technologies will enable us to reinvent our learning environments so that they are dynamically constructed in cooperation with our learners and the general public. Perhaps future learning environments can be engaging and collaborative places of ongoing formal and informal personalized learning. We may have exciting and fulfilling times ahead of us if we can adjust our mindsets and participate.

REFERENCES

Adler, R. (2013). *Connecting the edges: A report of the 2012 Aspen Institute Roundtable on Institutional Innovation*. Washington, D.C.: The Aspen Institute. Retrieved from http://www.aspeninstitute.org/sites/default/files/content/docs/pubs/ConnectingEdges-FINAL_0.pdf

Alexander, B. (2008). Social networking in higher education. In R. N. Katz (ed.), *The tower and the cloud: Higher education in the age of cloud computing* (pp. 197–201). Washington, D.C.: EDUCAUSE Publications.

Brown, J. S. (2008, October 17). How to connect technology and passion in the service of learning. *The Chronicle of Higher Education*. Retrieved from http://chronicle.com/weekly/v55/i08/08a09901.htm

Brown, J. S., & Adler, R. P. (2008, January 18). Minds on fire: Open education, the long tail, and learning 2.0. *Educause review online, 43*(1), 16–32. Retrieved from http://net.educause.edu/ir/library/pdf/ERM0811.pdfhttp://net.educause.edu/ir/library/pdf/ERM0811.pdf

Brown, J. S., Collins, A., & Duguid, P. (1989). Situated cognition and the culture of learning. *Educational Researcher, 18*(1), 32–42.

Carr, N. (2008, July 1). Is Google making us stupid? *The Atlantic*. Retrieved from http://www.theatlantic.com/magazine/archive/2008/07/is-google-making-us-stupid/306868/http://www.theatlantic.com/magazine/archive/2008/07/is-google-making-us-stupid/306868/

Carvin, A. (2008, January 11). Web 2.0 and education: Hot or not? *Learning Now*. Retrieved from http://www.pbs.org/teachers/learning.now/2008/01/web_20_and_education_hot_or_no.html#contenthttp://www.pbs.org/teachers/learning.now/2008/01/web_20_and_education_hot_or_no.html - content

Celizic, M. (2008, November 15). Father of brain-injured child offers hope to others. *Today Show*. Retrieved from http://www.msnbc.msn.com/id/27717674/http://www.msnbc.msn.com/id/27717674/

Downes, S. (2008, November 16). The future of online learning: Ten years on [Blog post]. Retrieved from http://halfanhour.blogspot.com/2008/11/future-of-online-learning-ten-years-on_16.htmlhttp://halfanhour.blogspot.com/2008/11/future-of-online-learning-ten-years-on_16.html

Finder, A. (2012, August 15). The joys and hazards of self-publishing on the Web. *The New York Times*. Retrieved from http://www.nytimes.com/2012/08/16/technology/personaltech/ins-and-outs-of-publishing-your-book-via-the-web.html?pagewanted=all&_r=1&

Flood, A. (2014, June 13). Self-publishing boom lifts sales by 79 percent in a year. *The Guardian*. Retrieved from http://www.theguardian.com/books/2014/jun/13/self-publishing-boom-lifts-sales-18m-titles-300m

Garrison, D. R. (1990). An analysis and evaluation of audio teleconferencing to facilitate education at a distance. *The American Journal of Distance Education, 4*(3), 16–23.

Ghosh, P. (2008, September 15). Warning sounded on Web's future. *BBC News UK*. Retrieved from http://news.bbc.co.uk/2/hi/technology/7613201.sthttp://news.bbc.co.uk/2/hi/technology/7613201.st

Johnson, L., Adams Becker, S., Estrada, V., & Freeman, A. (2014). *NMC horizon report: 2014 Higher education edition*. Austin, TX: The New Media Consortium. Retrieved from http://cdn.nmc.org/media/2014-nmc-horizon-report-he-EN-SC.pdf

Keen, A. (2007). *The cult of the* amateur: *How today's Internet is killing our culture*. New York: Doubleday.

——. (2012). *Digital vertigo: How today's online social revolution is dividing, diminishing, and disorienting us* (pp.14–18). New York: St. Martin's Press. Retrieved from https://archive.org/details/digitalvertigo00keen

Keohane, K. (2008). Unpopular opinion: Everyone's an expert on the Internet. Is that such a bad thing? *Communication World, 25*(1), 12.

Leadbeater, C. (2005). The era of open innovation [Video file]. Retrieved from http://www.ted.com/index.php/talks/charles_leadbeater_on_innovation.html

Lin, Y., & Ranjit, K. (2012). Using social media to create virtual interest groups in hospital libraries. *The Grey Journal*, *8*(1), 35–42. Retrieved from http://greynet.org/images/GL13-S1P,_Lin_and_Ranjit.pdf

Liston, D., Whitcomb, J., & Borko, H. (2009). The end of education in teacher education: Thoughts on reclaiming the role of social foundations in teacher education. *Journal of Teacher Education*, *60*(2), 107–11. doi: 10.1177/0022487108331004

Marques, J. (2013, April 17). A short history of MOOCs and distance learning. *MOOC News and Reviews*. Retrieved from http://moocnewsandreviews.com/a-short-history-of-moocs-and-distance-learning/

O'Hear, S. (2006). E-learning 2.0: How Web technologies are shaping education. Retrieved from http://readwrite.com/2006/08/08/e-learning_20

Perelman, L. J. (1993). *School's out: A radical new formula for the revitalization of America's educational system*. New York: Avon.

Putnam, R. D. (2000). *Bowling alone: The collapse and revival of American community*. New York: Simon and Schuster.http://en.wikipedia.org/wiki/Ravelry

Rosen, C. (2008, Spring). The myth of multitasking. *The New Atlantis*, *20*, 105–10. Retrieved from http://www.thenewatlantis.com/publications/the-myth-of-multitasking

———. (2013, October 25). Are Smartphones turning us into bad Samaritans? *The Wall Street Journal*. Retrieved from http://online.wsj.com/news/articles/SB10001424052702304402104579151850028363502

Scardamalia, M., & Bereiter, C. (1994). Computer support for knowledge-building communities. *Journal of the Learning Sciences*, *3*(3), 265–83.

Sherry, L. (1996). *Issues in distance learning. International Journal of Educational Telecommunications*, *1*(4), 337–65.

Shirky, C. (2008a). *Here comes everybody: The power of organizing without organizations*. New York: The Penguin Press.

———. (2008b, May 7). Gin, television, and social surplus. [Web log post]. Retrieved from http://www.worldchanging.com/archives/008009.html

———. (2008c, July 21). Why abundance should breed optimism: a second reply to Nick Carr. [Web log entry]. Retrieved from http://web.archive.org/web/20080729002436/http://www.britannica.com/blogs/2008/07/why-abundance-should-breed-optimism-a-second-reply-to-nick-carr/

———. (2010). *Cognitive surplus: Creativity and generosity in a connected age*. New York: The Penguin Press.

———. (2014, January 29). The end of higher education's Golden Age. [Web log entry]. Retrieved from http://www.shirky.com/weblog/2014/01/there-isnt-enough-money-to-keep-educating-adults-the-way-were-doing-it/

Siemens, G. (2005). Connectivism: A learning theory for the digital age. *International Journal of Instructional Technology and Distance Learning*, 2(1). http://www.itdl.org/Journal/Jan_05/article01.htm

Slocum, Z. (2008, November 9). Web 2.0 Summit videos: Huffington, Musk, Gore. *CNET News*. Retrieved from http://news.cnet.com/8301-17939_109-10092190-2.htmlhttp://news.cnet.com/8301-17939_109-10092190-2.html

Statistic Brain (2014, July 11). Twitter statistics. Retrieved from http://www.statisticbrain.com/twitter-statistics/http://www.statisticbrain.com/twitter-statistics/

Veletsianos, G. (2013). Open practices and identity: Evidence from researchers and educators' social media participation. *British Journal of Educational Technology*, 44(3), 639–51.

Wesch, M. (2008a). A portal to media literacy [Video file]. Retrieved from http://www.youtube.com/watch?v=J4yApagnros&feature=user

———. (2008b). A vision of students today [Video file]. Retrieved from http://youtu.be/dGCJ46vyR9o

———. (2009). From knowledgeable to knowledge-able: Learning in new media environments. Retrieved from http://www.academiccommons.org/commons/essay/knowledgable-knowledge-able

———. (2014, June 17). Learning as soul-making. *Digital ethnography @ Kansas State University*. Retrieved from http://mediatedcultures.net/presentations/learning-as-soul-making/

———. (2014, July 10). Learning worth crying about. *Digital ethnography @ Kansas State University*. Retrieved from http://mediatedcultures.net/thoughts/learning-worth-crying-about/

Wikipedia: About. (2014). In *Wikipedia: the free encyclopaedia*. Retrieved from http://en.wikipedia.org/wiki/Wikipedia:About

YouTube. (n.d.). Press room. Retrieved from https://www.youtube.com/yt/press/index.html

PART II

APPLICATIONS

6 Educational Data Mining and Learning Analytics

Potentials and Possibilities for Online Education

▶ *R. S. Baker and P. S. Inventado*

Over the last decades, online and distance education has become an increasingly prominent part of the higher educational landscape (Allen & Seaman, 2008; O'Neill et al., 2004; Patel & Patel, 2005). Many learners turn to distance education because it works better for their schedule, and makes them feel more comfortable than traditional face-to-face courses (O'Malley & McCraw, 1999). However, working with distance education presents challenges for both learners and instructors that are not present in contexts where teachers can work directly with their students. As learning is mediated through technology, learners have fewer opportunities to communicate to instructors about areas in which they are struggling. Though discussion forums provide an opportunity that many students use, and in fact some students are more comfortable seeking help online than in person (Kitsantas & Chow, 2007), discussion forums depend upon learners themselves realizing that they are facing a challenge, and recognizing the need to seek help. Further, many students do not participate in forums unless given explicit prompts or requirements (Dennen, 2005). Unfortunately, the challenges of help-seeking are general: many learners, regardless of setting, do not successfully recognize the need to seek help, and fail to seek help in situations where it could be extremely useful (Aleven et al., 2003). Without the opportunity to interact with learners in a face-to-face setting, it is therefore harder for instructors as well to recognize negative affect or disengagement among students.

Beyond a student not participating in discussion forums, ceasing to complete assignments is a clear sign of disengagement (Kizilcec, Piech, & Schneider, 2013), but information on these disengaged behaviors is not always available to instructors, and more subtle forms of negative affect (such as boredom) are difficult for an unaided distance instructor to identify and diagnose. As such, a distance educator has additional challenges compared to a local instructor in identifying which students are at-risk, in order to provide individual attention and support. This is not to say that face-to-face instructors always take action when a student is visibly disengaged, but they have additional opportunities to recognize problems.

In this chapter, we discuss educational data mining and learning analytics (Baker & Siemens, 2014) as a set of emerging practices that may assist distance education instructors in gaining a rich understanding of their students. The educational data mining (EDM) and learning analytics (LA) communities are concerned with exploring the increasing amounts of data now becoming available on learners, toward providing better information to instructors and better support to learners. Through the use of automated discovery methods, leavened with a workable understanding of educational theory, EDM/LA practitioners are able to generate models that identify at-risk students so as to help instructors to offer better learner support. In the interest of provoking thought and discussion, we focus on a few key examples of the potentials of analytics, rather than exhaustively reviewing the increasing literature on analytics and data mining for distance education.

DATA NOW AVAILABLE IN DISTANCE EDUCATION

One key enabling trend for the use of analytics and data mining in distance education is that distance education increasingly provides high-quality data in large quantities (Goldstein & Katz, 2005). In fact, distance education has always involved interactions that could be traced, but increasingly data from online and distance education is being stored by distance education providers in formats designed to be usable. For example, The Open University (UK), an entirely online university with around 250,000 students, collects large amounts of electronic data including student activity data, course information, course feedback and aggregated completion rates, and demographic data (Clow, 2014).

The university's Data Wranglers project leverages this data by having a team of analytics experts analyze and create reports about student learning, which are used to improve course delivery. The University of Phoenix, a for-profit online university, collects data on marketing, student applications, student contact information, technology support issue tracking, course grades, assignment grades, discussion forums, and content usage (Sharkey, 2011). These disparate data sources are integrated to support analyses that can predict student persistence in academic programs (Ming & Ming, 2012), and can facilitate interventions that improve student outcomes.

Massive Open Online Courses (MOOCs), another emerging distance education practice, also generate large quantities of data that can be utilized for these purposes. There have been dozens of papers exploiting MOOC data to answer research questions in education in the brief time since large-scale MOOCs became internationally popular (see, for instance, Champaign et al., 2014; Kim et al., 2014; Kizilcec et al., 2013). The second-largest MOOC platform, edX, now makes large amounts of MOOC data available to any researcher in the world. In addition, formats have emerged for MOOC data that are designed to facilitate research (Veeramachaneni, Dernoncourt, Taylor, Pardos, & O'Reilly, 2013).

Increasingly, traditional universities are collecting the same types of data. For example, Purdue University collects and integrates educational data from various systems including content management systems (CMS), student information systems (SIS), audience response systems, library systems and streaming media service systems (Arnold, 2010). This institution uses this data in their Course Signals project, discussed below.

One of the key steps to making data useful for analysis is to pre-process it (Romero, Romero, & Ventura, 2013). Pre-processing can include data cleaning (such as removing data stemming from logging errors, or mapping meaningless identifiers to meaningful labels), integrating data sources (typically taking the form of mapping identifiers—which could be at the student level, the class level, the assignment level or other levels—between data sets of tables), and feature engineering (distilling appropriate data to make a prediction). Typically, the process of engineering and distilling appropriate features that can be used to represent key aspects of the data is one of the most time-consuming and difficult steps in learning analytics. The process of going from the initial features logged by an online learning system (such as correctness and time, or the textual content of a post) to more semantic features (history of correctness on a specific skill; how fast an action is compared to typical time taken by other students on the same problem step; emotion expressed and context in a discussion of a specific discussion forum post) involves considerable theoretical understanding of the educational domain. This understanding is sometimes encoded in schemes for formatting and storing data, such as the MOOC data format proposed by Veeramachaneni et al. (2013) or the Pittsburgh Science of Learning Center DataShop format (Koedinger, Baker, Cunningham, Skogsholm, Leber, & Stamper, 2010).

METHODS FOR EDUCATIONAL DATA MINING AND LEARNING ANALYTICS

In tandem with the development of these increasingly large data sets, a wider selection of methods to distill meaning have emerged; these are referred to as educational data mining or learning analytics.

As Baker and Siemens (2014) note, the educational data mining and learning analytics communities address many of the same research questions, using similar methods. The core differences between the communities are in terms of emphasis: whether human analysis or automated analysis is central, whether phenomena are considered as systems or in terms of specific constructs and their interrelationships, and whether automated interventions or empowering instructors is the goal. However, for the purposes of this article, educational data mining and learning analytics can be treated as interchangeable, as the methods relevant to distance education are seen in both communities. Some of the differences emerge in the section on uses to benefit learners, with the approaches around providing instructors with feedback being more closely linked to the learning analytics community, whereas approaches to providing feedback and interventions directly to students are more closely linked to practice in educational data mining.

In this section, we review the framework proposed by Baker and Siemens (2014); other frameworks for understanding the types of EDM/LA method also exist (e.g., Baker & Yacef, 2009; Scheuer & McLaren, 2012; Romero & Ventura, 2007; Ferguson, 2012). The differences between these frameworks are a matter of emphasis and categorization. For example, parameter tuning is categorized as a method in Scheuer and McLaren (2012); it is typically seen as a step in the prediction modeling or knowledge engineering process in other frameworks. Still, mostly the same methods are present in all frameworks.

Baker and Siemens (in press) divide the world of EDM/LA methods into prediction modeling, structure discovery, relationship mining, distillation of data for human judgment, and discovery with models. In this chapter, we will provide definitions and examples for *prediction, structure discovery*, and *relationship mining*, focusing on methods of particular usefulness for distance education.

Prediction

Prediction modeling occurs when a researcher or practitioner develops a model, which can infer (or predict) a single aspect of the data, from some combination of other variables within the data. This is typically done either to infer a construct that is latent (such as emotion), or to predict future outcomes. In these cases, good data on the predicted variable is collected for a smaller data set, and then a model is created with the goal of predicting that variable in a larger data set, or a future data set. The goal is to predict the construct in future situations when data on it is unavailable. For example, a prediction model may be developed to predict whether a student is likely to drop or fail a course (e.g., Arnold, 2010; Ming & Ming, 2012). The prediction model may be developed from 2013 data, and then utilized to make predictions early in the semester in 2014, 2015, and beyond. Similarly, the model may be developed using data from four introductory courses, and then rolled out to make predictions within a university's full suite of introductory courses.

Prediction modeling has been utilized for an ever-increasing set of problems within the domain of education, from inferring students' knowledge of a certain topic (Corbett & Anderson, 1995), to inferring a student's emotional state (D'Mello, Craig, Witherspoon, McDaniel, & Graesser. 2008). It is also used to make longer-term predictions, for instance predicting whether a student will attend college from their learning and emotion in middle school (San Pedro, Baker, & Gobert, 2013).

One key consideration when using prediction models is distilling the appropriate data to make a prediction (sometimes referred to as feature engineering). Sao Pedro et al. (2012) have argued that integrating theoretical understanding into the data mining process leads to better models than a purely bottom-up data-driven approach. Paquette, de Carvalho, Baker, and Ocumpaugh (2014) correspondingly find that integrating theory into data mining performs better than either approach alone. While choosing an appropriate algorithm is also an important challenge (see discussion in Baker, 2014), switching algorithms often involves a minimal change within a data mining tool, whereas distilling the correct features can be a substantial challenge.

Another key consideration is making sure that data is validated appropriately for its eventual use. Validating models on a range of content (Baker, Corbett, Roll, & Koedinger, 2008) and on a representative sample of eventual students (Ocumpaugh, Baker, Gowda, Heffernan & Heffernan, 2014) is important to ensuring that models will be valid in the contexts where they are applied. In the context of distance education, these issues can merge: the population of students taking one course through a distance institution may be quite different than the population taking a different course, even at the same institution. Some prediction models have been validated to function accurately across higher education institutions, which is a powerful demonstration of generality (Jayaprakash, Moody, Lauría, Regan, & Baron, 2014).

As with other areas of education, prediction modeling increasingly plays an important role in distance education. Arguably, it is the most prominent type of analytics within higher education in general, and distance education specifically. For example, Ming and Ming (2012) studied whether students' final grades could be predicted from their interactions on the University of Phoenix class discussion forums. They found that discussion of more specialized topics was predictive of higher course grades. Another example is seen in Kovacic's (2010) work studying student dropout in the Open Polytechnic of New Zealand. This work predicted student dropout from demographic factors, finding that students of specific demographic groups were at much higher risk of failure than other students.

Related work can also be seen within the Purdue Signals Project (Arnold, 2010), which mined content management system, student information system, and gradebook data to predict which students were likely to drop out of a course and provide instructors with near real-time updates regarding student performance and effort (Arnold & Pistilli, 2012; Campbell, DeBlois, & Oblinger, 2007). These predictions were used to suggest interventions to instructors. Instructors who used those interventions, reminding students of the steps needed for success, and recommending face-to-face meetings, found that their students engaged in more help-seeking, and had better course outcomes and significantly improved retention rates (Arnold, 2010).

Structure discovery

A second core category of learning LA/EDM is structure discovery. Structure discovery algorithms attempt to find structure in the data without an a priori idea of what should be found: a very different goal than in prediction. In prediction, there is a specific variable that the researcher or practitioner attempts to infer or predict; by contrast, there are no specific variables of interest in structure discovery. Instead, the researcher attempts to determine what structure emerges naturally from the data. Common approaches to structure discovery in LA/EDM include clustering, factor analysis, network analysis, and domain structure discovery.

While domain structure discovery is quite prominent in research on intelligent tutoring systems, the type of structure discovery most often seen in online learning contexts is a specific type of network analysis called Social Network Analysis (SNA) (Knoke & Yang, 2008). In SNA, data is used to discover the relationships and interactions among individuals, as well as the patterns that emerge from those relationships and interactions. Frequently, in learning analytics, SNA is paired with additional analytics approaches to better understand the patterns observed through network analytics; for example, SNA might be coupled with discourse analysis (Buckingham, Shum, & Ferguson, 2012).

SNA has been used for a number of applications in education. For example, Kay, Maisonneuve, Yacef, and Reimann (2006) used SNA to understand the differences between effective and ineffective project groups, through visual analysis of the strength of group connections. Although this project took place in the context of a face-to-face university class, the data analyzed was from online collaboration tools that could have been used at a distance. SNA has also been used to study how students' communication behaviors in discussion forums change over time (Haythornthwaite, 2001), and to study how students' positions in a social network relate to their perception of being part of a learning community (Dawson, 2008), a key concern for distance education. Patterns of interaction and connectivity in learning communities are correlated to academic success as well as learner sense of engagement in a course (Macfadyen & Dawson, 2010; Suthers & Rosen, 2011).

Relationship mining

Relationship mining methods find unexpected relationships or patterns in a large set of variables. There are many forms of relationship mining, but Baker and Siemens (2014) identify four in particular as being common in EDM: correlation mining, association rule mining, sequential pattern mining, and causal data mining. In this section, we will mention potential applications of the first three.

Association rule mining finds if-then rules that predict that if one variable value is found, another variable is likely to have a characteristic value. Association rule mining has found a wide range of applications in educational data mining, as well as in data mining and e-commerce more broadly. For example, Ben-Naim, Bain, and Marcus (2009) used association rule mining to find what patterns of performance were characteristic of successful students, and used their findings as the basis of an engine that made recommendations to students. Garcia, Romero, Ventura, and De Castro (2009) used association rule mining on data from exercises, course forum participation, and grades in an online course, in order to gather data related to effectiveness to provide to course developers.

A closely related method to association rule mining is sequential pattern mining. The goal of sequential pattern mining is to find patterns that manifest over time. Like association rule mining, if-then rules are found, but the if-then rules involve associations between past events (if) and future events (then). For example, Perera, Kay, Koprinska, Yacef, and Zaiane (2009) used sequential pattern mining on data from learners' behaviors in an online collaboration environment, toward understanding the behaviors that characterized successful and unsuccessful collaborative groups. One could also imagine conducting sequential pattern mining to find patterns in course-taking over time within a program that are associated with more successful and less successful student outcomes (Garcia et al., 2009). Sequential patterns can also be found through other methods, such as hidden Markov models; an example of that in distance education is seen in Coffrin, Corrin, de Barba, and Kennedy (2014), a study that looks at patterns of how students shift between activities in a MOOC.

Finally, correlation mining is the area of data mining that attempts to find simple linear relationships between pairs of variables in a data set. Typically, in correlation mining, approaches such as post-hoc statistical corrections are used to set a threshold on which patterns are accepted; dimensionality reduction methods are also sometimes used to first group variables before trying to correlate them to other variables. Correlation mining methods may be useful in situations where there are a range of variables describing distance education and a range of student outcomes, and the goal is to figure out an overall pattern of which variables correspond to many successful outcomes rather than just a single one.

USES TO BENEFIT LEARNERS

As the examples above indicate, there are several potential uses for data mining and analytics in distance education. These methods can be used to learn a great deal about online and distance students, their learning processes, and what factors influence their outcomes. In our view, the primary uses can be categorized in terms of automated feedback and adaptation.

Automated feedback to students about their learning and performance has a rich history within online education. Many distance education courses today offer immediate correctness feedback on pop-up quizzes or other problem-solving exercises (see Janicki & Liegle, 2001; Jiang et al., 2014), as well as indicators of course progress. Research suggests that providing distance education students with visualizations of their progress toward completing competencies can lead to better outcomes (Grann & Bushway, 2014). Work in recent decades in intelligent tutoring systems and other artificially intelligent technologies shows that there is the potential to provide even more comprehensive feedback to learners. In early work in this area, Cognitive Tutors for mathematics showed students "skill bars," giving indicators to students of their progress based on models of student knowledge (Koedinger, Anderson, Hadley, & Mark, 1997). Skill bars have since been extended to communicate hypotheses of what misconceptions the students may have (Bull, Quigley, & Mabbott, 2006). Other systems give students indicators of their performance across a semester's worth of subjects, helping them to identify what materials need further study prior to a final exam (Kay & Lum, 2005). Some systems provide learners with feedback on engagement as well as learning, reducing the frequency of disengaged behaviors (Walonoski & Heffernan, 2006). These intelligent forms of feedback are still relatively uncommon within distance education, but have the potential to increase in usage over time.

Similarly, feedback to instructors and other university personnel has a rich history in learning analytics. The Purdue Signals Project (discussed above) is a successful example of how instructors can be empowered with information concerning which students are at risk of unsuccessful outcomes, and why each student is at risk. Systems such as ASSISTments provide more fine-grained reports that communicate to instructors which skills are generally difficult for students (Feng & Heffernan, 2007), influencing ongoing instructional strategies. In the context of distance education, Mazza and Dimitrova (2004) have created visualizations for instructors that represent student knowledge of a range of skills and participation in discussion forums. Another example is TrAVis, which visualizes for instructors the different online behaviors each student has engaged in (May, George, & Prévôt, 2011). These systems can be integrated with tools to support instructors, such as systems that propose types of emails to send to learners (see Arnold, 2010).

Finally, automated intervention is a type of support that can be created based on educational data mining, where the system itself automatically adapts to the individual differences among learners. This is most common in intelligent tutoring systems, where there are systems that automatically adapt to a range of individual differences. Examples include problem selection in Cognitive Tutors (Koedinger et al., 1997), where exercises are selected for students based on what material they have not yet mastered; pedagogical agents that offer students support for meta-cognitive reasoning (Biswas, Leelawong, Belynne, Viswanath, Schwartz, & Davis. 2004), engagement (Arroyo, Ferguson, Johns, Dragon, Meheranian, Fisher, Barto, Mahadevan, & Woolf, 2007), and collaboration (Dyke, Leelawong, Belynne, Viswanath, Schwartz, & Davis, 2013); and memory optimization, which attempts to return to material at the moment when the student is at risk of forgetting it (Pavlik & Anderson, 2008). Intelligent tutoring systems have been used at scale more often for K-12 education than for higher education, but there are examples of their use in the latter realm (Mitrovic & Ohlsson, 1999; Corbett et al., 2010). The use of intelligent tutor methodologies in distance education can be expected to increase in the coming years, given the acquisition of Carnegie Learning, a leading developer of intelligent tutoring systems, by the primarily distance education for-profit university, the University of Phoenix.

LIMITATIONS AND ISSUES TO CONSIDER

Educational data mining and learning analytics have been successful in several areas, but there are several issues to consider when applying learning analytics. A key issue, in the authors' opinion, is model validity. As discussed above, it is important that models be validated (tested for reliability) based on genuine outcome data, and that models be validated using data relevant to their eventual use, involving similar systems and populations. The invalid generalization of models creates the risk of inaccurate predictions or responses.

In general, it is important to consider both the benefits of a correctly applied intervention and the costs of an incorrectly applied one. Interventions with relatively low risk (sometimes called "fail-soft interventions") are preferable when model accuracy is imperfect. No model is perfect, however; expecting educational at-risk models to be more reliable than standards for first-line medical diagnostics may not be entirely realistic.

Another important consideration is privacy. It is essential to balance the need for high-quality longitudinal data (that enables analysis of the long-term impacts of a student behavior or an intervention) with the necessity to protect student privacy and follow relevant legislation. There is not currently a simple solution to the need to protect student privacy; simply discarding all identifying information protects privacy, but at the cost of potentially ignoring long-term negative effects from an intervention, or ignoring potential long-term benefits.

CONCLUSION

Data mining and analytics have potential in distance education. In general, as with many areas of education, distance education will be enhanced by the increasing amounts of data now becoming available. There is potential to enhance the quality of course materials, identify at-risk students, and provide better support both to learners and instructors. By doing so, it may be possible to create learning experiences that create a level of individual personalization better than what is seen in traditional in-person courses, instead emulating the level of personalization characteristic of one-on-one tutoring experiences.

REFERENCES

Aleven, V., Stahl, E., Schworm, S., Fischer, F., & Wallace, R. M. (2003). Help seeking and help design in interactive learning environments. *Review of Educational Research* 73(2), 277–320.

Allen, I. E., & Seaman, J. (2008). *Staying the course: Online education in the United States, 2008*. Needham, MA: Sloan Consortium.

Anderson, J. R., Matessa, M., & Lebiere, C. (1997). ACT-R: A theory of higher-level cognition and its relation to visual attention. *Human-Computer Interaction* 12(4), 439–62.

Arnold, K. E. (2010). Signals: Applying academic analytics. *Educause Quarterly, 33*(1).

Arnold, K. E., & Pistilli, M. D. (2012). Course signals at Purdue: Using learning analytics to increase student success. In *Proceedings of the 2nd International Conference on Learning Analytics and Knowledge*, LAK 2012 (pp. 267–70), New York: ACM.

Arroyo, I., Ferguson, K., Johns, J., Dragon, T., Meheranian, H., Fisher, D., Barto, A., Mahadevan, S., & Woolf, B. P. (2007, June). Repairing disengagement with non-invasive interventions. In *Proceedings of the 2007 Conference on Artificial Intelligence in Education: Building Technology Rich Learning Contexts That Work* (pp. 195–202). IOS Press.

Baker, R. S. (2014). *Big data and education*. New York: Teachers College, Columbia University.

Baker, R., & Siemens, G. (2014). Educational data mining and learning analytics. In K. Sawyer (Ed.) *Cambridge handbook of the learning sciences: 2nd Edition* (pp.253 – 274). New York, NY: Cambridge University Press.

Baker, R. S., & Yacef, K. (2009). The state of educational data mining in 2009: A review and future visions. *Journal of Educational Data Mining 1*(1), 3–17.

Baker, R. S. J. D., Corbett, A. T., Roll, I., & Koedinger, K. R. (2008). Developing a generalizable detector of when students game the system. *User Modeling and User-Adapted Interaction 18*(3), 287–314.

Ben-Naim, D., Bain, M., & Marcus, N. (2009). A user-driven and data-driven approach for supporting teachers in reflection and adaptation of adaptive tutorials. In the *Proceedings of Educational Data Mining 2009* (pp. 21–30).

Biswas, G., Leelawong, K., Belynne, K., Viswanath, K., Schwartz, D., & Davis, J. (2004). Developing learning by teaching environments that support self-regulated learning. In *Intelligent tutoring systems, 3220: Lecture notes in computer science,* pp. 730–40. Maceió, Brazil: Springer.

Buckingham Shum, S., & Ferguson, R., (2012). Social learning analytics. *Educational Technology and Society 15*(3), 3–26.

Bull, S., Quigley, S. & Mabbott, A. (2006). Computer-Based formative assessment to promote reflection and learner autonomy, engineering education. *Journal of the Higher Education Academy Subject Centre 1*(1), 8–18.

Campbell, J. P., DeBlois, P. B., & Oblinger, D. G. (2007). Academic analytics: A new tool for a new era. *Educause Review 42*(4), 40.

Champaign, J., Colvin, K. F., Liu, A., Fredericks, C., Seaton, D., & Pritchard, D. E. (2014). Correlating skill and improvement in 2 MOOCs with a student's time on tasks. In *Proceedings of the First ACM Conference on Learning @ Scale Conference* (pp. 11–20). ACM.

Clow, D. (2014). Data wranglers: Human interpreters to help close the feedback loop. In *Proceedings of the Fourth International Conference on Learning Analytics and Knowledge, LAK 2014* (pp. 49–53). New York: ACM.

Coffrin, C., Corrin, L., de Barba, P., & Kennedy, G. (2014). Visualizing patterns of student engagement and performance in MOOCs. In *Proceedings of the Fourth International Conference on Learning Analytics and Knowledge* (pp. 83–92). New York: ACM.

Corbett, A. T., & Anderson, J. R. (1995). Knowledge tracing: Modeling the acquisition of procedural knowledge. *User Modeling and User-Adapted Interaction 4*, 253–78.

Corbett, A., Kauffman, L., Maclaren, B., Wagner, A., & Jones, E. (2010). A cognitive tutor for genetics problem solving: Learning gains and student modeling. *Journal of Educational Computing Research 42*(2), 219–39.

d'Aquin, M., & Jay, N. (2013). Interpreting data mining results with linked data for learning analytics: Motivation, case study and directions. In *Proceedings of the Third International Conference on Learning Analytics and Knowledge, LAK 2013* (pp. 155–64). New York: ACM.

d'Aquin, M. (2012). Putting linked data to use in a large higher-education organisation. In *Proceedings of the Interacting with Linked Data (ILD) Workshop at Extended Semantic Web Conference (ESWC)*.

Dawson, S. (2008). A study of the relationship between student social networks and sense of community. *Educational Technology and Society 11*(3), 224–38.

Dennen, V. P. (2005). From message posting to learning dialogues: Factors affecting learner participation in asynchronous discussion. *Distance Education 26*(1), 127–48.

D'Mello, S. K., Craig, S. D., Witherspoon, A., McDaniel, B., & Graesser, A. (2008). Automatic detection of learner's affect from conversational cues. *User Modeling and User Adapted Interaction 18*, 45–80.

Dyke, G., Howley, I., Adamson, D., Kumar, R., & Rosé, C. P. (2013). Towards academically productive talk supported by conversational agents. In *Productive multimodality in the analysis of group interactions* (pp. 459–76). New York: Springer US.

Feng, M., & Heffernan, N. T. (2007). Towards live informing and automatic analyzing of student learning: Reporting in ASSISTment system. *Journal of Interactive Learning Research 18*(2), 207–30.

Ferguson, R. (2012). Learning analytics: drivers, developments and challenges. *International Journal of Technology Enhanced Learning 4*(5), 304–17.

García, E., Romero, C., Ventura, S., & De Castro, C. (2009). An architecture for making recommendations to courseware authors using association rule mining and collaborative filtering. *User Modeling and User-Adapted Interaction 19*(1–2), 99–132.

Goldstein, P. J., & Katz, R. N. (2005). Academic analytics: The uses of management information and technology in higher education. *Educause*. Retrieved from https://net.educause.edu/ir/library/pdf/ers0508/rs/ers0508w.pdf

Grann, J., & Bushway, D. (2014). Competency map: Visualizing student learning to promote student success. In *Proceedings of the Fourth International Conference on Learning Analytics And Knowledge* (pp. 168–72). ACM.

Haythornthwaite, C. (2001). Exploring multiplexity: Social network structures in a computer- supported distance learning class. *The Information Society: An International Journal 17*(3), 211–26.

Janicki, T., & Liegle, J. O. (2001). Development and evaluation of a framework for creating web-based learning modules: a pedagogical and systems perspective. *Journal of Asynchronous Learning Networks 5*(1), 58–84.

Jayaprakash, S. M., Moody, E. W., Lauría, E. J., Regan, J. R., & Baron, J. D. (2014). Early alert of academically at-risk students: An open source analytics initiative. *Journal of Learning Analytics 1*(1), 6–47.

Jiang, S., Warschauer, M., Williams, A. E., O'Dowd, D., & Schenke, K. (2014). Predicting MOOC Performance with Week 1 Behavior. *Proceedings of the 7th International Conference on Educational Data Mining* (pp. 273–75).

Kay, J., & Lum, A. (2005). Exploiting readily available web data for scrutable student models, *Proceedings of the 12th International Conference on Artificial Intelligence in Education* (pp. 338–45), Amsterdam, Netherlands: IOS Press.

Kay, J., Maisonneuve, N., Yacef, K., & Reimann, P. (2006) The big five and visualisations of team work activity. *Proceedings of the International Conference on Intelligent Tutoring Systems* (pp. 197–206).

Kim, J., Guo, P. J., Seaton, D. T., Mitros, P., Gajos, K. Z., & Miller, R. C. (2014, March). Understanding in-video dropouts and interaction peaks in online lecture videos. In *Proceedings of the First ACM Conference on Learning@ Scale Conference* (pp. 31–40). ACM.

Kitsantas, A., & Chow, A. (2007). College students' perceived threat and preference for seeking help in traditional, distributed, and distance learning environments. *Computers and Education 48*(3), 383–95.

Kizilcec, R. F., Piech, C., & Schneider, E. (2013). Deconstructing disengagement: Analyzing learner subpopulations in massive open online courses. In *Proceedings of the Third International Conference on Learning Analytics and Knowledge* (pp. 170–79). ACM.

Knoke, D., & Yang, S. (eds.). (2008). *Social network analysis (vol. 154)*, 2nd Ed. Thousand Oaks, CA: Sage.

Koedinger, K. R., Anderson, J. R., Hadley, W. H., & Mark, M. A. (1997). Intelligent tutoring goes to school in the big city. *International Journal of Artificial Intelligence in Education 8*, 30–43.

Koedinger, K. R., Baker, R.S. J. D., Cunningham, K., Skogsholm, A., Leber, B., & Stamper, J. (2010). A data repository for the EDM community: The PSLC DataShop. In C. Romero, S. Ventura, M. Pechenizkiy, & R. S. Baker, R. S. J. D. (eds.), *Handbook of educational data mining*. Boca Raton, FL: CRC Press (pp. 43–56).

Kovacic, Z. (2010). Early prediction of student success: Mining students' enrolment data. In *Proceedings of Informing Science and IT Education Conference (InSITE) 2010* (pp. 647–65).

Lam, W. (2004). Encouraging online participation. *Journal of Information Systems Education 15*(4), 345–48.

Macfadyen, L. P., & Dawson, S. (2010). Mining LMS data to develop an "early warning system" for educators: A proof of concept. *Computers and Education 54*(2), 588–99.

May, M., George, S., & Prévôt, P. (2011). TrAVis to enhance online tutoring and learning activities: Real-time visualization of students tracking data. *Interactive Technology and Smart Education 8*(1), 52–69.

Mazza, R., & Dimitrova, V. (2004, May). Visualising student tracking data to support instructors in web-based distance education. In *Proceedings of the 13th International World Wide Web Conference on Alternate Track Papers and Posters* (pp. 154–61). ACM.

Ming, N. C., & Ming, V. L. (2012). Predicting student outcomes from unstructured data. *Proceedings of the 2nd International Workshop on Personalization Approaches in Learning Environments* (pp. 11–16).

Mitrovic, A., & Ohlsson, S. (1999). Evaluation of a constraint-based tutor for a database. *International Journal of Artificial Intelligence in Education 10*, 238–56.

Ocumpaugh, J., Baker, R., Gowda, S., Heffernan, N., & Heffernan, C. (2014) Population validity for educational data mining models: A case study in affect detection. *British Journal of Educational Technology 45*(3), 487–501.

O'Malley, J., & McCraw, H. (1999). Students' perceptions of distance learning, online learning and the traditional classroom. Online Journal of Distance Learning Administration 2(4).

O'Neill, K., Singh, G., & O'Donoghue, J. (2004). Implementing elearning programmes for higher education: A review of the literature. *Journal of Information Technology Education Research 3*(1), 313–23.

Palazuelos, C., García-Saiz, D., & Zorrilla, M. (2013). Social network analysis and data mining: An application to the e-learning context. In J.-S. Pan, S.-M. Chen, & N.-T. Nguyen (eds.) *Computational collective intelligence. technologies and applications* (pp. 651–60). Berlin and Heidelberg: Springer.

Paquette, L., de Carvalho, A. M. J. A., Baker, R. S., & Ocumpaugh, J. (2014). Reengineering the feature distillation Process: A case study in the detection of gaming the system. In *Proceedings of the 7th International Conference on Educational Data Mining* (pp. 284–87).

Patel, C., & Patel, T. (2005). Exploring a joint model of conventional and online learning systems. *E-Service Journal 4*(2), 27–46.

Pavlik, P. I., & Anderson, J. R. (2008). Using a model to compute the optimal schedule of practice. *Journal of Experimental Psychology Applied 14*(2), 101.

Perera, D., Kay, J., Koprinska, I., Yacef, K., & Zaiane, O. R. (2009). Clustering and sequential pattern mining of online collaborative learning data. *IEEE Transactions on Knowledge and Data Engineering 21*(6), 759–72.

Rabbany, R., Takaffoli, M., & Zaïane, O. R. (2011). Analyzing participation of students in online courses using social network analysis techniques. In *Proceedings of Educational Data Mining* (pp. 21–30).

Romero, C., & Ventura, S. (2007). Educational data mining: A survey from 1995 to 2005. *Expert Systems with Applications 33*(1), 135–46.

Romero, C., Romero, J. R., & Ventura, S. (2013). A survey on pre-processing educational data. In *Educational data mining* (pp. 29–64). Berlin: Springer International Publishing.

San Pedro, M. O. Z., Baker, R. S. J. D., Bowers, A. J., & Heffernan, N.T. (2013) Predicting college enrollment from student interaction with an intelligent tutoring system in middle school. In *Proceedings of the 6th International Conference on Educational Data Mining* (pp. 177–84).

Sao Pedro, M., Baker, R. S. J. D., & Gobert, J. (2012). Improving construct validity yields better models of systematic inquiry, even with less information. *Proceedings of the 20th International Conference on User Modeling, Adaptation and Personalization (UMAP 2012)*, (pp. 249–60).

Scheuer, O., & McLaren, B. M. (2012). Educational data mining. In *Encyclopedia of the sciences of learning* (pp. 1075–79). New York: Springer US.

Sharkey, M. (2011). Academic analytics landscape at the University of Phoenix. In *Proceedings of the First International Conference on Learning Analytics and Knowledge, LAK 2011* (pp. 122–26). ACM.

Suthers, D., & Rosen, D. (2011). A unified framework for multi-level analysis of distributed learning. In *Proceedings of the 1st International Conference on Learning Analytics and Knowledge* (pp. 64–74).

Veeramachaneni, K., Dernoncourt, F., Taylor, C., Pardos, Z., & O'Reilly, U. M. (2013). Developing data standards for MOOC data science. In *AIED 2013 Workshops Proceedings* (p. 17). Berlin: Springer.

Walonoski, J. A., & Heffernan, N. T. (2006). Prevention of off-task gaming behavior in intelligent tutoring systems. In *Intelligent tutoring systems* (pp. 722–24). Berlin: Springer.

The Emergence of Practice

Two Case Studies of Moodle in Online Education

▶ *Andrew Whitworth and Angela D. Benson*

This chapter discusses how practices, as well as technologies, can be studied as "emerging" and why such a perspective is essential if both researchers and practitioners are to understand how a technology emerges into a specific workplace context, whether in higher education institutions (HEIs) or elsewhere. As with the original version of this chapter (Whitworth and Benson, 2010), we base these discussions on some results from our "Technology at the Planning Table" (TPT) project, which ran from 2005–2007 and conducted qualitative case studies of several distance learning programs from universities in the UK and US. These cases used a variety of course management systems (CMSs), including commercial, open access/open source, homegrown, and ad hoc (academic-created) systems. We then focused particularly on the two cases that used an open access/open source CMS, namely Moodle, to construct and deliver their distance learning programs. Since the original chapter was published, one of these cases, the Public Administration Program (or PAP), has also been discussed in detail in Benson and Whitworth (2014). We have also elaborated on our ideas of "responsiveness" and "directiveness," first mooted in Benson and Whitworth (2007) then explored in more detail in Whitworth and Benson (2014b). We use those expanded ideas here to reinterpret the analysis of the Moodle cases, which forms the second part of this chapter.

The original chapter (Whitworth and Benson 2010) presented the project's theoretical framework, derived from activity theory (such as Engeström, Miettinen & Punamäki, 1999), and recognized that CMSs, rather than simply being technological tools, also constituted *rules* and *divisions of labor* (roles) for the subjects of the activity system. Some of that prior discussion has been retained in this revised chapter. But there is also a need to consider work on the theory of e-learning, and technology within organizations more broadly that has been published since we originally wrote the chapter in 2009, particularly that which considers the nature of practice. We have therefore rewritten much of the theoretical part of this chapter in order to give more detailed consideration to the question of practice, as it is this that can be considered the truly emergent factor here. Wenger, whose ideas regarding communities of practice (Wenger, 1999) have been so influential, collaborated a decade later with White and Smith in their book *Digital Habitats* (Wenger, White, & Smith, 2009), and we draw on insights from that work, particularly the notion of *stewarding*, to better conceptualise the divisions of labour that exist within the course teams we studied.

EMERGING TECHNOLOGIES — OR EMERGING PRACTICES?

Even in 2009 it was stretching a definition to describe CMS technology as "emerging" in the sense of it being something new or innovative—but the discussion by Veletsianos (2010) showed that "newness" is not necessarily a characteristic of the emerging technology. We wanted to observe how a CMS *in context* is always emergent; that is, constantly formed and re-formed from interactions occurring in many micro-level contexts (De Wolf & Holvoet, 2005, p. 3), which are structured by and yet also structure the macro-level features of a given organizational setting.

Because this construction of practice is, in principle, a continuous process, the CMS — or any other sociotechnical system — is always something new. Ideally the practices that "intertwine" (Wenger et al., 2009, p. 19) with the technology emerge within communities of practice as a result of reflection (Schön, 1991) by users, managers, and other stakeholders, and are continuously being tested "on the ground" with reflections on one iteration fed back and used to enhance the next, making practices and technologies more effective. But this ideal is far from being consistently achieved. Generally, organizational life is as much characterized by the institutionalisation (Douglas, 1986) or reification (Wenger, 1999) of incumbent practices even after their time has passed, with further change being blocked in various ways. CMSs, even in 2009, were frequently derided as "undead" technologies, sucking resources out of institutions like vampires and giving little back (see Wheeler, 2009; Whitworth & Benson, 2014b, p. xii); at best, as *in*flexible (Kultur & Yazici 2014) rather than dynamic and constantly evolving.

As we said in response to this critique (Whitworth & Benson, 2014a), the CMS *can* evolve, but

> this transformation is one that does not just result in changes in software or interfaces, but the working practices that exist around the CMS . . . [these] are not givens, that is, wholly dependent on the technological features of the system. Instead, they are constructed through a combination of factors [and] . . . influenced by the diverse (and sometimes conflicting) interests of multiple stakeholders: faculty, students, administrators, IT services groups, managers, employers and governments. (p. xii)

These issues are intrinsically bound up with how practice, and the formation of knowledge, are managed and controlled within an organization. Thus how a technology "emerges" is a sociological question, and one that can only be answered with reference to specific contexts. This kind of study sheds light not only on how a CMS is used but also why there may be resistance to one's adoption and subsequent changes in practice (Veletsianos, 2010, p. 14).

STUDYING THE CMS AS A BOUNDARY OBJECT

A technology like a CMS originates from micro-level interactions, but once it achieves a certain finality of form and spreads outside its original context, it becomes the focus of multiple inquiries, taking place in many different contexts. It therefore resides on the *boundary* of different communities of practice.

Anderson (2010) invokes complexity theory as a way of understanding the contexts within which educational technology must emerge, particularly the social and structural norms in place. Anderson refers to McElroy's (2000) idea of "the edge of chaos," the transitional zone in which new practices can emerge. It is the "edge" because this zone is not so divergent from existing practice that the innovation can simply find no root, but there is also a required boundary interaction with something *other*, and through this interaction, new insights can at least potentially penetrate the structures which have formed within the institution. Fischer and Ostwald (2005) said that boundary objects have meaning

> within the conceptual knowledge systems of at least two communities of practice. The meaning need not be the same — in fact, the differences in meaning

are what lead to the creation of new knowledge. . . . The interaction around a boundary object is what creates and communicates knowledge, not the object itself. (p. 224–25)

A danger with any community is that it can become isolated and parochial, and as a result, struggle to incorporate new practices even when this would be beneficial to its operations. Boundary objects link communities of practice together, providing a conduit for information flows. Through engagement with them, communities are potentially exposed to new perspectives, giving them material for reflection and, eventually, absorption into their own practice. This is why Anderson (2010) says:

> Organizational structures aid to surf at the "edge of chaos," not function to eliminate or constrain the creative potential of actors engaged at this juncture. Further, this understanding can guide creation and management of these complex environments, not with goals to control or understand learning, but with an objective to create systems in which learning emerges rapidly and profoundly. (p. 29)

From this perspective, then, the development of new practices around a CMS is best facilitated not by the development of generic (that is, context-independent) set-piece training programs, but by creating an environment that brings together different stakeholders across the boundaries of different communities of practice, promotes reflective practice and is built around a CMS that is *responsive* to the learning that takes place in that environment. This latter point is crucial. As we said (Benson & Whitworth, 2014b, p. 185), if digital habitats are to be *transformed* as the result of learning in professional contexts, the "key tension is . . . between the outcomes of learning processes, and whether the technology can respond to that learning, or directs it."

We touched on this distinction, between responsiveness and directiveness, in the 2010 version of this chapter (and see also Benson & Whitworth, 2007), but have subsequently developed the ideas in more detail (Whitworth & Benson, 2014b). The case studies below consider how these tendencies played out in two real distance learning settings.

STEWARDING AS A LEARNING PROCESS

In their book *Digital Habitats*, Wenger, White and Smith (2009) draw attention to the phenomenon of *stewarding*. Stewarding is the process through which communities of practice maintain the technological environments — the digital habitats — that they use, but also continually construct, as they work and learn. It is a creative role, and a leadership one (Wenger et al., 2009).

Wenger et al. (2009) describe various processes that stewards should become involved in, including technology acquisition, supporting community members' use of the technology, identifying and spreading good practice, and ensuring continuity across any significant disruptions. For our purposes here, a key statement is that "stewards can help transform experiments, accidents or local discoveries into community-wide practices and agreements that advance the community's capacity" (p. 242). Stewards are thus, at least in part, responsible for maintaining the responsiveness of a technology. They should also "attend ... to community boundaries created by technology" (p. 243).

Wenger et al.'s book is written in a style directed at the individual practitioner, who has a relatively formalized mandate to work with the community's use of technology. Certainly such roles exist, with IT support offices in a university being an obvious example. But this also suggests the steward may not necessarily be located *within* the community they have a mandate to help. There are also different ways of distributing the authority that is invested in the role. The capacity to steward may be distributed widely throughout the members of the community, and not necessarily invested only in one or two people. Thus, stewarding may result in *divisions of labor* (see the reference to activity theory, above) but it also may not, depending on the context and its continual emergence. Stewarding may therefore become institutionalised and reified, but can also remain participatory and emergent.

Embedding values into technology is how organizations learn: "through the storage of individual knowledge in organizational structure and routines" (Tagliaventi & Mattarelli, 2006, p. 293). But reification occurs when different cognitive cultures that could potentially contribute to a system design are no longer communicating across their boundaries (Whitworth, 2007). What becomes embedded will then be a singular perspective, that of an isolated community of practice, which might be core—the managers', for instance—or peripheral. Douglas describes how these perspectives are more likely to become institutionalised, and thus cognitively locked within an organization, meaning they become unscrutinised and not open to review: "That's not the way we do things here."

On the other hand, a CMS that is negotiated between the centre and the periphery can be an *architecture of participation* (Garnett & Ecclesfield, 2008), promoting both professional practice and organizational learning. This would help the system to remain responsive, and truly emergent: that is, emerging from the broadest range of micro-level contexts, rather than having its nature directed by only a limited subset of stakeholders. For this to happen, ongoing processes of *negotiation* (Cervero & Wilson, 1998) are required between various stakeholder communities, which challenge "the limits of each [stakeholder] community's beliefs" (Brown & Duguid, 1998, p. 98). Such negotiation is more likely to take place in informal work settings "on the ground" than in formalized meetings (see Tagliaventi & Mattarelli, 2006). And, as noted by Wenger et al. (2009, p. 143), stewarding partly involves the bringing together of these different interests across their boundaries: thus maintaining their architecture of participation and not just their technology architecture.

How, then, can architectures of participation be facilitated in HEIs, in ways that are compatible with the loosely coupled nature of these institutions (Weick, 1976) and which do not encourage the reification and institutionalisation of existing practice but rather create CMSs that are responsive to the enquiries of the communities of practice that form around them?

MOODLE AS A BOUNDARY OBJECT

When multiple perspectives come together via a boundary object, it becomes the locus of a *community of interest*. Fischer and Ostwald (2005, p. 213–14) suggest that these communities of interest address "the challenges of collaborative design involving stakeholders from different practices and backgrounds"; promote "constructive interactions among multiple knowledge systems"; and rely "on boundary objects to mediate knowledge communication." Crucial to this process of collaborative design, which is simultaneously a process of knowledge formation and ultimately practice formation, is "the educational impact of participation itself" (Blaug, 2007, p. 41). A negotiated, participatory, and responsive CMS brings together the various cognitive cultures in an HEI (at both centre and periphery) within the boundary object that is the CMS, engaging them in a joint learning process, oriented to enable the continual emergence and evolution of practice.

As we have said, responsiveness in a CMS is not solely the province of open-source technologies such as Moodle, and it would be quite possible for a Moodle solution to be imposed from the centre, in a directive way. Nevertheless the open-source approach to CMS development does provide certain channels for participation that other types of CMS do not.

Many Moodles exist throughout the education sector. Moodle was specifically designed to be easy to adapt to different contexts (Dougiamas & Taylor, 2003), and it scales easily from single, one-off uses in a particular course to serving the need of large HEIs. In principle, *any* user can design a Moodle-based innovation that could be adapted into the central technological architecture, the kernel. Therefore, as well as being a boundary object at the organizational level, wherein various stakeholders can come together to review and develop Moodle (Bower, McNeill, & Hedberg, 2014), the moodle.org community works at an even broader macro-level to develop a shared understanding about the architecture on which local Moodles are then based. This is partly a technical programming task, but it is also a matter of developing shared understandings about the pedagogical (or other) principles that underpin the technology (Dougiamas & Taylor, 2003; Moodle, 2008). In theory, through the "free market" operations of open-source software, these principles are being constantly validated and dynamically updated by a global community of users; stewarding is thus widely distributed.

In practice, however, Moodle is susceptible to distortions that affect any community that "focuses heavily on building a body of quality resources" (Stuckey & Barab, 2007, p. 446); "the 'grab and run' action of many new members becomes counter-productive to dialogue" (Stuckey & Barab, 2007, p. 446). Moodle could be passively consumed by users rather than being actively generated and stewarded by them. This places the burden of development on only a small proportion of users. Also, work at the community of practice level will also be subject to distortions that originate outside the community; for example, pressures placed on course teams by institutional management.

A TALE OF TWO MOODLE SITES

Our research included two program sites where the open-source Moodle software was the CMS of choice. PAP (Public Administration Programme) is a wholly online UK Master's program. It originated and was funded as part of the UKeU project and survived that institution's collapse (Conole, Carusi, & de Laat, n.d.). E-TECH is a wholly online US Master's program in educational technology. The program originated with funding from the Sloan Foundation. The programs were very similar in organizational structure but very different in philosophies of online teaching and learning (see also Benson, Lawler, & Whitworth, 2008).

Program goals

Two primary goals drove the E-TECH program: to provide a site for research into online learning tools, technologies, and strategies; and to provide a stable and effective online E-TECH program. PAP's primary goal was to provide a stable and effective online program that was self-supporting.

Program and campus technology

E-TECH's selection of the open-source Moodle software as its course management system is reflective of the program's goal to be a research bed where instructor-researchers could perform trials and demonstrate online technology tools and strategies. PAP's selection of Moodle was more practical. They had to quickly move from the vanishing UKeU platform, and Moodle was a reasonable alternative that was available on a local server. They were assisted in this emergency move by a colleague in a different department who had used Moodle himself in his own teaching: a clear example of stewarding.

E-TECH used Moodle and several other commercial and open-source supporting technology tools in its courses, while PAP was a strict user of Moodle-only tools. Both the PAP and E-TECH campuses adopted Blackboard as the campus-wide commercial course management system. PAP's university did so despite PAP staff lobbying for Moodle. After this decision, the PAP program was directed to move PAP to Blackboard. PAP staff had to make a case for why they should not move to the new system. The process was contentious, but PAP was allowed to continue its use of Moodle, though not indefinitely.

E–TECH staff have not been directed to move E-TECH to the campus system. In fact, the campus office that administers external programs provides E-TECH with technical support for Moodle and the other technology tools the program uses. The research objective of the program and the researcher roles that instructors play may keep E-TECH shielded from such influence in the future.

Program cultures

Because of the twofold objective of the E-TECH staff, the E-TECH philosophy tends toward an open and nonstandardized course design. Instructors are encouraged to experiment in their course designs, which results in students having drastically different experiences in each course in the program. E-TECH operates its own budget, using funds generated by student enrolment and subsidized by the academic department in which it is housed. Finally, E-TECH staff fully supports Moodle.org and participates frequently in its forums.

The PAP culture tends toward standardization of course design and tutor practice with the use of compliance documents, such as course development guides, tutor contracts, and student guides. PAP sponsors a yearly conference for tutors to further enhance the community aspect. PAP operates its own budget, using funds generated by student enrolment and subsidized by the academic department in which it is housed. PAP also fully supports Moodle.org and submits each new feature it develops to Moodle.org for inclusion in the base Moodle product. However, this is not quite as inclusive a process as it is with E-TECH, as the next section will show.

Program communities

Several stakeholder groups participate in the development and ongoing administration of both programs, but the divisions of labour of each differ (here, see also Benson et al., 2008). For example, in E-TECH, instructors and developers work together to provide course content and activities. E-TECH staff (teaching and development assistants) build the courses and instructors teach them. E-TECH staff and developers serve as the first line of technology and administrative support for instructors and students. E-TECH also benefits from a university-level academic support organization, which works with them to provide advanced software support, including fixes and new feature development.

Likewise, several stakeholder groups participate in the development and ongoing administration of PAP, but the relationships are different. While PAP staff remain the builders of courses, content and content experts provide activities, and then tutors, full-time and part-time, teach the courses. PAP staff is the first line of technology and administrative support for tutors and students, but advanced software support is less integral to PAP than it is in (and around) E-TECH. An external contractor provides advanced software support, including software fixes, new feature development, and Moodle.org liaison for submitting locally developed features. The university's technical support staff only supports the university's standard virtual learning environment, Blackboard (eLearning), not Moodle.

RESPONSIVENESS AND DIRECTIVENESS IN E-TECH AND PAP

Responsiveness and directiveness are not uniform. A digital habitat can be responsive in some ways and directive in others. E-TECH and PAP are primarily responsive digital habitats. E-TECH can be characterized as responsive at the content, pedagogy, architecture, and system levels; while PAP can be characterized as directive at the content level and responsive at the pedagogy, architecture, and system levels. At each level, team members use a variety of strategies (accommodation, evaluation, and subversion) to learn about and/ or handle inconsistencies between the system and the environment in which it is was deployed. Likewise, parties external to the team may employ strategies (relaxation, acknowledging feedback, and blocking) to address these inconsistencies.

Accommodation occurs when team members change ways of working or teaching to align with system standards; *relaxation* occurs when tight system procedures are allowed to slip, or management "turns a blind eye" to them. *Evaluation* occurs when team members, systematically or informally, gather data, reflect, conduct action research, deliberate, and thus make informed decisions about a technology that may enter or has entered the digital habitat; *acknowledging feedback* occurs when, in response to user feedback, a new version of the system, technology, or procedure is released or the current one upgraded. *Blocking* occurs when system changes cannot be made due to extant procedures, with architecture or systems taking precedence over user demands; *subversion* occurs when team members ignore or bypass the imposed system change, possibly giving the appearance of compliance but not actually changing behaviour. The primary types of responsiveness exhibited in E-TECH were acknowledging feedback and evaluation, while PAP exhibited all types except subversion.

System

At the system level, team members may choose the CMS they use (responsive) or the CMS may be chosen for them at a higher level in the organization (directive). E-TECH faculty chose Moodle as their CMS (or other online medium, such as wikis or blogs), and thus had a responsive digital habitat at the system level. While instructors were subtly encouraged to gravitate toward Moodle because it provided certain administrative benefits such as reducing support costs, having a single access point for records of student logins, they were not forced to do so. The type of responsiveness exhibited by E-TECH was evaluation.

Likewise with PAP, Moodle was the team's choice for CMS, making PAP also responsive at the system level. When "Churchampton" (a pseudonym), PAP's host institution, tried to compel PAP to move to the Blackboard system that it had purchased, PAP made a strong case for why it should be allowed to continue Moodle use. The type of responsiveness exhibited by PAP was also evaluation.

Had Churchampton succeeded in making PAP move to Blackboard, PAP would have been considered a directive habitat of the blocking type.

Architecture

At the architecture level, team members can make changes to the technical features of the CMS (responsive) or be restricted from making such changes (directive). Since Moodle is open-source software, by definition E-TECH and PAP can make changes to its technical features, making both responsive at the architecture level.

E-TECH (which uses Moodle significantly but not exclusively) does not just consume the expertise of the Moodle community but actively contributes to it, having developed enhancements that have been incorporated into the Moodle kernel. E-TECH has also made financial contributions to the Moodle community. The team recognizes that its participation in the Moodle community helps the CMS actively respond to its needs. The type of responsiveness demonstrated from the Moodle community perspective was acknowledging feedback and evaluation from E-TECH's perspective.

Likewise, PAP team members can, and have, proposed changes to its architecture, and engaged contract programmers to create these changes, which were embedded in the Moodle kernel. As noted for E-TECH, this is a form of responsiveness, through evaluation and acknowledgement of feedback within the wider community of users, and is unique to the open-source CMSs.

Content

At the content level, team members may be able to create and/or adapt the teaching materials (responsive) or the teaching materials may be prescribed or created outside the team (directive). Teachers on PAP (known as e-tutors) are not content creators. External consultants who are content area experts write PAP courses, making PAP directive at the content level. Since PAP teachers cannot make content changes, the type of directiveness exhibited is blocking. E-TECH took a different approach. Members of the E-TECH instructional team write E-TECH courses and individual teachers are allowed to change course content, making E-TECH responsive at the content level.

Pedagogy

At the pedagogy level, team members can change instructional methods and delivery modes (responsive) or methods and delivery modes may be assigned (directive). In its first few years, PAP imposed standardized course templates on e-tutors, and thus was directive (blocking) at the pedagogy level. This requirement has recently been relaxed, allowing e-tutors more freedom to experiment and evaluate new methods. As an example, in PAP, tutors who earlier in the program's history had no ability to choose pedagogical methods were, over time, given more freedom to do so, but no obligation to do so. Thus, PAP changed from a directive (blocking) habitat to a directive (relaxation) habitat at the pedagogy level.

No obligation was placed on E-TECH faculty to teach in particular ways and the laissez-faire managerial ethos of the team resulted in support being offered, or at least investigated, by the in-house team for any approach the faculty wished to explore. Irina, the course manager, said their approach to tech support was "proactive." Like PAP, E-TECH had a research interest in educational technology and this strongly influenced the approach, which is best characterized as responsive at the pedagogy level. E-TECH placed great reliance on the ongoing evaluation of new technologies, whether by the faculty or the technical support staff (who are actively tasked, via job descriptions, to anticipate tensions before they arise, hence the idea of "proactive" tech support). Thus the type of directiveness exhibited by E-TECH was evaluation.

LESSONS LEARNED

While E-TECH and PAP have similar organizational structures, their reasons for choosing Moodle, an open-source CMS, and their philosophies of using it are very different. This section presents several lessons learned about open-source CMS selection, implementation and use from the PAP and E-TECH experiences. The lessons relate to responsiveness/directiveness, cost, centralization/localization, and standardization/individualization.

Responsive vs. directive habitats

A key feature of open-source systems makes them more likely to result in a responsive digital habitat: they can be standardized for users who want standardization and they can be individualized for users who prefer customization. This feature, which sets open-source CMS apart from commercial CMS, made PAP and E-TECH responsive habitats. E-TECH was characterized as responsive at the content, pedagogy, architecture, and system levels; while PAP was characterized as directive at the content level and responsive at the pedagogy, architecture, and system levels. The differences between the two programs have been reviewed in detail above.

The E-TECH example suggests that while it is possible to sustain a highly responsive system, which thus creates a participatory architecture, where the stewarding role is widely distributed throughout the community, one must remain aware of the resourcing implications of doing so. E-TECH's program objectives offered incentives, for the program and institutional managers, to directly or indirectly allocate a certain amount of the program's resources to this end, and thus to support evaluation, acknowledge feedback, and consequently revise the continuously emerging technologies and practices of the team. Programs or departments, which do not have such an objective, will undoubtedly welcome a certain amount of directiveness, particularly where a proportion of the budget has already been "top-sliced" to fund these kinds of centralised activities. But the danger in this latter case is that stewarding could be completely separated from the community. PAP was largely able to retain control over its emerging CMS precisely because it had retained within the team significant amounts of knowledge about its digital habitat (technology and practice), and was then able to express this not just within itself but across the boundary, making arguments that other stakeholder groups could engage with, for instance that Moodle was an essential element of sustaining teaching quality and student satisfaction scores. A more directive architecture would have been less likely to allow this.

No cost vs. different costs

Often people think of the open-source option for course management systems as a free or low-cost alternative to the major commercial systems. While it is true that the source code may be free or less expensive, there are hidden costs associated with the use of open-source course management systems. The biggest of these costs is technology support and administration. E-TECH employed a Moodle programmer and technology support staff, while PAP purchased a Moodle programming and technology support contract from an external provider. In addition, these programs require pedagogical expertise in online course design and delivery. These skills are not necessarily found in Moodle programmers or technical support, so additional pedagogical support staff is also needed.

Although the operational proximity (see Tagliaventi & Mattarelli, 2006) between instructors, developers, and Moodle itself was slightly less in PAP than E-TECH, both teams were active users of Moodle, not just passive consumers of its benefits. In both cases, these teams did succeed in having the results of their reflective practice—their learning about the system-in-use—embedded not only into their local Moodle but also into the Moodle kernel. Particularly for PAP, in which members of the course team had less freedom and fewer resources with which to experiment and innovate with alternative technologies, this was a way of stabilizing the system-in-use, rendering the team as a whole less vulnerable to updates to the system coming in from outside, that is, being imposed on them as a result of changes to the Moodle kernel developed elsewhere. Their reflective practice, therefore, has increased the knowledge base of the team as a whole, and embedded that knowledge, at least partly, into the technological architecture. Active use of the CMS, therefore, leads to a more negotiation-based, participatory, and responsive system, as opposed to a directive one.

Centralization vs. localization

One observation that can be made from the PAP and E-TECH programs' use of Moodle is the tension that exists between campus-level administrators and systems and program-level administrators and systems. This tension exists because campus-level administrators and program-level administrators have different primary goals. In both E-TECH and PAP, campus-level administrators were concerned about security and the integration of course management systems with other campus systems for registration, security, and grading. These were not the primary goals of either of the programs.

The tensions suggest a question that campus administrators must address: what is gained from the centralization of course management systems and their support as opposed to what is gained from decentralization? There are no easy answers. Benson and Whitworth (2007) determined that centralized systems tended to be less responsive to their users at the program level than decentralized systems managed locally by the programs themselves. As a result, program-level administrators tended to use subversion tactics—employing workarounds to address system shortcomings instead of working with campus-level staff to address them—when required to use campus-level systems. Examples of subversive tactics include using the centralized CMS as a front-end to the program courses, but providing the actual content directly on the Web or with locally managed external applications. As we noted above, this is an example of the workarounds becoming the object of activity rather than the CMS, and the learning that these course teams engage in is consequently not feeding back into the system. In situations where this "subversion" happens—which included all three of the directive systems we researched (Benson & Whitworth, 2007)—the system cannot be said to be truly emergent.

This did not happen so obviously with either of our Moodle case studies. Both were self-contained in technological terms, and both expressed a commitment to a management style that they self-termed "laissez-faire" (E-TECH's course director) and "inclusive . . . enabling the people who work on the team to have as much responsibility and as much ownership as possible for their work" (PAP's course director). E-TECH's director continued:

> You bring your best ideas in for your course, and we'll help you mix and match and merge that with the best ideas from technology, and we'll get the course up. And if you wanna ask some questions of us, we're there to help you. But we're not there to pass muster on your ideas, [your] pedagogical and course information ideas.

A research student, who is also paid to act as the local Moodle developer, facilitates E-TECH's policy. As noted above, this person also has an active relationship with the kernel and Moodle.org. There is thus an ongoing process of negotiation occurring here, not only among members of the E-TECH team but through this brokerage (see Fischer & Ostwald, 2005, p. 225), E-TECH and other activity systems that share its technological architecture. For E-TECH, Moodle is a genuine boundary object working at both the micro-level and the wider macro-level structure. Though divisions of labour are stronger in PAP, this is at least in part explained by its courses being targeted at civil servants rather than at educational technologists. Deliberate policy decisions were taken to standardize certain practices, as it was believed this would make the technology easier to use for its students. Teaching staff is also not expected to engage with CMS technology at the level of research and active use. Nevertheless, over time, a more participatory system is emerging at the micro scale, and Moodle has always been a boundary object between PAP and other systems.

Ideally, campus-level administrators must be sensitive to the different types of CMS users. Users who are delivering full programs online have different needs than users who are supplementing their traditional campus courses with online content, activities, and resources. The campus-level administrators on the E-TECH campus were sensitive to the needs of the program and supported the open-source system. The campus-level administrators on the PAP campus were also sensitive to program needs but they felt the campus security needs overrode them. As noted above, however, PAP has been able to defend itself from top-down directives to change. Indeed, as a result of the case made by the staff, the campus-level e-learning administrator has requested certain changes be made to the Blackboard system before PAP's host institution fully adopts it. The investments made in learning about the technology have, in this case, been able to change practices in other parts of this loosely coupled HEI, albeit indirectly.

We suggest that one way campus-level administrators can address the centralization-decentralization question for fully online programs is to centralize the course management function but decentralize the technical support. By definition, open-source systems can be responsive to user needs, but that responsiveness requires a strong set of technology skills and a high level of knowledge of the systems' features and processes. Unless this knowledge and skill sets are made available locally to the online program, the system will not be fully utilized by the program or made fully compatible with the program's needs. This corresponds to Tagliaventi and Mattarelli's (2006) suggestion that operational proximity—literally, sharing a context—is most helpful for facilitating the transfer of knowledge and innovation between different stakeholder groups.

Standardization vs. individualization

PAP and E-TECH adopted different philosophies for course design and delivery. The operating practices of the PAP staff yield a structured and controlled online course environment in which students face a consistent interface and operation in each module in the course. As noted above, since students are not technology experts and courses are not technology-related, this standardization is a positive characteristic of the program. There is, though, a downside to this standardization: it severely limits tutor decision-making when teaching a course. Thus, even though the PAP use of Moodle was responsive (Benson & Whitworth, 2007), standardization in course design limits that responsiveness at the tutor level. The PAP staff has recognized this unintended consequence and is working toward loosening some of the course standards.

E-TECH's course design philosophy, on the other hand, is that course design should reflect the interests and preferences of teaching faculty, yielding a set of courses with designs that vary by course and instructor. This philosophy is effective in E-TECH since the program's content is related to teaching with technology, so the students are enriched by the variety of course designs. The philosophy may not be appropriate, though, for programs where the content is not related to technology use. In those cases, the philosophy could become a hindrance to student learning.

Online program administrators would be better served by staking out a middle position along the standardization-individualization continuum, since neither PAP's extreme standardization nor E-TECH's extreme individualization is ideal. A better solution would be one that balances the need for instructor flexibility in meeting course objectives with the student need for a nonintrusive use of technology. Once again, this is an example of how negotiation, participation, and responsiveness could be designed into an activity system and, thus, a digital habitat.

CONCLUSION

Open-source course management systems seem to be low-cost, flexible solutions to online course delivery, but that appearance can be deceiving. The cost of the required programming and technical support must be added to the low cost of the source code. The inherent ability to customize an open-source system for a particular use must be balanced with the need to provide students with an interface that does not detract from their learning. Finally, the ease of acquisition of open-source systems by programs within institutions challenges the economies of scale that many institutions gain with centralized systems. Campus-level concerns can lead to distance educators being directed toward solutions that are less appropriate for their specific contexts.

In both our case studies, however, learning processes were taking place that were facilitated by the design of both the CMS itself and the sociotechnical activity system that surrounded the technology. Both case studies were differently configured, but both configurations were clearly the result of conscious design decisions made by program managers and (in E-TECH's case only) campus-level administrators. Operational proximity helped create "knowledge brokers," who were able to feed the reflective practices of course team members back into an emergent system. In each case, however, this was more apparent vis-à-vis Moodle itself than vis-à-vis each program's host institution. Though these examples show that loose coupling does not necessarily have to lead to "bottom-up" reification by isolationist communities of practice, they do suggest that it remains easier to develop communities of interest between different HEIs than within a single one. Stuckey and Barab (2007) write that community design is never final: it requires a commitment to ongoing and sustained design, and management focus should be on community as a negotiation process (p. 442).

Our research has led us to believe that to truly address the issue of organizational learning within HEIs, such a commitment is required both from management and the communities of practice, and is easier to sustain with a system that is responsive. Online learning course teams should be aware that responsiveness within any system is not a given. It can be designed in as a factor of management style, but it may also be challenged from without or it could decay, if not continuously refreshed by professional practice. The result may be a more directive system that ultimately could retard both the teams' and their host institutions' ability to learn about, and adapt to, the changes wrought by emergent technologies. Investing in operational proximity, which can create both knowledge brokers and boundary objects, and thus increase the knowledge base of the team as a whole, may be a significant investment for distance learning teams wishing to maintain their autonomy in the face of campus-level concerns.

REFERENCES

Anderson, T. (2010). Theories for learning with emerging technologies. In G. Veletsianos (ed.), *Emerging technologies in distance education*. Edmonton: Athabasca University Press (pp. 23–39).

Benson, A., Lawler, C., & Whitworth, A. (2008). Rules, roles, and tools: Activity theory and the comparative study of e-learning. *British Journal of Educational Technology* 39(3), 456–67.

Benson, A. D., & Whitworth, A. (2007). Technology at the planning table: Activity theory, negotiation, and course management systems. *Journal of Organisational Transformation and Social Change* 4(1), 65–82.

———. (2014a). The Public Administration Program at Churchampton College, UK. In A. P. Mizell and A. A. Piña (eds.), *Real-life E-learning: Case studies in research and practice*. Charlotte, NC: IAP

———. (2014b). The evolution of the CMS: Learning, social shaping and professional development. In Benson, A. D. and Whitworth, A. (eds.), *Research on course management systems in higher education* (pp. 239–51). Charlotte, NC: IAP.

Blaug, R. (2007). Cognition in a hierarchy. *Contemporary Political Theory*, 6(1), 24–44.

Bower, M., McNeill, M., & Hedberg, J. (2014). Evaluating extensions for a university course management system. In Benson, A. D. and Whitworth, A. (eds.), *Research on course management systems in higher education* (pp. 203–20). Charlotte, NC: IAP.

Brown, J. S., & Duguid, P. (1998). Organizing knowledge. *California Management Review* 40(3), 90–111.

Carr, W., & Kemmis, S. (1986). *Becoming Critical: Knowing Through Action Research*. Geelong, Australia: Deakin University Press.

Cervero, R., & Wilson, A. (1998). *Working the planning table: The political practice of adult education*. San Francisco: Jossey-Bass.

Conole, G., Carusi, A., & de Laat, M. (n.d.). *Learning from the UKeU experience* [e-Learning Research Centre working paper]. Retrieved from http://www. researchgate.net/publication/42792450_Learning_from_the_UKeU_ experience/file/60b7d51f9162a4a2fb.pdf

de Wolf, T., & Holvoet, T. (2005). Emergence vs. self-organisation: Different concepts but promising when combined. In S. A. Brückner (ed.), *Engineering self-organising systems: Methodologies and applications* (pp. 1–15). New York: Springer.

Dougiamas, M., & Taylor, P. (2003). *Moodle: Using learning communities to create an open source course management system*. Paper presented at EDMEDIA 2003 Honolulu, HI, USA.

Douglas, M. (1986). *How institutions think*. Syracuse, NY: Syracuse University Press.

Engeström,Y., Miettinen, R., & Punamäki, R. L. (1999). *Perspectives on activity theory*. Cambridge, UK: Cambridge University Press.

Fischer, G., & Ostwald, J. (2005). Knowledge communication in design communities. In R. Bromme, F. Hesse, & H. Spada (eds.), *Barriers and biases in computer-mediated knowledge communication*. New York: Springer.

Garnett, F., & Ecclesfield, N. (2008). Developing an organisational architecture of participation. *British Journal of Educational Technology 39*(3), 468–74.

Kultur, C., & Yazici, C. (2014). Adoption, diffusion and implementation of course management systems: A faculty focus. In A. D. Benson & A. Whitworth (Eds.) *Research on course management systems in higher education* (pp. 21–46). Charlotte, NC: IAP.

McElroy, M. (2000). Integrating complexity theory, knowledge management and organizational learning. *Journal of Knowledge Management 4*(3), 195–203.

Moodle. moodle.org (2008). *Philosophy*. Retrieved from http://docs.moodle. org/en/Philosophy

Schön, D. (1991). *The reflective practitioner: How professionals think in action*. Aldershot, UK: Ashgate.

Stuckey, B., & Barab, S. (2007). New conceptions for community design. In R. Andrews & C. Haythornthwaite (eds.), *The Sage handbook of E-learning research* (pp. 439–65). London: Sage.

Tagliaventi, M., & Mattarelli, E. (2006). The role of networks of practice, value sharing, and operational proximity in knowledge flows between professional groups. *Human Relations 59*(3), 291– 319.

Veletsianos, G. (2010). A definition of emerging technologies for education. In G. Veletsianos (ed.), *Emerging technologies in distance education* (pp. 3–22). Edmonton, AB: Athabasca University Press.

Weick, K. E. (1976). Educational organisations as loosely coupled systems. *Administrative Science Quarterly 21*(1), 1–19.

Wenger, E. (1999). *Communities of practice: Learning, meaning and identity.* Cambridge, UK: Cambridge University Press.

Wenger, E., White, N., & Smith, J. D. (2009). *Digital habitats: Stewarding technology for communities.* Portland, OR: CPSquare.

Wheeler, S. (2009). The VLE sucks. [Blog post]. Retrieved from http://steve-wheeler.blogspot.co.uk/2009/11/vle-sucks.html

Whitworth, A. (2007). Researching the cognitive cultures of e-learning. In R. Andrews & C. Haythornthwaite (eds.), *The Sage handbook of E-learning research* (pp. 202–20). London: Sage.

Whitworth, A., & Benson, A. D. (2010). Learning, design and emergence: Two case studies of Moodle in distance education. In G. Veletsianos (ed.), *Emerging technologies in distance education* (pp. 195–213). Edmonton, AB: Athabasca University Press.

——. (2014a). Introduction. In A. D. Benson & Whitworth, A. (eds.) *Research on course management systems in higher education* (pp. xi–xxi). Charlotte, NC: IAP.

——. (2014b). Reflective practice and digital habitats: Responsiveness and directiveness in course management systems. In A. D. Benson & A. Whitworth (eds.), *Research on course management systems in higher education* (pp. 183–201). Charlotte, NC: IAP.

8 Issues in Research, Design, and Development of Personal Learning Environments

▶ *Trey Martindale and Michael Dowdy*

Over the course of the last twenty years or so, use of the World Wide Web (the web) has grown—evolving from a hobbyist's tool to an indispensable resource for social interaction, education, commerce, and entertainment, among other uses. The web evolved into a tool for self-directed personal development and has become a vast resource that enables one to learn and grow outside the parameters of what is considered formal learning (courses, degrees, and other offerings). Adherents of a constructivist viewpoint on learning might be pleased at the many opportunities for one to construct one's learning opportunities from web resources (Wilson & Lowry, 2000). But the challenge for learners is to be able to create meaning from the vast amounts of information available for informal learning—learning that occurs outside of an education or training program. This challenge has created a significant need for a better way to organize self-directed personal development.

To meet this need, tools have continued to evolve as well, partly in order to help users organize and contribute to this vast informational resource. The concept of "Web 2.0" has been used to describe the evolution of the web from an information source to a "read/write" medium (O'Reilly, 2005). Individuals use these tools, sometimes known as social software, to interact, organize resources, and contribute new content. Social software can be defined simply as software that supports group interaction (Allen, 2004). Learners can thus organize and share content along with their own interpretation of the content. Some of this organizing, sharing, and interpreting is being done by persons with particular learning goals. It is in this context that the concept of the personal learning environment (PLE) has emerged.

The PLE qualifies as an emerging technology as defined in the opening chapter of this book. It is a new and evolving construct, not yet fully understood, and its unfulfilled potential means it can be disruptive. The concept of the PLE has emerged in recent years via the work of online theorists, researchers, and developers, as a result of the limitations of learning management systems (LMS), recognition of the importance of informal learning, and the growth of social software.

In this chapter we will describe the history of the PLE, explain why the PLE is useful, present PLE examples, examine the affordances of the PLE as compared to the LMS, describe barriers to the PLE, and present directions for future PLE development. Our work builds on the earlier version of this chapter published in Martindale and Dowdy (2010).

DEFINING THE PLE

Defining the PLE is a challenge, because the term has been used in several contexts to describe tools, processes, and sometimes both. Some define the PLE as a conceptual way of working to accomplish (usually informal) learning goals. In this case, the PLE is a collaborative ad hoc set of procedures learners use to interact and share resources that further the expertise and competence of the individual (and group, in some cases). Conversely, some define the PLE as a specific tool or set of tools (usually software) that a learner employs to interact with and manipulate online learning environments and resources. Buchem (2010) collected some commonly cited definitions for a PLE and we direct the reader to this useful resource for further study of the evolving definition of the concept. To demonstrate the diversity of thought, the following are some definitions of a PLE:

> Personal learning environments are systems that help learners take control of and manage their own learning. This includes providing support for learners to: set their own learning goals; manage their learning . . . both content and process; communicate with others in the process of learning; and thereby achieve learning goals. A PLE may be composed of one or more sub-systems: As such it may be a desktop application, or composed of one or more web-based services. (van Harmelen, 2008)

[A] facility for an individual to access, aggregate, configure and manipulate digital artifacts of their ongoing learning experiences. (Lubensky, 2006)

A collection of social software tools that take on a learner-centered approach (Schaffert & Hilzensauer, 2008).

It is tempting to think of it as a content management device or as a file manager. But the heart of the concept of the PLE is that it is a tool that allows a learner (or anyone) to engage in a distributed environment consisting of a network of people, services and resources. It is not just Web 2.0, but it is certainly Web 2.0 in the sense that it is (in the broadest sense possible) a read-write application. (Downes, 2006)

The PLE is not a single piece of software, but instead the collection of tools used by a user to meet their needs as part of their personal working and learning routine. So, the characteristics of the PLE design may be achieved using a combination of existing devices (laptops, mobile phones, portable media devices), applications (newsreaders, instant messaging clients, browsers, calendars) and services (social bookmark services, weblogs, wikis) within what may be thought of as the practice of personal learning using technology. (Wilson et al., 2006, p. 36)

The PLE concept has evolved with the development of social software. Web 2.0 and social software tools have gradually expanded and are now a significant part of the online world. These tools include blogs, wikis, podcasting, social networking, RSS, microblogging, instant messaging, virtual worlds, and others. It is worth noting that some researchers make a distinction between the PLE itself and the personal toolkit that one uses to act upon this environment.

The phrase "personal learning environment" appears to have first been mentioned at the annual JISC-CETIS conference in 2004 (Schaffert & Hilzensauer, 2008). The history of the PLE concept has been documented in a number of sources (e.g., van Harmelen, 2008) and we refer the reader to this source for more detail on the history of PLEs. A key event in PLE history was Scott Wilson's presentation of "the VLE of the future" (Wilson, 2005). Soon afterward, the PLE became a theme in the 2005 JISC-CETIS annual conference.

As the PLE concept gained exposure, researcher Scott Leslie solicited and posted a collection of PLE models (Leslie, 2008) that would receive significant attention. Four years after posting the original diagrams, Leslie subsequently posted some observations about the collection, including some commentary on commonalities among the posts (Leslie, 2012). This collection of PLE diagrams was categorized by entries that were generally tool oriented, action oriented, person oriented, or consisted of a hybrid approach to all these. Figure 8.1 and 8.2 are two examples of such diagrams.

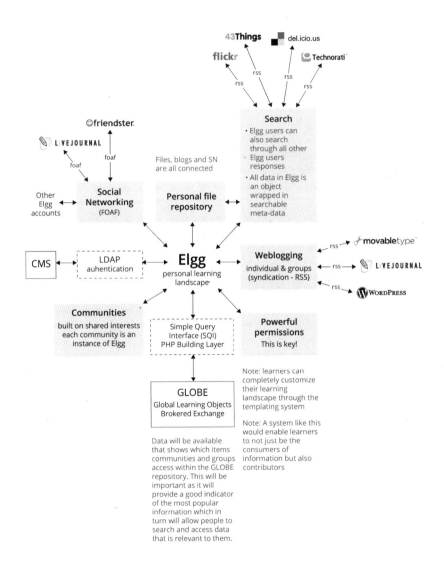

Figure 8.1 David Tosh PLE Diagram (Tosh, 2005).

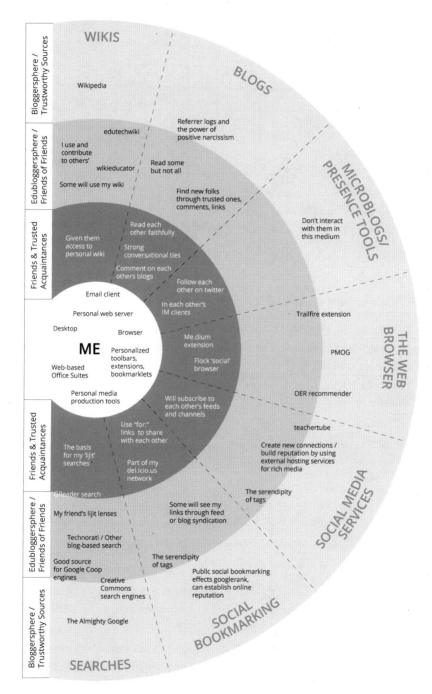

Figure 8.2 Scott Leslie, PLE Diagram (Leslie, n.d.).

In the years since the publication of our previous version of this chapter on PLEs (Martindale & Dowdy, 2010), there have been three notable additions to the PLE landscape. First, a series of academic conferences focusing on PLEs have been held, beginning in 2011 (http://pleconf.org). These conferences have facilitated the publication of many articles pertaining to the concept. For example, the conference proceedings from the 2013 PLE Conference (Buchem, Attwell, & Tur, 2013) focused on PLEs and "smart cities." Second, there have been special issues in academic journals concentrating on PLEs such as the ones in *eLearning Papers* (http://openeducationeuropa.eu/en/paper/personal-learning-environments) and the *Journal of Literacy and Technology* (http://www.literacyandtechnology. org/volume-15-number-2-june-2014.html). Third, the International Journal of Virtual and Personal Learning Environments (IJVPLE) was launched in 2010 and has since published over eighty articles (http://www.igi-global.com/journal/ international-journal-virtual-personal-learning/1134).

INSTANCES OF PLES

Sclater (2008) identified three perspectives on what PLEs should consist of and how PLEs should function. The first perspective is that the PLE should be client software that mediates between the learner and whatever resources the learner wants or requires. The second perspective is that a web-based portal can be an effective PLE without the need for client software. The third perspective is that PLEs are present in the form of physical and electronic resources learners can manipulate and customize to learn effectively (Sclater, 2008). The following is a brief summary of tools that can function as all or part of a PLE given these three perspectives:

PLEX (http://www.reload.ac.uk/plex/) is an open-source PLE prototype application developed at the University of Bolton. PLEX allows the user to seek out learning opportunities and manage them. PLEX supports standards such as RSS, Atom, and FOAF.

Colloquia (http://www.colloquia.net/) is a software application developed for group work. Once installed on each user's computer, Colloquia allows a user to create workgroups based on contexts or projects. These contexts allow for sharing of resources, messaging, and project management. Colloquia was released as version 1.3 in September 2001 and transitioned to open source in September of 2002. This platform has been described as a conversation-based PLE (van Harmelen, 2006).

Elgg (http://www.elgg.org/) is an open-source social networking platform and e-portfolio tool. Elgg is server-based, meaning one can download, install, and host an instance of Elgg.

Responsive Open Learning Environments (ROLE) (http://www.role-project.eu) is a European collaborative project with the goal to provide and support open learning environments, and organize a central repository of "widgets" that could be present in a PLE.

EyeOS (http://www.eyeos.org) is a "private-cloud" application platform that resides within one's web browser. One's files, applications, and settings are available at any networked computer.

Facebook (http://facebook.com) is a proprietary web-based social networking platform, but has enough components and flexibility to be considered as a form of PLE, even though it was not built primarily as a learning tool. Facebook includes a somewhat open API, extensibility, file sharing, forums, microblogging, instant messaging, and RSS feeds.

43 Things (http://www.43things.com) was a web-based service where users post lists of resolutions or life goals they wish to accomplish. Users can find others with shared goals and form an ad hoc community for encouragement and accountability along the way. Many of the posted goals involve learning in some way. The site and service was discontinued in 2014.

Netvibes (http://www.netvibes.com) is a web portal (sometimes referred to as a "webtop") where users can personalize pages. Individuals can assemble favorite widgets, websites, blogs, email accounts, social networks, search engines, instant messengers, photos, videos, podcasts, and more in one place. Netvibes is primarily an information-gathering service, but one can see in this service the semblance of a PLE.

LePress is an example of a customized plugin for the WordPress blogging platform. This plugin has been used by instructors in an attempt to balance the control issues of conducting a course while allowing students the freedom of using a blogging platform as their PLE (Tomberg, Laanpere, Ley, & Normak, 2013).

Two other examples include a model for an interactive logbook PLE (Chan, Corlett, Sharples, & Ting, 2005) and a "personal learning planner" (Havelock, Gibson, & Sherry, 2006). In addition, there have been attempts to describe a framework of what a PLE could consist of (see Figure 8.3), in terms of components and connections (Chatti, Agustiawan, Jarke, & Specht, 2010). Finally, Labrović and colleagues studied students' use of learning tools for informal learning to develop a "map" of how these tools coalesce to form a PLE (Labrović, Bijelić, & Milosavljević, 2014).

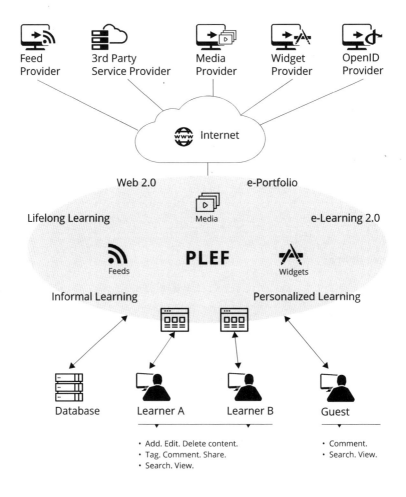

Figure 8.3 PLEF Framework (Chatti et al., 2010).

Another development has been the investigation of the "mash-up personal learning environment" (MUPPLE). This consists of collections of tools that users assemble and modify to construct PLEs in unique configurations. There have been a series of MUPPLE conferences (https://sites.google.com/site/muppleworkshop/) and also a code project called MUPPLE II within the Mozilla Developers Network (https://wiki.mozilla.org/Education/Projects/JetpackForLearning/Profiles/MUPPLE).

BENEFITS AND AFFORDANCES OF A PLE

In recent years there has been an increasing acceptance of the idea that informal learning will be the primary avenue for a person's learning experience, while formal learning programs make up a much smaller portion of the time one spends learning over a lifetime (Cross, 2007). The PLE can be seen as a manifestation of how one learns informally from a variety of sources and networks, both online and offline. With the growth of social software and social networking online, the web has become a place for connecting with other persons and communities rather than just a large repository of data and information. Dabbagh and Kitsantas (2012) have described how a PLE augments one's informal learning opportunities, and have described a pedagogical framework for social media use within a PLE to support student self-regulated learning, as students face a number of challenges with self-regulation when constructing and learning with PLEs (Kravcik & Klamma, 2012).

One of the perceived strengths of the PLE is that, as generally conceived as a learning environment; it is similar to what persons experience in real life—at least those persons who have access to Internet resources. Internet users are becoming accustomed to regularly using web-based resources and also contributing as producers of information for the networked world. The web has evolved to the point that it is unusual for a web resource to not have some opportunity for feedback and comments, if not extension, sharing, and reuse of information.

Another favorable aspect of PLEs is the perceived value of learner-centered instruction. Constructivist proponents contend that PLEs encourage learners to construct their own environments and communities, and create, share, and remix resources (Attwell, 2006).

In a report on PLEs, researchers with the Center for Educational Technology and Interoperability Standards (CETIS) derived these principles when examining current learning technologies (JISC-CETIS, 2007).

Learning opportunities should be accessible to students irrespective of constraints of time and place.

Learning opportunities should be available continually over the period of an individual's life.

Effective teaching should have as its central concern the individual learning needs and capabilities of a student.

The social component of learning should be prioritized through the provision of effective communication tools.

Barriers to learning, whether they are institutional, technical, or pedagogical should be removed.

In a similar report (Johnson, Liber, Wilson, Sharples, Milligan, & Beauvoir, 2006), five major themes were identified as a critique of current learning environments. These can be contrasted with how the PLE is typically described conceptually in terms of its affordances.

Desire for great personal ownership of technology.

Desire for more effective ways to manage technological services.

Desire for the integration of technological activity across all aspects of life.

Removal of barriers to the use of tools and services.

Desire to facilitate peer-based working.

In a frequently referenced post about the "anatomy of a PLE" Wheeler (2010) describes how proposed components of a PLE interact, and how they might interface with a university or workplace learning environment. Figure 8.4 represents the components he discusses.

Tu and colleagues have written about PLEs as part of open-network learning environments (ONLE). These authors described the advantages of such environments, including opportunities for student-generated and student-structured communities, multiple modes and dimensions for discourse, and cloud-based collaboration (Tu, Sujo-Montes, Yen, Chan, & Blocher, 2012).

Anderson (2006) summarizes the advantages of the PLE over the traditional LMS. With PLEs, the learner has a sense of self or identity beyond the classroom. As they direct their own learning, learners control the environment in which they work. The learner personally organizes the environment instead of operating within an environment that makes sense to the instructor or institution. The learner has responsibility for his or her own content. No longer a passive consumer, the learner is in an ownership role. The learner's reach extends much farther than the traditional classroom and LMS. While taking part in various online communities of practice, the learner develops an online personality.

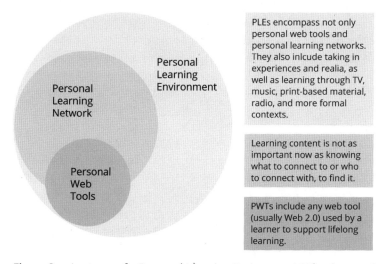

PLEs encompass not only personal web tools and personal learning networks. They also inlcude taking in experiences and realia, as well as learning through TV, music, print-based material, radio, and more formal contexts.

Learning content is not as important now as knowing what to connect to or who to connect with, to find it.

PWTs include any web tool (usually Web 2.0) used by a learner to support lifelong learning.

Figure 8.4 Anatomy of a Personal Learning Environment (Wheeler, 2010).

It is apparent from the conceptual definitions and the examples cited that the PLE is a response to the limitations of current learning environments. Consider the following scenario of a hypothetical university student's use of a PLE:

Liam is a "traditional learner," equipped with his own laptop computer, who makes the most of Web2.0 services . . . coordinated via his PLE. . . . As a student at University his course information, including resources, assignments, tutor feedback, etc. is made available to him via services provided by the institution, which interoperate with his PLE. In addition, he has access to further services, which support reflective activity and provide a repository for interesting items. Many of these services are provided outside the institution. All of these elements can be integrated and organized in whichever way Liam finds useful. Finally, his environment allows him to set up collaborative social groups, and to coordinate activity within these groups with other groups of which he is a member. . . . He is mindful of the fact that the performance of such a range of tasks without his PLE would present considerable obstacles for him—not least in simply remembering how to use all the different tools he would have to negotiate. In fact, Liam might go so far to say that his PLE is very much his "tool for dealing with life." (JISC-CETIS, 2007)

The following is a second scenario of a student using a PLE.

John is a twenty-year-old college student studying European history. He is enrolled in three courses at three different universities. Each university has its own LMS, but every part of each LMS can be accessed by his own web-based application (part of his PLE). He does not have to "go" to each university's system—rather the information comes to him. He is a frequent user of social networking software, and by his decision he regularly receives "learning opportunity notices" from trusted people and organizations based on his interests and career goals. These learning opportunities are structured around a standard set of fields or metadata that his PLE can interpret. For instance, he wants to learn to play the acoustic guitar, and his PLE interacts with his social network to find opportunities and resources to help him learn along with others who also want to learn to play. His PLE also connects with various open courseware sites to access open educational content, and can manage his interaction with others using the same content. John's PLE helps him maintain an online portfolio of his products and competencies. He can easily configure this portfolio for the appropriate audience(s) when he needs to demonstrate what he knows and what he can do. From informal interests to formal degree programs, John's PLE can interact with the various systems via one familiar and personally configurable interface.

THE PLE COMPARED AND CONTRASTED WITH THE LMS

Researchers and theorists investigating PLEs sometimes frame a philosophical debate in which the PLE is positioned against the learning management system (LMS). The LMS in some ways is an easy target in that it is frequently a large, somewhat inflexible environment that is chosen and implemented by formal educational organizations rather than by the learners (see chapter 7). An LMS offers control, tracking, and management by the institution and by the instructor in a particular course, and therefore is quite different in nature and purpose from the PLE as described in this chapter.

In terms of "market reach" and scope of adaptation, the LMS has been very successful in higher education. The LMS meets certain needs of the institution, such as tracking student enrollment, participation, assessment (grading), and completion. It allows for discussion and other types of interaction, and is a relatively quick and easy way for an instructor or entire program to "put courses

Trey Martindale and Michael Dowdy

online." The LMS has been popular in business and industry as a way to quickly deliver and track employee training, particularly in terms of compliance training and meeting regulatory requirements (Avgerinou, Papasalouros, Retalis, & Skordalakis, 2003). Having achieved success in business and in higher education, the LMS vendors are rapidly moving into secondary and primary education, for both in-person and online education.

Wilson et al. (2006) examined the design of LMSs and the alternative design presented by PLEs. The researchers compared LMSs to standards such as the VHS videotape and the QWERTY keyboard, and proposed that the LMS had become the de facto standard in online learning. Here is a summary of LMS characteristics.

LMSs concentrate on the course context.

All resources are loaded and linked within the overall structure of a course.

LMSs have an inherent asymmetric relationship between instructor and learner in terms of control of the learning experience.

The learner's role is one of passive acceptance of content and limited permissions set by the LMS.

Every learner experiences content exactly the same way. Each learner interacts with content in identical fashion.

Most LMS implementations are focused on managing rights and permissions in terms of access, which further restricts the learner's experience. And generally these rights and permissions do not extend beyond the hosting institution. An LMS by nature is concerned with managing learning and learners, and learners may prefer not to be managed; they may prefer to be encouraged, challenged, motivated, and inspired. Attwell (2006) posits that the predominant focus on managing via the institutional LMS has not resonated with modern learners, and that the educational system is in danger of being perceived as irrelevant or as an imposition. Outside the LMS, the modern learner has access to a wide variety of online information, experiences, and communities, the combination of which may make the LMS appear quite limited or impoverished as a learning environment (Sclater, 2008).

LMSs have been criticized for being so large and standardized that they become inflexible, and in fact prescribe a certain kind of learning environment.

From the learner's point of view, the limitations of an LMS have become more pronounced as social networking and related software has risen in prominence. The ease and flexibility afforded by a combination of tools mostly under the learner's control can make the university LMS seem too rigid and out of touch.

Researchers have identified the following perceived failures of the state of online learning environments in higher education:

> Accessibility has only partially been achieved by moving the medium of dissemination onto the web. However, Barriers to accessibility remain in the form of institutional procedures and usability.

> The institutionalization of learning technology presents a further barrier, because with institutional ownership of technology comes the requirement for students to re-learn the technologies of access to learning at each education provider.

> Current pedagogical practice is still teacher-centric. The promise of e-learning in enabling effective management of a diverse student population has only seldom been realized. At its worst, the VLE [virtual learning environment] can be characterized as a giant photocopier!

> The process of education is primarily institution-centric, rather than learner-centric. (JISC-CETIS, 2007)

A PLE brings with it many changes for the learner, the institution, and the content. The following table (Schaffert & Hilzensauer, 2008) identifies how seven facets of online learning differ in an LMS compared to a PLE. The table specifies these differences as well as the challenges and changes that PLEs represent.

Table 8.1 The shift from LMS to PLE (Schaffert & Hilzensauer, 2008).

		LMS	PLE	Challenges and Shifts
1	Role of the learner	learner as consumer of pre-defined learning materials, dependent on the "creativity" of the teacher	active, self-directed, creator of content	shift from consumer to "prosumer," self-organization is possible AND necessary

		LMS	PLE	Challenges and Shifts
2	Personaliza-tion	. . . is an arrange-ment of learning assignments and materials accord-ing to a (proposed or pre-defined) learner's model, based on an under-lying expert system	. . . means to get information about learning opportu-nities and content from community members and learning services fitting to the learn-er's interests (via tags/RSS)	competence for usage of several tools and self-orga-nization is needed
3	Content	developed by domain experts, special authors, tutor and/or teachers	the infinite "bazaar" of learn-ing content in the Web, exploring learning opportuni-ties and services	necessary compe-tences to search, find and use appro-priate sources (e.g., weblogs [blogs])
4	Social involvement	limited use of group work, focus on the closed learner group (e.g. in the LMS), collaboration and exchange not pri-marily in the focus	the community and the social involvement (even in multiple com-munities) is the key for the learning process and the recommendations for learning oppor-tunities	community and collaboration as the central learning opportunities
5	Ownership	content is gen-erally owned by the educational institutions or the students, due to technological reasons, this ownership cannot always be realized	content is orga-nized in multiple web-based tools, ownership is controlled by the learners themselves and/ or (commercial) service providers	awareness of personal data is needed

		LMS	PLE	Challenges and Shifts
6	Educational & organizational culture	imitation of classroom learning, course-oriented, teacher-oriented features	self-organized learner is the focus	change of learning culture and perspective—move toward self-organization and self-determination
7	Technical aspects	classical learning content needs interoperability between LMS and data repositories	Social software tools and aggregation of multiple sources	required interoperability between LMS and the social software

The PLE's accommodation of new tools and services makes it difficult for LMS developers and vendors to keep pace. There are instances of LMSs employing social media. Tensions arise, however, because social media are outward manifestations of an underlying ethos—of social learning, communities of practice, and open resources (Downes, 2005). For example, some LMSs offer student blogs, but the blogs may not be accessible to readers outside the LMS. While an LMS can include Web 2.0 elements in its systems, it is rooted in the traditional instructor-centric model of instruction. Curricula are determined, courses are designed, networks extend only to the boundaries of the institution, and participation is limited to students paying tuition, and often only the students in a particular course. In a PLE, the learner is not restricted to only institutionally approved groups and resources. The PLE becomes the gateway to the web where learners evaluate resources and make meaning of content. This type of activity aligns with the concept of communities of practice (Wenger, 1998). We contend that communities of practice have more potential to be realized with the PLE than the LMS.

LIMITATIONS AND FUTURE ISSUES

PLEs are attractive for a number of reasons, and yet currently face significant issues that would need to be overcome to see broad implementation of the environment as described in this chapter. As we mentioned, the LMS has become a dominant feature of formal learning environments, and it is a large and lucrative market. Despite the criticisms, we predict that LMS use will continue long into the future. One of the key issues will be determining where PLEs fit in terms of relationship with the LMS. Is it an augmentation, a competitor, a replacement, or something else?

There are three scenarios in which PLEs could coexist with LMSs. The first scenario would be the PLE existing in a "parallel life," dominating the informal learning space while the LMS continues to dominate formal education. The second scenario would see LMSs gradually open their structures to include interoperability with PLEs. The third scenario would be the LMS attempting to co-opt elements of the PLE. One study was conducted to bring the PLE into the LMS through the use of widgets (OpenSocial applications), which could be integrated into Moodle. The researchers found that these widgets were perceived to be useful by the students. However, students not being able to fully or extensively personalize the environment detracted from the acceptance and utility of this blending of the PLE and the LMS (Bogdanov, Ullrich, Isaksson, Palmer, & Gillet, 2012). This can be compared to a related project in which the researchers eschewed the LMS completely and constructed their own cloud-based environment using OpenSocial applications (Gillet & Bogdanov, 2012).

Sclater (2008) raised a number of PLE implementation issues. Why would a LMS vendor allow a PLE client to access the LMS functions without the user directly using the LMS? How would the PLE reconcile with the traditional elements of formal education such as syllabi, assignments, grades, and schedules? Finally, the PLE "movement" lacks a recognized charismatic leader or champion to push the development of PLE standards.

LMSs provide boundaries between approved institutional users and the outside community. However, online communities can contain many thousands of participants and resources. Wilson et al. (2006) contended that emerging PLE technology might solve the issue of limitless resources by facilitating local filtering within a learner's PLE. In effect, trusted persons and processes become the "personal librarians" for the learner, mining through mountains of information and directing the learner to valuable resources (Martindale, 2007). We see instances of this with blogrolls and RSS feed collections, in which users can show "who" and "what" they are reading. Tools such as Twitter show whom a user is following and who is following the user.

Beyond the clearly marked boundaries of the institutional LMS (with its clear delineation between the expert instructor and the novice learner), the PLE learner must master skills beyond self-regulation. These skills also include evaluation of online resources (Bouchard & Qc, 2013). Schaffert and Hilzensauer (2008) described the need for media-literate learners:

> The change from content that was developed by expert and/or teachers towards possibilities and challenges to make use of the bazaar of learning opportunities and content leads to the necessity of advanced self-organizing and searching in the Web—in other words: media competent learners (Schaffert & Hilzensauer, 2008).

PLEs generally comprise several social software applications. The rate at which these applications arrive, expand, and sometimes disappear creates a challenge to learners looking for new components for their PLEs. Successful PLE learners must be able to navigate multiple systems, passwords, and content formats to benefit from the myriad offerings on the Web. PLE users must spend higher proportions of their time learning and relearning user interfaces of emerging Web 2.0 personal technologies (JISC-CETIS, 2007; Johnson et al., 2006).

There are several technologies and initiatives that could affect the prominence of the PLE. For instance,

> The Open Courseware Consortium (http://ocwconsortium.org/) is a collaboration of over 200 institutions to share open learning resources.

> The e-Framework for Education and Research (http://e-framework. org) is an attempt to create standards of interoperability for LMSs and related tools.

> Moodle (http://moodle.org/) is a free and widely used open-source LMS that has the potential to be more learner-centered than the typical LMS.

> Mahara (https://mahara.org) is an open-source e-portfolio application that allows a person to construct an electronic portfolio, and interact with others. Mahara interacts well with Moodle.

> Google Open Social (http://code.google.com/apis/opensocial/) is a set of common APIs (application program interfaces) for building social applications across many websites.

> Google Classroom (https://www.google.com/edu/classroom/) appears to be aimed at K-12 teachers, and might be characterized as a very lightweight LMS for document sharing, grading, assessments, etc.

The Open ID project (http://openid.net/) is a shared identity project that allows Internet users to log on to many different web sites using a single username and password (an identity).

Attwell (2006) specified that PLEs should operate online and offline, work on multiple devices, allow granular permissions control, and support multiple learning contexts. PLEs need to be open to multiple sources, provide powerful searches, be easily updated, be easily installed and maintained, be extensible, provide multiple presentation options, have built-in interoperability, be based on standards, and help learners sequence their own content (Attwell, 2006; Attwell & Costa, 2008). With this as a checklist, clearly there is much work to be done for the PLE to be realized. As a good example of the type of work needed, Fournier and Kop (2010) described a study in which participants ranked experiences with tools they used, and the desired features in a proposed PLE.

There are many opportunities for future research and development in terms of investigating PLEs for learning. Buchem (n.d.) has collected a number of research and conceptual articles, and Cosgrave (2014) has curated a list for further reading on the subject of PLEs. In summary, the scholarly community needs a greater understanding of:

Identity management and privacy issues across multiple sites and services;

Selecting social software applications for effective learning;

The practical, legal, and financial implications of decentralized learning environments for institutions such as universities; and

The implications of learners being responsible for their own environments, and in many instances, regulating their own learning.

This is an exciting time for research and exploration of personal learning environments, as researchers and educators are investigating the emergence of the PLE and its relationships to and impacts on education and learning.

REFERENCES

Allen, C. (2004, October 14). Tracing the evolution of social software. [Blog post]. Retrieved from http://www.lifewithalacrity.com/2004/10/tracing_the_evo.html

Anderson, T. (2006, June 8). PLEs versus LMS: are PLEs ready for prime time? [Blog post]. Retrieved from http://terrya.edublogs.org/2006/01/09/ples-versus-LMS-are-ples-ready-for-prime-time/

Attwell, G. (2006, December 12). Personal learning environments. [Blog post]. Retrieved from http://www.knownet.com/writing/weblogs/Graham_Attwell/entries/6521819364

Attwell, G., & Costa, C. (2008). Integrating personal learning and working environments. *Pontydysgu-bridge to learning*. Retrieved from http://pontydysgu.org/wp-content/uploads/2008/11/workandlearning.pdf

Avgerinou, P., Papasalouros, A., Retalis, S., & Skordalakis, M. (2003). Towards a pattern language for learning management systems. *Educational Technology and Society*, 6(2), 11–24.

Bogdanov, E., Ullrich, C., Isaksson, E., Palmer, M., & Gillet, D. (2012). From LMS to PLE: a step forward through opensocial apps in Moodle. *Advances in Web-based learning-ICWL 2012* (pp. 69–78).

Bouchard, P., & Qc, M. (2013). *The problem of learner control in Networked Personal Learning Environments*. Paper presented at the Special Edition: Papers from the 2013 PLE Conference Personal Learning Environments: Learning and Diversity in Cities of the Future, Berlin, Germany.

Buchem, I. (n.d.). PLE. Retrieved from http://ibuchem.wordpress.com/ple/

———. (2010, May 9). Definitions of personal learning environment (PLE). [SlideShare presentation]. Retrieved from http://www.slideshare.net/ibuchem/definitions-of-personal-learning-environment-ple-4029277

Buchem, I., Attwell, G., & Tur, G. (2013). The PLE conference 2013: Learning and diversity in the cities of the future. *The Proceedings of the 4th International Conference on Personal Learning Environments* (pp. 1–340). Berlin, Germany. Retrieved from https://ibuchem.files.wordpress.com/2014/07/pproceedings-ple13.pdf

Chan, T., Corlett, D., Sharples, M., & Ting, J. (2005). Developing interactive logbook: a personal learning environment. *IEEE International Workshop on Wireless and Mobile Computing*.

Chatti, M. A., Agustiawan, M. R., Jarke, M., & Specht, M. (2010). Toward a personal learning environment framework. *International Journal of Virtual and Personal Learning Environments (IJVPLE)* 1(4), 66–85.

Cosgrove, M. (2014, July 30). PLE personal learning environmnts. Retrieved from https://www.zotero.org/groups/plepersonallearningenvironments

Cross, J. (2007). *Informal learning: Rediscovering the natural pathways that inspire innovation and performance*. San Francisco: Pfeiffer/Wiley.

Dabbagh, N., & Kitsantas, A. (2012). Personal Learning Environments, social media, and self-regulated learning: A natural formula for connecting formal and informal learning. *The Internet and Higher Education* 15(1), 3–8.

Downes, S. (2005). E-learning 2.0. *elearn Magazine.* Retrieved from http://www.elearnmag.org/subpage.cfm?section=articles&article=29-1

———. (2006). Learning networks and connective knowledge. *Instructional Technology Forum.* [Blog post]. Retrieved from http://it.coe.uga.edu/itforum/paper92/paper92.html

Fournier, H., & Kop, R. (2010). *Researching the design and development of a Personal Learning Environment.* Paper presented at the 2010 PLE Conference, Barcelona, Spain.

Gillet, D., & Bogdanov, E. (2012). Personal learning environments and embedded contextual spaces as aggregator of cloud resources. In *Proceedings of the 1st International Workshop on Cloud Education Environments (WCLOUD)*, Antigua, Guatamala, November 15, 2012.

Havelock, B., Gibson, D., & Sherry, L. (2006). The personal learning planner: Collaboration through online learning and publication. *Computers in the Schools, 23*(3/4), 55–70.

JISC-CETIS (2007). The personal learning environment: A report on the JISC CETIS PLE project. Retrieved from http://wiki.cetis.ac.uk/Ple/Report

Johnson, M., Liber, O., Wilson, S., Sharples, P., Milligan, C., & Beauvoir, P. (2006). *Mapping the Future: The personal learning environment reference model and emerging technology.* Paper presented at the 13th Association for Learning Technology Conference (ALT-C 2006), Heriot-Watt University, Scotland, UK.

Kravcik, M., & Klamma, R. (2012). *Supporting self-regulation by personal learning environments.* Paper presented at the Advanced Learning Technologies (ICALT), IEEE 12th International Conference, Rome, Italy, July 4–6, 2012.

Labrović, J. A., Bijelić, A., & Milosavljević, G. (2014) Mapping students' informal learning using personal learning environments. *Management, 71,* 73–80.

Leslie, S. (n.d.). PLE Diagrams. Retrieved from http://edtechpost.wikispaces.com/PLE+Diagrams

———. (2008, June 4). A collection of PLE diagrams. [Blog post]. Retrieved from http://edtechpost.wikispaces.com/PLE+Diagrams.

———. (2012, December 9). Some observations on PLE diagrams. [Blog post]. Retrieved from http://www.edtechpost.ca/wordpress/2012/12/19/ple-diagrams-observations/

Lubensky, R. (2006). The present and future of personal learning environments (PLE). *eLearning and Deliberative Moments*. Retrieved from http://members.optusnet.com.au/rlubensky/elearningmomentsarchive/2006_12_01_elearningmomentsarchive.html

Martindale, T. (2007). Assembling your own personal learning environment. Memphis, TN: Institute for Intelligent Systems Cognitive Science Seminar.

Martindale, T., & Dowdy, M. (2010). Personal learning environments. In G. Veletsianos (ed.), *Emerging technologies in distance education* (pp. 177–93). Edmonton, AB: Athabasca University Press.

O'Reilly, T. (2005). What is Web 2.0?: Design patterns and business models for the next generation of software. Retrieved from http://www.oreillynet.com/pub/a/oreilly/tim/news/2005/09/30/what-is-web-20.html

Schaffert, S., & Hilzensauer, W. (2008). On the way towards personal learning environments: Seven crucial aspects. *eLearning Papers* (9)2.

Sclater, N. (2008). *Web 2.0, Personal learning environments, and the future of learning management systems* (Research Bulletin, Issue 13). Boulder, CO: EDUCAUSE Center for Applied Research.

Tomberg, V., Laanpere, M., Ley, T., & Normak, P. (2013). Sustaining teacher control in a blog-based personal learning environment. *The International Review of Research in Open and Distance Learning 14*(3), 109–33.

Tosh, D. (2005, August 21). Elgg—A personal learning landscape. Retrieved from http://tesl-ej.org/ej34/m1.html

Tu, C.-H., Sujo-Montes, L., Yen, C.-J., Chan, J.-Y., & Blocher, M. (2012). The integration of personal learning environments and open network learning environments. *TechTrends 56*(3), 13–19.

van Harmelen, M. (2006). Personal learning environments. Paper presented at the Sixth International Conference on Advanced Learning Technologies (ICALT'06), Kerkrade, Netherlands, Vol. 6 (pp. 815–16).

———. (2008). *Personal learning environments*. Retrieved from http://octette.cs.man.ac.uk/jitt/index.php/Personal_Learning_Environments

Veletsianos, G. (2010). A definition of emerging technologies for education. In G. Veletsianos (ed.), *Emerging technologies in distance education*. Edmonton, AB: Athabasca University Press.

Wenger, E. (1998). *Communities of practice: Learning, meaning, and identity*. Cambridge, UK: Cambridge University Press.

Wheeler, S. (2010, July 11). Anatomy of a PLE. [Blog post]. Retrieved from http://steve-wheeler.blogspot.com/2010/07/anatomy-of-ple.html

Wilson, B., & Lowry, M. (2000). Constructivist learning on the Web. *New Directions for Adult and Continuing Education 88*, 79–88.

Wilson, S. (2005, October 4). Architecture of virtual spaces and the future of VLEs. [Blog post]. Retrieved from http://zope.cetis.ac.uk/members/scott/blogview?entry=20051004162747.

Wilson, S., Liber, O., Johnson, M., Beauvoir, P., Sharples, P., & Milligan, C. (2006). Personal learning environments: Challenging the dominant design of educational systems. In E. Tomadaki & P. Scott (eds.), *Innovative approaches for learning and knowledge sharing*, EC-TEL 2006 (pp. 173–82).

9 Designing for Open and Social Learning

▶ *Alec Couros and Katia Hildebrandt*

In January 2008, Alec Couros led an open-access, graduate level, educational technology course at the University of Regina titled "Education, Curriculum, and Instruction (EC&I) 831: Open, Connected, Social." In the book *Emerging Technologies in Distance Education* we documented the initial run of the course (Couros, 2010). Since then, Couros has taught the course an additional six times. While the overall philosophy and structure have remained largely the same, the course has evolved in light of emerging technologies, student feedback, and societal trends in the use of social media. The revised version of this chapter includes an updated description of the technologies that are central to the course's structure and a new how-to section that includes strategies and suggestions for developing an open course based on past student feedback.

EC&I 831 is a fully online course that was developed and facilitated using primarily free and open-source software (FOSS) or freely available services. Additionally, the course demonstrates emerging practice of open teaching: educational practice inspired by the open-source movement, complementary learning theory, and networked theories of knowledge. The course challenges typical boundaries common to more traditional distance education courses as students build personal learning networks (PLNs) to collaboratively explore, negotiate, and develop authentic and sustainable knowledge networks. This latter focus becomes a catalyst that, as one student described emphatically, "blew the doors of this course right off their hinges." As a result, the context for learning shifts from the potentially mundane to an open environment where the registered students freely interact with hundreds of other educators, theorists, and students from around the world.

EC&I 831 has received considerable attention from academic researchers and educational bloggers. Dave Cormier (2008) wrote that the course provides "an ideal example of the role social learning and negotiation can play in learning." Young (2008) listed the course as one of three examples of a "growing movement" toward experimenting with open teaching in higher education. Siemens (2008) described the design of the course as "an important source of insight" that served to inspire the development of the "Connectivism and Connective Knowledge" (CCK08) course, the inaugural Massive Open Online Course (MOOC) facilitated by Siemens and Downes. It is our hope in writing this chapter that we capture and document relevant reflections and activities to provide starting points for those considering open teaching as educational innovation.

This chapter is divided into four sections. In the first, we briefly outline key theoretical foundations that influenced the design and development of the course. This section combines philosophical, pedagogical, and practical considerations to inform a model for open teaching. In the second section, we describe the course experience in detail. This discussion includes an updated overview of emerging technologies used in the course and an outline of the various course activities and assessments. The third section summarizes discoveries related to the role of personal learning networks (PLNs), outlines techniques for developing and leveraging PLNs in distance education courses, and describes the role of emerging technologies in building and facilitating networked interactions. Finally, the fourth section provides suggestions for developing open courses.

THEORETICAL FOUNDATIONS

Several overlapping bodies of theory and practice informed the development and facilitation of EC&I 831. This section briefly identifies relevant points from the following areas: the open movement, complementary learning theories, and connectivism. The section ends with a description of how these areas informed a model of open teaching for the course.

The open movement

In 2003, Alec Couros initiated a two-year-long study that examined the perceptions, beliefs, and practices of educators who participated in free and open-source software (FOSS) communities (Couros, 2006). Through data collection and analysis, it was revealed that the majority of participants were strongly influenced by the dominant philosophical views inherent within these FOSS communities. Participants identified strong tendencies toward collaboration, sharing, and openness in their classroom activities and through professional collaborations. Generally, these individuals identified themselves as part of a larger phenomenon, later defined as the "the open movement":

> The open movement is an informal, worldwide phenomenon characterized
> by the tendency of individuals and groups to work, collaborate and publish
> in ways that favour accessibility, sharing, transparency and interoperability.
> Advocates of openness value the democratization of knowledge construc-
> tion and dissemination, and are critical of knowledge controlling structures.
> (Couros, 2006, p. 161)

In the early stages of this study, participants expressed frustration with perceived barriers that limited the adoption of openness in their practice. Several technical barriers were identified (software not available, suitable, or mature; sparsely available content), but soon, many of these issues improved or were resolved. One of the most advantageous developments was perceived to be the sudden popularization and availability of Web 2.0 tools. Study participants and their students alike had now gained the ability to *easily* create, share, and collaborate through emerging technologies such as blogs, wikis, podcasts, and social networks. Along with this greater access to publishing came the greater availability of educationally relevant content. Participants gained access to information resources such as Wikipedia, course content through initiatives such as MIT OpenCourseWare and the OER Commons, and multimedia and video content through services such as YouTube. The dilemma of the educator shifted quickly from a perceived lack of choice and accessibility to having to acquire the skills necessary to choose wisely from increased options.

Other relevant discoveries from this study included differences in the practical and philosophical beliefs of participants. The positioning of each individual ranged from open-source zealot to hobbyist, from those who refused to use *any* proprietary software to others who voiced more practical beliefs regarding the adoption of tools. To a FOSS purist, the perceptions of the latter group would likely be considered unacceptable. For the professional educator, these more practical beliefs supported greater options for the adoption of emerging technologies. It is this latter, more general, view of openness that informs the emerging practice and framework of open teaching.

Complementary learning theories

Several learning theories have influenced this approach to distance education and online learning. These include social cognitive theory, social constructivism, and adult learning theory (andragogy). As much has been written regarding each of these theories, this section serves only to highlight key points of each theory as it relates to open teaching.

Social cognitive theory (SCT), also known as social learning theory, suggests that a combination of behavioural, cognitive, and environmental factors influences human behaviour. SCT posits that humans learn through their observations of other individuals. If one observes particular behaviours that become associated with favourable outcomes, such behaviours are more likely to be adopted by the observer (Albert & Bandura, 1963). Another relevant feature of SCT is Bandura's (1997) concept of self-efficacy, which he defines as "people's judgment of their capabilities to organize and execute courses of action required to attain designated types of performances" (p. 391). Bandura considered self-efficacy beliefs to be the most influential arbiter of human activity and an important element in conceptualizing student-centred learning environments (Lorsbach, 1999).

The theory of social constructivism, attributed to Vygotsky, is related to social cognitive theory in that both theories emphasize the importance of the sociocultural context and the role of social interaction in the construction of knowledge (Woolfolk & Hoy, 2002; Derry, 1999). Instructional models influenced by social constructivist perspectives highlight the importance of collaboration among learners and practitioners in educational environments (Lave & Wenger, 1991). Another important feature of social constructivism is the concept of the zone of proximal development (ZPD). The ZPD is commonly expressed as the difference between what a learner can do independently and what the same learner can do when tutored (Vygotsky, 1978). Moving beyond tutoring, Tabak (2004) introduced the concept of distributed scaffolding, an emerging approach of learning design that incorporates multiple forms of support that respond to the diversity of learner needs and to the complexity of given learning environments. Through a greater understanding of how individuals construct knowledge and skills, the role of the social environment, and the design of flexible learner support, educators can increase student performance in both face-to-face and distance learning environments.

Adult learning theory, also known as andragogy, is based on the perception that adults learn differently from children and that these differences should be acknowledged and accommodated. Knowles (1970), primary developer of this theory, argued that adults generally possess different motivations for learning and have acquired significant life experiences; both of these factors greatly influence the learning process. Knowles proposed the following principles for adult learning:

Adults need to be involved in the planning and evaluation of their instruction.

Experience (including mistakes) provides the basis for learning activities.

Adults are most interested in learning subjects that have immediate relevance to their job or personal life.

Adult learning is problem-centred rather than content-oriented. (p. 43)

These general principles proved to be beneficial in supporting the learning of the participants of EC&I 831.

Connectivism

Connectivism, originally developed by Siemens (2004), is a "net aware" theory of learning and knowledge (chapter 3) that is heavily influenced by theories of social constructivism (Vygotsky, 1978), network theory (Barabási, 2002; Watts, 2004), and chaos theory (Gleick, 1987). Connectivism emphasizes the importance of digital appliances, hardware, software, and network connections in human learning. The theory stresses the development of "metaskills" for evaluating and managing information and network connections, and notes the importance of pattern recognition as a learning strategy. Connectivists recognize the influences that emerging technologies have on human cognition and theorize that technology is reshaping the ways that humans create, store, and distribute knowledge.

The following principles of connectivism were most relevant to the development and facilitation of EC&I 831:

Learning and knowledge rests in diversity.

Dynamic learning is a process of connecting "specialized nodes" (people or groups), ideas, information, and digital interfaces.

Capacity to know more is more critical than what is currently known.

Fostering and maintaining connections is critical to knowledge generation.

A multidisciplinary, multiliteracy approach to knowledge generation is a core of human learning.

Decision-making is both action and learning: "Choosing what to learn and the meaning of incoming information is seen through the lens of a shifting reality" (Adapted from Siemens, 2005).

A connectivist approach to course design acknowledges the complexities of learning in the digital age. The theory offers insight into how learning can be managed through the better understanding of emerging technologies and their relationship to knowledge networks.

Open teaching

Through an exploration of the above influences, Couros developed a definition for the concept of open teaching. This definition helped to inform the epistemological, philosophical, and pedagogical considerations for EC&I 831.

Couros defines open teaching as the facilitation of learning experiences that are open, transparent, collaborative, and social. Open teachers are advocates of a free and open knowledge society, and support their students in the critical consumption, production, connection, and synthesis of knowledge through the shared development of learning networks. Typical activities of open teachers may include some or all of the following:

- advocacy and use of free and/or open source tools and software wherever possible and beneficial to student learning;

- integration of free and open content and media in teaching and learning;

- promotion of copyleft content licences for student content production and publication;

- facilitation of student understanding regarding copyright law (e.g., fair use/fair dealing, copyleft/copyright);

- facilitation and scaffolding of student personal learning networks for collaborative and sustained learning;

- development of learning environments that are reflective, responsive, student-centred, and that incorporate a diverse array of instructional and learning strategies;

- modelling of openness, transparency, connectedness, and responsible copyright/copyleft use and licensing; and,

- advocacy for the participation and development of collaborative gift cultures in education and society.

Open teaching is an emerging practice, but the general framework described above was one that guided the design, development, and evolution of EC&I 831.

EC&I 831 IN DETAIL

This section provides thorough detail of the development and facilitation of EC&I 831. Covered areas include a general overview of the course, details of the project's initiation, a description of the course learning environment and facilitation model, an overview of the role of PLNs in distance education environments, and a final section on lessons learned that provides suggestions for developing open/networked courses.

Overview of the course

EC&I 831 is a graduate studies course in education that focuses on the appropriate and critical integration of technology and media in the K–12 classroom environment. The course is not new — it has been around since 2001 — but when originally submitted to the university calendar, it was written broadly enough to provide sufficient flexibility for future course development. This feature has allowed it to be tailored to changes in the field of educational technology, from the shifting focus (such as from eLearning to social learning) to the types of emerging technologies available to universities and colleges.

This section describes the foundations of the course and its present iteration. Typically the course has between twenty-five and forty registered students, most of whom are practicing teachers (K–12) or educational administrators. The graduate courses in our faculty have a typical maximum of eighteen students, but this course generally operates with a significant overload (25-40+ students) due to the peer-supported, networked pedagogical model.

Project initiation

In the past, the Government of Saskatchewan offered Technology Enhanced Learning grants for the development of online courses, and $30,000 was awarded for the initial development of EC&I 831 in 2007. While such courses were typically assigned instructional design and multimedia support personnel, the area of support most needed for EC&I 831 was in the development and support of the participants' personal learning networks. Thus, in lieu of support personnel, two teaching assistants were hired to act as social connectors, and their primary responsibilities were to support students in the development of PLNs. These connectors were not tied to a tool or to a learning environment, but directly to the participants — their technical experience, their unique needs for support, and their learning goals.

Course learning environment

While several different learning environments (such as WebCT, Moodle, and Ning) were considered as the primary learning environment for the initial run of the course, the first few iterations of the class utilized a Wikispaces education wiki (see Couros, 2010 for a discussion of this choice). However, since 2011, the course has moved even further away from a centralized learning environment; instead, EC&I 831 is based on the philosophy of "small tools, loosely joined" so that learning is distributed across various platforms and spaces. Below, we outline the key tools and spaces utilized most recently in the course.

Student blogs

Each participant is responsible for developing a digital space to document his or her learning through readings and activities, to provide a space for personal reflection, and to create a personal hub for networked connections. In most cases, these spaces quickly become showcases of student professional activity and act as distributed communication portals — alternatives to centralized, managed discussion forums. Students typically choose from a number of free services to host their spaces (e.g., WordPress.com, Edublogs.org, Blogger.com, self-hosted) and each blog is customized by the user, both functionally and aesthetically. In most cases, these blogs continue to be maintained and remain active well beyond the official end date of the course.

Feed aggregator

One of the convenient features of a learning management system (LMS) is the ability for the instructor to structure and organize content for student consumption. However, given the choice to decentralize the learning environment in EC&I 831, students are instead encouraged to utilize a content aggregator such as Feedly that allows them to subscribe to content related to their course and their personal interests. In addition, content aggregation is modelled through the use of FeedWordPress, a WordPress-based aggregator, which allows for the subscription and republication of participant blogs to one central location. In both cases, emphasis is placed on the assumption that content creation happens outside of the LMS and that aggregation is a form of new literary practice.

Twitter

Students are strongly encouraged to develop and maintain a professional Twitter account. Twitter, a microblogging platform, has become increasingly popular as a tool for professional development and resource sharing amongst educators. For the course, students are asked to share content and connect with others via a specific course hashtag. In doing so, Twitter becomes a vehicle for establishing open conversations with a global audience, thus allowing for a high degree of pedagogical serendipity. The use of a shared hashtag allows for conversations to be targeted, followed, and discovered. Finally, weekly Twitter chats are organized to provide an opportunity for an open and concentrated discussion and interrogation of course content along with networking and relationship building.

Google+ community

While the majority of interactions in EC&I 831 occur on the open web, the course also utilizes a Google+ community to allow for more private conversations and the sharing of resources. The inclusion of both public and private spaces within the course provides an opportunity for students to interrogate the social differences between these spaces. Additionally, it allows course participants to gain a better understanding of how degrees of privacy relate to issues of digital citizenship and affect both their voices and the voices of their students.

Course model

The following section outlines and describes the course facilitation model through a description of the major assessments and related activities performed by course participants.

Major assessments

Three major student assessments guide the activities of participants for EC&I 831: the development of a personal blog/digital portfolio; the completion of a student-chosen, major digital project; and a final summary of learning. Activities related to each of these assessments have been designed to require and/or result in the development of a personal learning network. Thus, PLNs are both the prerequisite to and the outcome of successful completion.

Networked professional learning. As mentioned, one of the main goals of the course is to have students participate in networked learning environments and to critically, and continually, reflect upon those experiences. In practice, this means students utilize a number of social tools (e.g., blogs, aggregators, curation tools), read widely from a number of traditional (e.g., academic journals) and non-traditional sources (e.g., educational blogs, Twitter), and connect with other educators who are already "connected," as a mechanism for developing their own personal learning networks.

Major digital project. The major digital project was designed so that students could develop a relevant resource for their specific professional context. Students have produced videos, instructional resources, and other multimedia. Others have engaged in social networking activities: participation in global collaborative projects, development of private social networks, and development of localized professional development workshops or courses. The completed activities represent a vast range of student technological competencies as well as professional and personal interests.

Summary of learning. As a final assignment, students produce an artifact (e.g., digital story, narrative, slide deck, audio, video, concept map) that summarizes the learning experience in EC&I 831. The artifacts produced reference significant course experiences (reflections, assessments, readings, presenters, networking, experimentation, etc.) that contributed to the greater understanding of educational technology and media. Students present these materials at the end of the course and are also encouraged to share them via their blogs or Twitter. This summary encourages and allows students to develop a high-level, concise, digital artifact that positioned itself as an alternative to the traditional written essay or final examination.

Course Interactions
There are a number of synchronous and asynchronous interactions designed throughout the course. This section outlines these interactions and describes the tools used.

> *Synchronous activities*: Two synchronous events are planned weekly. The first session of the week, which runs approximately 1.5 hours, is focused on developing student content knowledge and in connecting students to leaders in the educational technology community. Each semester, various guest presenters are invited to speak to class participants. The sessions are offered using Blackboard Collaborate,

a video-conferencing tool that includes various options for student interaction such as a collaborative whiteboard, a chat function, and polling tools. Additionally, all sessions are recorded and then posted in various formats, including an audio-only podcast version. As we described above, the second session of the week is a Twitter chat, which allows both for additional discussion of course content and for the development of students' personal learning networks through interactions with people within and outside of the course.

Asynchronous activities: Participants also engage in a number of asynchronous activities in addition to weekly sessions. Some of the most common activities include:

- reading, reviewing, and critiquing course readings through participant blogs;
- sharing and reviewing articles, tools, and readings through participant blogs or through posting to the Google+ community or to Twitter using the course hashtag;
- creation of screencasts, tutorials, or other resources for self-referencing or to assist other participants' understanding;
- reading, reviewing, commenting, and subscribing to blogs from outside of the course community;
- participation in open, viral professional development opportunities (e.g., additional Twitter chats, Classroom 2.0, the Educator's PLN);
- posting created content to YouTube, Voicethread, Google Drive, or other collaborative, social media services;
- microblogging through Twitter; and
- collaborative design and development of lesson plans or instructional sets.

Many of the asynchronous activities are completely unplanned. Participants work with individuals in the course community, but strong bonds often form with individuals outside of the course due to common interests. Through both the synchronous and asynchronous activities, personal learning networks develop as individuals freely connect with those interested in the content and collaboration, and not solely because of the identification with a specific course. Social interactions become authentic, dynamic, and fluid.

The first synchronous session of EC&I 831 each semester is a private session with only the registered course participants. In this session, students are briefed about the open nature of the course and are informed that nonregistered participants will be brought in to give presentations, to comment on student blogs, and to interact in other unanticipated ways. In the first iteration of the course, it was initially unclear how these interactions with outsiders would be solicited and facilitated. Yet, only two to three weeks into the first run of the course, it became evident how important the development and utilization of the instructor's PLN would be in supporting the pedagogical model. To share these understandings, this section will provide a brief definition of personal learning networks and online strategies for leveraging PLNs in distance education courses.

Conceptualizing the PLN

In conceptualizing the PLN, it is important first to distinguish the idea of a personal learning network from that of a personal learning environment (PLE). Couros (2010) includes a more detailed discussion of the process of differentiating between these two concepts. For our purposes in this chapter, it is enough to outline the commonly understood definitions of each. PLEs are the tools, artifacts, processes, and physical connections that allow learners to control and manage their learning. This definition supports Martindale and Dowdy's (chapter 8) definition of the PLE as:

> a collaborative ad hoc set of procedures learners use to interact and share resources that further the expertise and competence of the individual (and group, in some cases). Conversely, some define the PLE as a specific tool or set of tools (usually software) that a learner employs to interact with and manipulate online learning environments and resources. (p. 124)

Definitions of PLNs, however, seem to extend the PLE framework to more explicitly include the human connections that are mediated through the PLE. In this framework, PLEs become a subset of the substantially humanized PLN. For reference in the remainder of this section, our PLN definition is simple: personal learning networks are the sum of all social capital and connections that result in the development and facilitation of a personal learning environment.

In his doctoral work, Couros (2006) discovered a variation of the concept of the PLN as it emerged in the practice of the participants of the study; he noted a significant increase in the social connectivity related to the practice of study participants. This phenomenon was a vast departure from what was understood as a "typical teacher network," one often bound by local curriculum, school district, and geography. Based on this discovery, he developed two diagrams (Figure 9.1 and Figure 9.2) informed by the aggregate data, which describe the differences in the two networks.

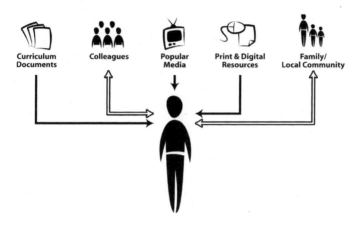

Figure 9.1 Typical teacher network (from Couros, 2006).

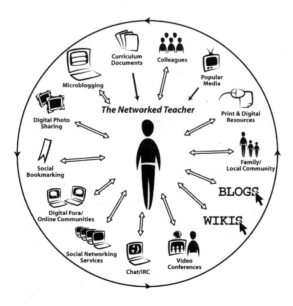

Figure 9.2 The networked teacher (from Couros, 2006).

The "networked teacher" representation is a personal learning environment (PLE) diagram. It describes an individual's connectivity through participation in social media activities (e.g., blogging, wikis, social networking), and the arrows represent both the consumption and production of content.

PLNs for teaching and learning

The following is a short list of strategies for developing a personal learning network and for leveraging the PLN in distance education courses. These points have been effective in the facilitation of EC&I 831, as evidenced by personal reflection and student feedback.

Immerse yourself

The entire PLN strategy depends on the use and understanding of social media in the formation of human networks. The essential tools in our experience are blogging platforms (self-hosted WordPress), social bookmarking (Delicious, Diigo), photo sharing (Flickr, Instagram), video sharing (YouTube), microblogging (Twitter), and other social networking platforms (Google+). Understanding how these tools work, how they can be used together, and how your students can utilize them is essential. Moreover, human connections in PLNs are strengthened through various degrees and forms of interaction. In addition to the creation of content, feedback on the contribution of others is also equally important for social bonding and bridging. Providing feedback and comments, participating in digital conferences, or contributing to community resources strengthens your PLN.

Learn to read social media

Social media is read much differently than traditional media. Although the situation is improving, traditional search engines are not ideal for reading social media; instead, there are a number of social media search engines and tools available that are important to understand. Tools such as TweetDeck, Hootsuite, Feedly, Paper.li, Flipboard, and Zite have been developed for those who primarily view, produce, and interact with social media; these tools allow for content curation, aggregation, and sharing.

Know and leverage your connections

Through interaction and research, one is able to get a sense of the backgrounds and skills of the individuals within one's PLN. This is of great benefit to an instructor of an open course, as it allows him or her to refer students to educators who may be willing to assist and provide expertise in particular areas of study or interest. Over time, and through sustained interactions with others in networked spaces, students will develop their own authentic PLN connections.

PLNs are central to learning

PLNs can be critical for sustained, long-term learning, for students and facilitators alike. The ability to build a vehicle for continued learning is one of the major advantages of an open pedagogical model. With the use of a traditional closed LMS, a tremendous amount of time and effort is put into the development of local, time-based, course-centric communities, but the resultant communities die, usually only days after the official end-of-course date, because they are communities based around courses, not communities based around communal learning. For students who develop PLNs in EC&I 831, the learning communities still exist. The individuals are active and interactive and continue to form and negotiate the connections they need to sustain long-term learning for themselves and for their students.

LESSONS LEARNED

A few suggestions based on student feedback and personal experience for instructors who currently teach open courses or who hope to develop them are listed below.

Importance of student feedback

In the early stages of network development, students often report feeling isolated; until they have developed a PLN, what they tweet, blog, or otherwise share online will likely receive little or no feedback. Thus, it is important for instructors to ensure that students receive feedback on the content that they create and share, particularly early on in the course. However in a large class, it is often not feasible for the instructor to provide substantial feedback to every student; it is important, then, to engage both the other students in the course (by encouraging them to comment on each other's' work) and those outside the course (for instance, by sharing student blog posts with members of the instructor's PLN via social media) in order to increase the amount of feedback received. When blogging, students should also be encouraged to use strategies that will increase readership and promote commenting, such as tagging posts, including questions that incite discussion, and sharing their work with their own growing networks.

Structures to lessen the messiness of networks

The non-traditional structure (or lack of structure) of the learning environment can frustrate students and create anxiety. Students should be oriented to the complexity of the learning environment, and be provided with structures and supports for sense-making and discovery (chapter 2). The instructor-developed course blog aggregator, for instance, provides a tool for the selection and subscription of selected content while modelling the importance of aggregation methods for networked knowledge. A course calendar with detailed event descriptions can help students keep track of synchronous events by time and place. Tools such as TweetDeck can help students make sense of the course and communicate through the course hashtag or within other related communities. Instructors should also be mindful of the possibilities of linking and building connections among the various course spaces whenever possible (for instance, by installing a Twitter widget that displays tweets with the course hashtag on the course blog aggregator).

Providing options that account for varying student comfort zones

When planning an open course, instructors should take into account differences in comfort with of privacy and sharing. For many students, the idea of sharing created content in networked publics can initially be overwhelming and intimidating; additionally, the pedagogical model of peer-centred, networked learning is often unfamiliar to students. By providing a variety of options for both public and private interactions (for instance, Twitter vs. the closed Google+ community in EC&I 831), instructors can vary the degree of openness to allow students to develop a level of comfort while allowing them to practice self-directed, networked learning in safe spaces (for example, with only the members of the Google+ community) before venturing onto the open web.

Use of exemplars

Given the non-traditional nature of assignments and activities in these types of courses, it is helpful to provide exemplars of past student work or of content created by individuals outside the course. This can aid students in imagining the possibilities of what might be created using various forms of media. Exemplars can also provide starting points or some level of structure to what can feel like nebulous expectations to students who are often more familiar with assignments such as written essays or tests.

FINAL THOUGHTS

Two commonly perceived barriers to the development of open courses are the issue of finding support for non-traditional models of teaching and concerns over time commitment. In regard to the first concern, the importance of institutional support for open teaching cannot be overemphasized. Fortunately EC&I 831 was developed in an environment where faculty members are constructively critical of technology but strongly supportive of innovation in teaching and learning. Additionally, social justice is an integral theme in our faculty programming, and open teaching supports similar philosophies and the need for more accessible learning in our communities and in our greater society. With respect to the second concern, we posit that *good* teaching always requires more time. This viewpoint is often not well received, considering the "publish or perish" mantra evident in contemporary universities. If we truly embrace the ideals of open teaching and learning, however, the activities of teaching, learning, and research become increasingly interlaced and are supported in myriad ways by our personal learning networks, which are richly comprised of members of the greater academic community. While developing a PLN requires a significant time commitment initially, these losses can be regained quickly through networked efficiencies, enhanced learning experiences, and new opportunities.

Many developments around open courses have occurred in academia since the initial offering of EC&I 831. Hundreds of MOOCs have been offered by universities around the world, collectively engaging millions of students. The proven successful model utilized in EC&I 831 may offer an intriguing approach that blends traditional aspects of a graduate level course with the pedagogical affordances and scale of massive human networks. To add a disclaimer, this model is most suited to instructors who are willing to or have already begun to develop and shape their personal learning networks and have become savvy with social networking tools.

This chapter highlighted some of the key processes involved in the development and facilitation of EC&I 831. Careful attention to the course's theoretical foundations, use of emerging technologies, and personal network building assure the success of this course for its students. However it is important to note, that given the constantly evolving nature of technology, this chapter provides a snapshot of this course at a particular time; just as previous iterations of the course have shifted to reflect changes in the field, future versions will have to be adapted to ensure that the course remains relevant and up-to-date. Indeed, one of the most simultaneously exciting and challenging aspects of teaching an open course is that the course structure does not operate based on a static formula but instead shifts in response to societal and technological change. Nevertheless, regardless of structure, the principles of peer-centred, networked, and self-directed learning are what underpin these courses and make them successful and unique. Perhaps the most telling quote regarding the success of the course comes from a student who wrote, "The best part of this course is that it's not ending. With the connections we've built, it never has to end."

REFERENCES

Bandura, A. (1997). *Self-efficacy: The exercise of control*. New York: Worth Publishers.

Bandura, A., & Walters, R. H. (1963). *Social learning and personality development*. Austin, TX: Holt, Rinehart and Winston.

Barabási, A. (2002). *Linked*. New York: Penguin Group USA.

Cormier, D. (2008). Rhizomatic education: Community as curriculum. *Innovate*, 4(5). Retrieved from http://www.innovateonline.info/index.php?view=article&id=550

Couros, A. (2006). Examining open (source) communities as networks of innovation: Implications for the adoption of open thinking by teachers [Unpublished doctoral dissertation]. University of Regina, Regina, SK, Canada.

———. (2010). Developing personal learning networks for open and social learning. In G. Veletsianos (ed.), *Emerging technologies in distance education* (pp. 109–28). Edmonton, AB: Athabasca University Press.

Derry, S. J. (1999). A fish called peer learning: Searching for common themes. In A. O'Donnell & A. King (eds.), *Cognitive perspectives on peer learning* (pp. 197–211). Mahwah, NJ: Lawrence Erlbaum.

Gleick, J. (2002). *What just happened: A chronicle from the learning frontier*. London: Fourth Estate.

Knowles, M. (1970). *The modern practice of adult education: Andragogy versus pedagogy*. Washington, DC: Association Press.

Lave, J., & Wenger, E. (1991). *Situated learning: Legitimate peripheral participation (Learning in doing: Social, cognitive and computational perspectives)*. New York: Cambridge University Press.

Lorsbach, A. (1999). Self-efficacy theory and learning environment research. *Learning Environments Research*, 2(2), 157–67.

Siemens, G. (2004). *Connectivism: A learning theory for the digital age*. Retrieved from www.elearnspace.org/Articles/connectivism.htm

————. (2008). On finding inspiration. Retrieved from http://ltc.umanitoba.ca/connectivism/?p=25

Tabak, I. (2004). Synergy: A complement to emerging patterns of distributed scaffolding. *The Journal of the Learning Sciences, 13*(3), 305–35.

Vygotsky, L. (1978). *Mind in society: Development of higher psychological processes.* Cambridge, MA: Harvard University Press.

Watts, D. J. (2004). *Six degrees: The science of a connected age.* New York: W.W. Norton.

Woolfolk, A., & Hoy, W. (2002). *Instructional leadership: A learning-centered guide.* Boston, MA: Allyn and Bacon.

Young, J. (2008, 26 September). More "open teaching" courses, and what they could mean for colleges. *The Chronicle of Higher Education.* Retrieved from http://chronicle.com/wiredcampus/article/3349/more-open-teaching-courses-and-what-they-could-mean-for-colleges

The Phenomenal MOOC

Sociocultural Effects of a Marginal Learning
Model

▶ *Rolin Moe*

Four years after Stanford University's Computer Science 271, taught by Dr.
Sebastian Thrun, enrolled 160,000 students and became the archetype of what
popular culture considers a massive open online course (MOOC), discussion of
the acronym remains widespread and disparate. MOOC, in this chapter defined
as what Rodriguez (2012) classified as an xMOOC, has evolved into MOOC 2.0
(Thrun, 2013a), MOOC 3.0 (Sandeen, 2013), returned back to MOOC 2.0 (Scott,
2014), been buried (Borden, 2014), and been given a thriving bill of health (Pratt,
2014), and even expanded to MOOC 4.0 (Scharmer, 2015). Both the abundance
and vacillation of MOOC prognoses signify that the MOOC is an emerging concept that researchers and practitioners alike are struggling to make sense of
(chapter 1).

Little attention has been paid to the MOOC as an emerging practice or as a
reflection of how society conceptualizes and practices education. Lewin's article in the *New York Times*, "MOOCs, large courses open to all, topple campus
walls" (2012), created a torrent of press and publicity. His article was significant
because it (a) equated MOOCs to the type of courses developed in the guise of
Thrun's courses, ignoring earlier MOOC designs such as the ones described in
chapters 2 and 9; and (b) ignored pedagogy and theory, focusing instead on hype
and hope (Daniel, 2012). Since then, there have been numerous debates between
education scholars and practitioners and MOOC developers and adherents,

arguing for and against the manner in which scholars, practitioners, and society conceptualize the practice of higher education.

To better understand the impact of the MOOC phenomenon on education discourse, I conducted a Delphi Study, bringing together twenty experts to discuss the past, present, and future of MOOCs, as an agent of change in how society views and organizes education. Through twelve paraphrased quotations from the MOOC literature, experts engaged with one another on the issues around and implications for education in the wake of the MOOC movement. The conversations that emerged from this study provide a unique insight into how experts view the MOOC. In the pages that follow, I report on expert responses that identified four cultural and social implications in how the MOOC phenomenon is changing the manner in which we discuss and practice education. These responses demonstrate that the concept and practice of the MOOC is emerging, and even though a lot of these responses focus on the United States, I hope these are illuminating in understanding the MOOC phenomenon itself.

THE ARRIVAL OF THE MOOC AND ITS CONNECTION TO EDUCATION THEORY AND PRACTICE

Popular MOOC discussion, as first noted from outlets such as the *New York Times* (Lewin, 2012), revolved heavily around anointing the MOOC learning model as a sorely needed revolution (Friedman, 2012) and avoiding a link to existing research or historical precedents in education (Waldrop, 2013). MOOC developers described their work as a random opportunity or a bold experiment (Rodriguez, 2012) while failing to clarify the existence or importance of prior work. Rather, MOOC developers pointed to former hedge fund analyst Salman Khan (2012), whose YouTube videos led to his creation of education venture Khan Academy, as inspiration. Khan himself has chosen not to link his influences to prior educational research or historical theories, choosing to refer to his educational engagement as intuition-based (Khan, 2012). As a result, the MOOC has emerged as an ahistorical event, a learning model whose successes are earned but whose failures must be considered as growing pains (Bady, 2013).

The revolutionary attitude of MOOC developers and adherents in the early days of the phenomenon led to a common refrain presented as fact in light of the learning model: MOOCs would provide the highest quality education from the best teachers in the world (Friedman, 2012), lowering the cost of education while improving student experience and outcomes (Thrun, 2013a, 2013b). From this perspective, the MOOC's features would allow for its adoption across campuses and communities, rendering middle- and lower-tier courses obsolete and freeing up not only student money but institutional funds as well (Ferenstein, 2013). Thrun went so far as to claim that in the future there would only be need for ten universities, consisting of top professors as actor-producers creating and distributing higher education (Leckart, 2013).

Many of these comments have been denounced by education researchers and practitioners (Bady, 2013); however, such denunciation has not received the same attention as the anticipated positive impacts of the MOOC. While the MOOC can be both heralded and castigated in research-based education discussions, the popular discussion about MOOCs continues to grow and adapt without strong input from critical education voices.

METHODOLOGY

The research protocol used for this study was the Delphi method, a research design created to provide a space for field experts to discuss issues involving a central topic and to spur feedback from one another, forecasting potential outcomes and in some cases reaching consensus (Linstone & Turoff, 2002). In a Delphi study, experts protected through confidentiality discuss a topic through a defined instrument, reacting to the instrument over the course of three rounds, their responses taking into account the responses of others over the course of subsequent rounds. Delphi studies are designed to help gauge the impact of a recent phenomenon, and while many seek to gain consensus and potential future outlooks, its role as a standard for discussion is widely accepted (Linstone & Turoff, 2002). Delphi was used for this study because the MOOC is an emerging practice and technology of which little is known (chapter 1). The Delphi panel consisted of twelve men and eight women and was composed of four of each: MOOC professors, MOOC developers, online and/or distance education scholars, journalists and authors who had published extensively on the MOOC, and political/government voices involved in MOOC discourse.

DISCUSSION

Four specific issues arose in the Delphi study.

A battle between computer science and education theory

At a 2013 presentation for international educators, Sebastian Thrun noted that online learning was a field bereft of expertise, based upon anecdotes and small-sample empirical results but not grounded in what he called "big data"

(Alexander, 2013). This line of thinking, while questioned and subsequently disproven by education researchers (Siemens, 2013a), was evident in early MOOC discourse; the rise of MOOCs came with an ahistorical lens that claimed the learning model was unique and pioneering. To gauge expert response to this lens, Thrun's quotation was paraphrased for the Delphi study.

In the first round of the study, the twenty experts were unable to come to a consensus on whether or not online education was a field with a history and expertise. Despite the fact that the field has over fifty years of history (Garrison, 2009), twenty-five of which included telecommunications-based distance education (Nipper, 1989), MOOC experts were unable to agree on whether the field that rendered them an expert for the Delphi study was in fact a field of experts and history. The responses of those disagreeing with Thrun's statement were strong, and the prompt gained consensus in the negative for Round 2. However, those Round 1 statements agreeing with Thrun's assertion focused on the lack of quantitative data-driven models for online education.

Since 2011, those at the forefront of developing MOOCs have either linked their structures with recent technological phenomena such as Khan Academy (Vanderbilt, 2012), or avoided making a link to the history of education at all (Koller, 2013). Recent scholarship has linked the artificial intelligence and machine learning backgrounds of the primary MOOC developers to the cognitive principles at the foundation of their academic disciplines and in turn extended to how those frameworks merge with existing learning theory literature (Stanton & Harkness, 2014).

Such developments might be ideal if, as Marvin Minsky (1979) put it, the brain happens to be a meat machine. The evolution of educational psychology, generations removed from the dawn of theories of cognition in the 1960s and 1970s, has rendered cognitive learning theory archaic (Siemens, 2013a). While cognitive theory remains popular in computer science and among some educators, the work of educational psychologists and social scientists has identified the limits of cognitive learning theory while using its strengths to create new theories of learning (chapter 3). A theoretical return to ideas of cognitive learning creates a rift in the field of educational research, where a focus on the MOOC phenomenon as a learning model gives precedence to artificial intelligence theories on learning, a field removed from the more psychological theories of the past thirty years. Moreover, the ahistorical attitude of the MOOC movement implicitly invalidates prior education research, discarding prior initiatives and ignoring valuable lessons.

The dismissal of education as a field of study and subsequent re-adoption of cognitive learning theory has already been given prominence in public policy debates. California Governor Jerry Brown, who as Governor is an Ex-Officio Regent for the University of California system, recently pushed for the adoption of college courses designed to run without a professor or teaching staff:

> If this university can probe into "black holes," he said, "can't somebody create a course—Spanish, calculus, whatever—totally online? That seems to me less complicated than that telescope you were talking about," referring to an earlier agenda item.
>
> After receiving pushback from UC provost Aimée Dorr, who delivered the presentation, that students are "less happy and less engaged" without human interaction, Brown said those measurements were too soft and he wanted empirical results. (Koseff, 2014, para. 3)

This development is not novel; the State of California has engaged in a number of cognitive-heavy policy initiatives (such as the drafting of SB520 state legislation designed to promote and encourage the development and implementation of scalable online lower-level undergraduate courses). What is unique to the above quotes is Governor Brown's desire to remove the human element from courses entirely, shown through a belief that such an endeavour would be easier than *hard science* initiatives such as an astronomy telescope, as well as a desire to measure efficacy through back-end learning analytics rather than what Brown alludes to as soft educational measurements. These and other recent public policy discussions, in conjunction with Delphi experts coming to consensus on a belief that the MOOC could provide solutions to education problems through data mining, shows a societal shift toward learning analytics as preferential data for education policy, data derived from cognitive models of learning.

Despite the rich history of education as an academic discipline and field of research, education discussion and political movement throughout the MOOC phenomenon has largely been driven by outside voices, by individuals who have celebrated their lack of theoretical and pedagogical expertise within the education discipline (e.g., Khan, 2012). In this context, the lack of immediate consensus on the Thrun quotation makes sense, as the social spaces where education has been debated have erased expertise and replaced it with education newcomers with a cognitive worldview and dependent on a specific brand of quantitative data to solidify their theoretical lenses.

Educators fail to find consensus on the purpose of higher education

The following quote from a study respondent reveals a growing conflict in higher education:

> Blah blah blah tenured humanities professor sanctimony. Explain to me how you occupy the moral high ground when your students graduate $30,000 in debt and have no marketable skills.

The superstructure of higher education has been unable to create and align with a unifying purpose for why citizens should engage in higher education. This inability, in conjunction with the rising cost of attendance, has led to a cultural and political backlash against traditional higher education. Higher education authors (Bennett & Wilezol, 2013; Kamanetz, 2010) have advocated for individuals to join the workforce and/or become entrepreneurs rather than enrol in a higher education institution. This sentiment has gained political traction. In a speech designed to promote policy on education, President Barack Obama called for more young people to engage in skills and manufacturing trades in lieu of college, referencing the earnings of a tradesperson as superior to a person with a degree in art history (Horsley, 2014).

The media and policy push away from college has not been readily adopted by learners or families; a recent study on attitudes regarding the purpose of higher education notes a disconnect between politicians clamouring for job skills and STEM subjects, and citizens who see college as a space for developing broader skills that provide a foundation for workforce preparation (Lederman, 2014). Societal beliefs could be due to the longstanding notion that a college education is a ticket to the middle class (Carnevale, 2012), while politicians could see the erosion of the middle class as a reason to focus on trades and skills, either in a collegiate setting or outside of the academy (LeBlanc, 2013).

As tuition and expenses continue to rise, economics will grow as a factor in an individual's decision making on further education and career choices. While no economists predict that higher education costs will decline, there are several intervention strategies being discussed; in 2014 Oregon and Tennessee lawmakers proposed two years of free tuition to students enroled in a state community or technical college. In Oregon, the cost of tuition would then be repaid through the graduates' future earnings (Cooper, 2014). In Tennessee, tuition would be covered by the state after all other financial aid options have been exhausted. In supporting the initiative, American Association of Community Colleges Senior Vice President David Baime noted, "Many of the jobs in our economy these days don't require a four-year degree. An associates degree, a two-year degree, or even, in some cases, a one-year certificate . . . give people very good jobs" (FoxNews.com, 2014). The lack of vision and articulation concerning the importance of a college degree from a postsecondary institution has allowed for skills-and-competencies voices to gain a foothold in the debate (Veletsianos, 2014), and without a clear vision or government financial intervention, the decision will become more difficult as costs rise.

Imagining higher education as a space designed for the development of job skills that create employment opportunities marks an historic shift in what society considers the purpose of higher education. Advocates for education that emphasizes gainful employment stress the necessity of employability in today's evolving society (Thrun, 2013b). Clay Shirky has utilized an historical argument to further this ideology, casting the growth of federal-based education initiatives between World War II and the Civil Rights Era as the "Golden Age of Education," one that was unsustainable and that has been gone for forty years and thus should be viewed as an aberration rather than the basis for judging education policy and initiatives (Shirky, 2014).

Shirky's criticism has factual accuracies, but his lens fails to account for the historical push behind the purpose of education (Wagoner, 2004). The purpose of higher education since the mid-eighteenth century has been to produce an intelligent, vibrant, and critical citizenry, and by defining historical political initiatives as an unsustainable golden age rather than the inevitable result of over 200 years of philosophical and cultural thought, abstracts policy from its history and context. Such Shirky thinking provides an opportunity to advocate for initiatives that lessen the importance of education by casting the initiatives as far-reaching rather than expectant of historical progress.

Economics will play an ever-increasing role in the development of higher education

The role of economics in the MOOC phenomenon was highly evident through most prompts within the Delphi study. Discussions across prompts noted the rising cost of higher education, the inability of state or federal governments to offset those costs, and the value of a degree in relation to its financial cost to the student. Many experts opted to advocate for pragmatism in developing solutions to address student debt rather than engage economics in a different fashion, seeing the existing landscape of rising costs and decreasing subsidies as indicative of the future.

One place of economic agreement in the Delphi study was the cost of producing a MOOC. Participants discussed the monetary costs of time and labour to create a MOOC, as well as the time commitment from the instructional team in facilitating the first week of a MOOC. Others furthered this discussion by estimating the point where a MOOC can turn a profit: between its fourth and fifth iteration: "even if the direst prediction of time overhead here is true, a 4x time increase for a version of a course translates to a course reducing the need for human resources starting in semester #5." This leaves the question of who will pay for the initial iterations of these courses. Much of this money has come from venture capital or institutional endowment: in the second quarter of 2015 Coursera raised $49.5 million in venture capital (Billings, 2015), making the total VC investment in educational technology just under $600 million, nearly as much as was invested for all of 2014. While conversation continues on how these investments will be paid back, the history of venture capital through Udacity shows a desire by venture capital firms to recoup their investment (Garg, 2013).

On top of signature tracks and tier-based pricing, commercial MOOC providers are making money from higher education institutions, both those they work for as well as those who solicit their content. Kolowich (2013) details the relationship between edX and its two institutional customer bases: schools who collaborate to build edX courses, and schools who solicit edX courses for their use:

> edX offers its university affiliates a choice of two partnership models. Both models give universities the opportunity to make money from their edX MOOCs—but only after edX gets paid.
>   . . . Once a self-service course goes live on the edX Web site, edX will collect the first $50,000 generated by the course, or $10,000 for each recurring course. The organization and the university partner will each get 50 percent of all revenue beyond that threshold.
>   The second model, called the "edX-supported model," casts the organization in the role of consultant and design partner, offering "production assistance" to universities for their MOOCs. The organization charges a base rate of $250,000 for each new course, plus $50,000 for each time a course is offered for an additional term, according to the standard agreement.
>   Although the edX-supported model requires cash up front, the potential returns for the university are high if a course ends up making money. (para. 6)

The example discussed in the Delphi study was edX's partnership with the California State University system and San Jose State University in particular (Cheal,

2013), a school at the time with budget issues so severe it sought to make $16 million in baseline budget cuts between the Fall 2013 and Spring 2014 semester, notifying department chairs of the change only a few weeks prior to the end of semester (Murphy, 2013). The California State University system publicly subsidizes education institutions, yet a school looking to cut $16 million from its budget outsourced a portion of its academics to Massachusetts-based edX for curriculum and course content, and nearly $28 million in uncontested educational technology funds have been spent on programs and initiatives that have yet to benefit students (Murphy, 2014). While the Delphi panel was unable to agree whether or not the institution of education is a public good, the economics of its public subsidy are a decreasing part of both the student tuition as well as the social discussion.

Disagreement on definitions of education terms

The expert Delphi panel encountered a number of difficulties in finding agreed-upon definitions for education and research terms. Within the three rounds of discussion, terms such as *data, open, student, pedagogy, personalization, sufficient,* and *online education* were used in divergent ways to describe similar variables or phenomena. Historically some have argued that such disagreement stems from education as a moving profession basing itself within the sociocultural milieu of the time (Harvey, 2005), so definitions outside of an educator's primary discipline would be more negotiated than those within a field of study. However, experts quickly converged on definitions for the business and technological terms used in the study, such as *disruptive technology* and *learning analytics.*

Finding spaces of agreement or disagreement is predicated upon establishing the rules and parameters for a conversation. The Delphi study was designed to create a space for various experts associated with the MOOC phenomenon to freely discuss the social, historical, political and educational impact and future of the MOOC and higher education. This is the traditional method for a Delphi study: experts in a subject have a space to discuss a rising phenomenon amongst other experts, and the panellist design mitigates the levels of expertise so that conversation can begin at a high level (Linstone & Turoff, 2002). The experts chosen for this Delphi study were influential scholars and practitioners tied to MOOCs, but the varying definitions provided by experts in wrestling with prompts and topics created a space where conversation was dedicated to shoring up vocabulary misconceptions rather than debating the topics. It is possible, however, that the problems with terminology were in fact explorations and negotiations of an ill-understood emerging phenomenon.

For online education to remain a viable field from which to explore the MOOC, the field must agree upon terms as basic as data, open, and student, as well as complex topics such as pedagogy and personalization, and emergence.

CONCLUSION

While the speed with which the MOOC phenomenon gained traction in educational conversations was unprecedented, many educators and critics have expected the MOOC to follow the trajectory of previous waves of educational technology (Watters, 2012). These arguments often cite failed institutionally backed online initiatives of the past, or Gartner's Hype Cycle (Neal, 2013) to reasonably account for the excitement while justifying a belief that the technology cannot meet expectations. For these educators and critics, the MOOC phenomenon is yet another example of organizations and businesses with a limited understanding of education and pedagogy failing to adequately provide solutions.

The failures of prior online education efforts and subsequent reforms are important to consider as part of the MOOC phenomenon. The MOOC phenomenon born of CS 271 includes elite universities, multinational organizations, news media, public policy, commerce, and venture capital. While educators may see the MOOC under increased scrutiny as a learning model, its footprint in society and policy continues to grow, launching a new reality for online learning, one that appears to be unfamiliar with the field's past.

The results of the Delphi study show an interest in using MOOCs as well as other technologies and data formats to offer different and potentially better opportunities for learning, but they also show a reticence to engage the topic of education in a sociocultural manner, focusing instead on abstracting the institution of higher education from society and attempting to pinpoint progress. Higher education has long been an intersection of various stakeholders with varying understandings of history and research in education, and MOOC stakeholders new to the historical and research-based aspects of the discipline have made missteps and encountered knowledge gaps consistent with prior iterations of educational technology and educational solutionism. The prior ventures were not supported from outside by a web of power and sphere of influence, though; this has allowed the MOOC to enjoy an unprecedented rise in notoriety and popularity despite no research-based positive effect on the broken higher education system it purports to fix.

Where the MOOC has been successful is in shaping debate and setting discussion parameters outside the traditional higher education structure: redefining existing education vernacular while establishing new terms for the field, offering cognitive learning as the focal point of learning theory, focusing non-structural MOOC discussion on economics and thereby defining education as a product and a private good, and labelling the purpose of education as the development of careers and skills. From this perspective, MOOC success has less to do with course completion and more with renegotiating the manner in which society talks about education. It is those conversations that will continue to dictate the course of higher education practice and policy, rather than the intricacies of the learning model.

REFERENCES

Alexander, S. [SAlexander_UTS]. (2013, October 9). @mweller Thrun: there are no experts in online learning. Lots of anecdotes and here are 60 ways of learning but few who base work on big data [Tweet]. Retrieved from https://twitter.com/SAlexander_UTS/status/388022568013549568

Bady, A. (2013). The MOOC bubble and the attack on public education. *AcademicMatters: The Journal of Higher Education, 8*(1). Retrieved from http://www.academicmatters.ca/2013/05/the-mooc-bubble-and-the-attack-on-public-education/

Bennett, W., & Wilezol, D. (2013). *Is college worth it? A former United States Secretary of Education and a liberal arts graduate expose the broken promise of higher education*. Nashville, TN: Thomas Nelson Publishers.

Billings, M. (2015, August 25). The daily startup: Coursera picks up $49.5M as edtech funding continues. *The Wall Street Journal*. Retrieved from http://blogs.wsj.com/venturecapital/2015/08/25/the-daily-startup-coursera-picks-up-49-5m-as-edtech-funding-continues/

Borden, J. (2014, August 26). MOOCs are dead—long live the MOOC. *Wired* [Web Periodical]. Retrieved from http://www.wired.com/2014/08/moocs-are-dead-long-live-the-mooc/

Carnevale, A. (2012, April 9). For a middle-class life, college is crucial. *New York Times*. Retrieved from http://www.nytimes.com/roomfordebate/2012/03/01/should-college-be-for-everyone/for-a-middle-class-life-college-is-crucial

Cheal, C. (2013, August 14). Creating MOOCs for college credit: SJSU's partnership with edX and Udacity. *Educause Center for Analysis and Research* [Research Bulletin]. Retrieved from https://net.educause.edu/ir/library/pdf/ERB1307.pdf

Cooper, J. (2014, February 4). Oregon looks at free community college tuition. *The Washington Times*. Retrieved from http://www.washingtontimes.com/news/2014/feb/4/oregon-looks-at-free-community-college-tuition/

Daniel, J. (2012). Making sense of MOOCs: Musings in a maze of myth, paradox and possibility. *Journal of Interactive Media in Education, 16*(3). Retrieved from http://www.academicpartnerships.com/docs/default-document-library/moocs.pdf?sfvrsn=0.

Ferenstein, G. (2013, January 15). How California's online education pilot will end college as we know it. *TechCrunch* [Web Periodical]. Retrieved from http://techcrunch.com/2013/01/15/how-californias-new-online-education-pilot-will-end-college-as-we-know-it/

FoxNews.com (2014, February 10). Tennessee governor proposes free community college for high school graduates. Retrieved 11 February 2014 from http://www.foxnews.com/us/2014/02/10/tennessee-governor-proposes-free-community-college-for-high-school-gradua

Friedman, T. (2012, May 15). Come the revolution. *The New York Times*. Retrieved from http://www.nytimes.com/2012/05/16/opinion/friedman-come-the-revolution.html

Garg, A. (2013, November 21). Udacity's pivot. *The Online Economy: Strategy and Entrepreneurship* [Web Log]. Retrieved from http://www.onlineeconomy.org/udacitys-pivot

Garrison, R. (2009). Implications of online learning for the conceptual development and practice of distance education. *The Journal of Distance Education 23*(2): 93–104. Retrieved from http://files.eric.ed.gov/fulltext/EJ851906.pdf

Harvey, D. (2005). *A brief history of neoliberalism*. New York: Oxford University Press.

Helper, L. (2013, November 22). Coursera lands $20 million in new funding, despite online education turmoil. *Silicon Valley Business Journal* [Web Periodical]. Retrieved from http://www.bizjournals.com/sanjose/news/2013/11/22/coursera-lands-20-million-in-new.html

Horsley, S. (2014, January 31). Obama: We've got to move away from "train and pray." *NPR Morning Edition* [Audio File]. Retrieved from http://www.npr.org/2014/01/31/269216917/obama-weve-got-to-move-away-from-train-and-pray

Kamenetz, A. (2010). *DIY U: Edupunks, edupreneurs, and the coming transformation of higher education.* White River Junction, VT: Chelsea Green.

Khan, S. (2012). *The one-world schoolhouse: Education reimagined.* New York: Twelve.

Koller, D. (2013). The online revolution: Learning without limits. Presentation at Sloan-C 19th International Conference for Online Learning. Orlando, FL: November 2013.

Kolowich, S. (2013, February 21). How edX plans to earn, and share, revenue from its free online courses. *Chronicle of Higher Education* [Web Periodical]. Retrieved from http://chronicle.com/article/How-EdX-Plans-to-Earn-and/137433/

Koseff, A. (2014, January 23). Jerry Brown pushes UC to find "outer limits" of online education. *Sacramento Bee: Capitol Alert* [Web Log]. Retrieved from http://blogs.sacbee.com/capitolalertlatest/2014/01/am-alert-302.html

LeBlanc, P. (2013, October 18). Disaggregation and innovation in higher education: Charting a course through turbulent times. Keynote presentation at 2013 Educause Annual Meeting. Anaheim, CA.

Leckart, S. (2012, March 12). The Stanford education experiment could change higher learning forever. *Wired* [Web Periodical]. Retrieved from http://www.wired.com/wiredscience/2012/03/ff_aiclass/

Lederman, D. (2014, February 4). Tennessee Governor seeks free community college tuition. *Inside Higher Ed* [Web Periodical]. Retrieved from http://www.insidehighered.com/quicktakes/2014/02/04/tenn-governor-seeks-free-community-college-tuition

Lewin, T. (2012, March 4). MOOCs, large courses open to all, topple campus walls. *The New York Times.* Retrieved from http://www.nytimes.com/2012/03/05/education/moocs-large-courses-open-to-all-topple-campus-walls.html

Linstone, H., & Turoff, M. (2002). *The Delphi Method: Techniques and applications.* Reading, MA: Addison-Wesley. Retrieved from http://is.njit.edu/pubs/delphibook/delphibook.pdf

Minsky, M. (1982). Why people think computers can't. *AI Magazine, 3*(4). Retrieved from http://web.media.mit.edu/~minsky/papers/ComputersCantThink.txt

Murphy, K. (2013, November 6). San Jose State departments forced to cut classes for spring term. *San Jose Mercury News.* Retrieved from http://www.mercurynews.com/ci_24460539/san-jose-state-departments-forced-cut-classes-spring

———. (2014, October 4). San Jose State's costly high-tech upgrade with Cisco faces setbacks, questions. *San Jose Mercury News*. Retrieved from http://www.mercurynews.com/education/ci_26666181/san-jose-states-costly-high-tech-upgrade-cisco

Neal, M. (2013, December 19). MOOCs are a total bust, according to the hype cycle. *Motherboard* [Blog post]. Retrieved from http://motherboard.vice.com/blog/moocs-are-a-total-bustaccording-to-the-hype-cycle

Nipper, S. (1989). Third generation distance learning and computer conferencing. In R. Mason & A. Kaye (eds.) *Mindweave: Communication, computers and distance education.* Oxford: Pergamon. Retrieved from http://web.archive.org/web/20030412062614/http://icdl.open.ac.uk/literaturestore/mindweave/chap5.html

Pratt, T. (2014, August 27). New degree program is big test for MOOC-style higher ed. *PBS NewsHour* [Web Periodical]. Retrieved from http://www.pbs.org/newshour/updates/new-degree-program-big-test-mooc-style-higher-ed/

Rodriguez, C. (2012). MOOCs and the AI-Stanford like courses: Two successful and distinct course formats for massive open online courses. *European Journal of Open, Distance and E-Learning, 15*(2). Retrieved from http://www.eurodl.org/materials/contrib/2012/Rodriguez.pdf

Sandeen, C. (2013, July 18). From hype to nuanced promise: American higher education and the MOOC 3.0 era. *Huffington Post* [Web Periodical]. Retrieved from http://www.huffingtonpost.com/cathy-sandeen/from-hype-to-nuanced-prom_b_3618496.html

Scharmer, O. (2015, May 4.) MOOC 4.0: The next revolution in learning and leadership. *Huffington Post* [Web Periodical]. Retrieved 15 May 2015 from http://www.huffingtonpost.com/otto-scharmer/mooc-40-the-next-revoluti_b_7209606.html

Scott, A. (2014, March 25). MOOC 2.0: Open online education moves forward. *Marketplace* [Web Periodical]. Retrieved from http://www.marketplace.org/topics/business/education/mooc-20-open-online-education-moves-forward

Siemens, G. (2013a, March 10). Group work advice for MOOC providers. *elearnspace* [Blog post]. Retrieved 11 March 2013 from http://www.elearnspace.org/blog/2013/03/10/group-work-advice-for-mooc-providers/

———. (2013, November 15). The failure of Udacity. *Elearnspace* [Blog post]. Retrieved from http://www.elearnspace.org/blog/2013/11/15/the-failure-of-udacity/

Shirky, C. (2014, January 29).The end of higher education's golden age. *Clay Shirky* [Blog post]. Retrieved from http://www.shirky.com/weblog/2014/01/there-isnt-enough-money-to-keep-educating-adults-the-way-were-doing-it/

Stanton, J., & Harkness, S. (2014). Got MOOC?: Labor costs for the development and delivery of an Open Online Course. *Information Resources Management Journal (IRMJ)*, *27*(2), 14–26. doi:10.4018/irmj.2014040102

Thrun, S. (2013a, November 14). Launching our data science and big data track built with leading industry partners. *Udacity Blog* [Blog post]. Retrieved from http://blog.udacity.com/2013/11/sebastian-thrun-launching-our-data.html

———. (2013b, October 9). #highered @udacity: MOOC 2.0 is live: MOOCs with personalized mentoring and college credit, at 1980s tuition levels. [Tweet]. from https://twitter.com/SebastianThrun/status/324660481367363585

Vanderbilt, T. (2012). How artificial intelligence can change higher education. *Smithsonian Magazine*, December 2012. Retrieved from http://www.smithsonianmag.com/people-places/how-artificial-intelligence-can-change-higher-education-136983766/?c=y%3Fno-ist

Veletsianos, G. (2014, February 10). ELI 2014, learner experiences, MOOC research, and the MOOC phenomenon. *George Veletsianos* [Blog post]. Retrieved from http://www.veletsianos.com/2014/02/10/mooc-research-mooc-phenomenon/

Wagoner, J. (2004). *Jefferson and education*. Washington, D.C.: Thomas Jefferson Foundation.

Waldrop, M. (2013). Online learning: Campus 2.0. *Nature*, *495*(7440). Retrieved from http://www.nature.com/news/online-learning-campus-2-0-1.12590

Watters, A. (2012). Top ed-tech trends of 2012: MOOC. *Hack Education* [Blog post]. Retrieved from http://hackeducation.com/2012/12/03/top-ed-tech-trends-of-2012-moocs/

11 Arts-Based Technologies Create Community in Online Courses

▶ *Beth Perry and Margaret Edwards*

How can educators and learning designers enhance a sense of community in online courses? Exemplary online educators employ emerging technologies and practices that optimize meaningful interaction, facilitating an ongoing social experience to help create community (Perry, Janzen, & Edwards, 2012). In our experience many pedagogical strategies that facilitate this culture of community share one aspect: they are arts-based. Arts-based approaches include literary, visual, musical, or dramatic elements. We have labelled these *artistic pedagogical technologies* (APTs). APTs are distinguished from traditional online technologies in part by their emphasis on aesthetics and their link to creativity. How do APTs encourage interaction, create social presence, and facilitate a culture of community in the online educational milieu? Vygotsky's (1978) Social Development Theory (SDT) and Janzen, Perry, and Edwards's (2012a) Quantum Perspective of Learning provide some clues regarding the effects of APTs. Additionally, philosophical, theoretical, and pedagogical shifts influence the development, adoption, and use of APTs and need to be considered by educators and learning designers who may use APTs to facilitate online community building.

Advances in Internet technology continue to change the social and pedagogical perspectives of online learning (Pamuk, 2012). Many online educators have moved philosophically from objectivism to constructivism, theoretically from behaviourism to sociocognitive views of education, and pedagogically from supporting direct instruction to championing interactive learning (Bertin

& Nancy-Combes, 2012; chapter 3). There is a shift from teacher-centered pedagogy to more personalized, social, and participatory pedagogies that emphasize community in the postsecondary online classroom (Sun, 2011; McLoughlin & Lee, 2010; chapter 9). Often, the goal is transformative learning (Mayes, Ku, Akarasriworn, Luebeck, & Korkmaz, 2011).

Discussions regarding the theoretical underpinnings of APT techniques and the factors that influence their development and implementation remain sparse. Published literature regarding online teaching strategies often focuses on pedagogical practices such as computer-mediated conferencing (Baran & Correia, 2014; Mayes et al., 2011). Other relevant literature centres on emerging technologies on a macro level, describing how digital technologies can support pedagogy and create innovation (Aldosemani & Shepherd, 2014; Andersen & Ponti 2014; Li, Verma, Skevi, Zufferey, Blom, & Dillenbourg, 2014). In contrast, this chapter focuses on APTs as an emerging technology on a micro level, as we examine specific pedagogical strategies to enhance interaction, facilitate a shared social experience, and create a culture of community in online classes.

BACKGROUND

Exemplary online educators infuse a sense of presence into the classes they teach (Janzen, Perry, & Edwards, 2012). This sense of presence is both created and conveyed through the incorporation of interactive APT teaching strategies such as Photovoice, virtual reflective centres, and conceptual quilting (Perry & Edwards, 2010). Studies found that these APTs help stimulate interaction between students and teachers, among students, and between students and course materials. The result of such interactions is the enhancement of the experience of social presence in the virtual class, creating what we have labelled a "culture of community" (Perry & Edwards, 2010). Repeated experiences of an authentic shared presence help establish shared values, norms, and beliefs for a collective culture in the online class.

A plethora of literature supports the importance of interaction, social presence, and community in online education (Kang & Im 2013; Huahui, Sullivan, & Mellenius, 2014; Yuan & Kim, 2104). In foundational work, Moore (1989) defined interaction in online education as a student-content, student-student, or student-teacher exchange. Others added the interaction between student and self (Ornelles, 2007), and between student and technology (Paul & Cochran, 2013). In chapter 3 of this book, Anderson has further expanded the notion of interaction to include individuals, technology, and content. Positive outcomes of interaction in online courses include creativity and collaboration (Hendry & Tomitsch, 2014), increasing higher-order thinking and retention (Pecka, Kotcherlakota, & Berger, 2014), and increased learner motivation and academic success (Hawkins, Graham, Sudweeks, & Barbour, 2013).

Social presence is the ability of students and teachers to project their personal characteristics into the online class, thereby presenting themselves as "real people" (Rourke et al., 2000). The value of social presence for effective online teaching and learning is commonly highlighted. For example, social presence is one cornerstone of the widely supported Community of Inquiry Model (Rourke et al., 2000). The positive consequences of social presence in the online learning environment are many, such as the promotion of a sense of caring and belonging (Plante & Asselin, 2014), the creation of a warm and collegial environment that encourages participation and collaboration (Huahui, Sullivan, & Mellenius, 2014), and the development of increasing quality of cognitive *presence and higher order thinking* (Lee, 2014). Nevertheless, Kehrwald (2008) and Lowenthal (2009) cautioned that despite the general agreement among researchers that social presence is a key element for effective online teaching and learning, a shared understanding of social presence remains elusive.

The effective online classroom is a social environment that enacts community values such as the exchange of beliefs and ideas (Plante & Asselin, 2014). We define community as shared culture in the online classroom, including shared values, norms, and beliefs (Perry & Edwards, 2010). Others have defined community as a classroom in which knowledge is mutually constructed (Chang, 2012). The creation of an online learning community serves as the foundation for a successful learning environment (Chang, 2012). Learners in a community are able to make meaning from their learning experiences (Ziegler, Paulus, & Woodside, 2014), are encouraged to collaborate and provide reflection on their learning (Holmes, 2013), are more productive learners (Meyer, 2014), and have a sense of belonging or reduced feelings of isolation that may enhance the quality of their learning (Phelan, 2012). Moisey, Neu, and Cleveland-Innes (2008) found significant positive correlations between students' satisfaction with their courses and programs and levels of the sense of community cohesion.

To facilitate the goals of increased interaction, social presence, and community in online learning environments, Hawks (2014) called for pedagogical changes and stated that new models of online education should be considered. Others agreed: Hou (2012) argued that innovative strategies, such as online role playing, are needed to assist learners in attaining a deeper level of interaction and higher cognitive skills; and Mayne and Qiang (2011) suggested that personal emails from instructors and the presence of a "coffee shop" informal discussion forum were effective strategies for enhancing interaction and social presence.

Beyond these examples, however, research on instructional strategy development and course materials design for effective online learning remains limited. Educators are left to create interactive teaching technologies to achieve these goals, yet the literature suggests that they are often not successful (Allen & Seaman, 2012). Ashbaugh (2013) reported that the current abundance of "less than excellent online courses threatens to undermine the value of the educational opportunities afforded by the Internet" (p. 97). Ashbaugh (2013) concluded there have been advances in instructional technologies; however, online pedagogies lack quality and fail to enhance learning. Often teaching strategies are developed and utilized without being first subjected to rigorous research-based assessment.

In summary, interaction, social presence, and community are widely accepted as important to effective online teaching and learning. Interaction and social presence are linked to creation of a sense of online community in educational environments. Educators are often without evidence-based guidance as to what teaching technologies will help to facilitate these goals. Artistic pedagogical technologies seem to help accomplish these outcomes in online postsecondary classrooms.

DEFINITION AND DESCRIPTION OF ARTISTIC PEDAGOGICAL TECHNOLOGIES

Online instructors need to develop, implement, and evaluate new and creative teaching technologies to maximize interaction, social presence, and community online. Our team published findings related to three such teaching technologies (Photovoice, virtual reflective centres, and conceptual quilting) demonstrating positive educational outcomes (Perry & Edwards, 2005). Specifically, both students and teachers reported that their virtual classrooms were effective learning environments, in part because of the inclusion of these teaching technologies (Perry & Edwards, 2005). Students reported benefitting scholastically from the sense of community that arose when they participated in these learning activities. One finding from our preliminary studies that requires further analysis is the link between Photovoice, virtual reflective centres, and conceptual quilting teaching strategies — they are all founded in the arts (visual arts and drama). Why do artistic approaches, which value aesthetics as well as reason (Maguire,

Donovan, Mishook, Gaillande, & Garcia, 2012), seem to facilitate community in the online class?

The worth of the arts has been recognized in face-to-face education. Specifically, art, photography, literature, poetry, music, and drama have been reported as contributing positively to the face-to-face classroom educational experience by stimulating reflection, improving intellect, promoting creativity and helping to achieve affective objectives (Logsdon, 2013; Turketo & Smith, 2014). However, these claims for the value of art-based teaching strategies are primarily anecdotal.

The translation of artistic-based pedagogy to the online classroom seems to be an untested idea. Brown, Kirkpatrick, Magnum, and Avery (2008) declared a need to move on from established online pedagogies that no longer fully satisfy today's learner and to "develop and implement alternative interpretative pedagogies" (p. 283). APTs represent such pedagogical practices.

Recent research conducted by Perry and Edwards (2012) explored how APTs influenced postsecondary online learning environments and student learning. They helped provide a real and authentic medium for instructors and students to engage with one other, with technology, and with educational content (Janzen, Perry, & Edwards, 2011); created inviting learning environments; initiated, sustained, and enhanced interaction between students and instructors; and helped develop community (Perry & Edwards, 2012). Further, APTs stimulated creative thinking, captured student attention, extended the application of course content, contributed to positive learning outcomes, and helped develop a sense of professional fulfilment for instructors (Perry & Edwards, 2010). They also contributed to students establishing a sense of group identity, supported course engagement, enhanced the learning environment, and developed social connectedness (Perry, Dalton, & Edwards, 2009). Finally, students reported a positive influence on not only course interactions but their sense of community, as well as increased comfort in the educational milieu. They noted that APTs aided them in getting to know themselves, classmates, and instructors (Edwards, Perry, Janzen, & Menzies, 2012).

Photovoice

Wang and Burris (1997) developed Photovoice as a participatory-action research methodology. Perry (2006) transformed this research methodology into an interactive online teaching technology, which involves the instructor posting a digital image and a reflective question at the onset of each unit in the course. With this platform, students are encouraged to discuss the question in a dedicated forum. Photovoice is not graded and optional.

Positive outcomes included encouraging engagement and interest in the course content; making the learning environment more appealing, creative, and interesting; and facilitating the development of social cohesiveness (Perry et al., 2008).

Virtual reflective centres

An example of an APT that involves the artistic element of drama is the virtual reflective centre (Ronaldson, 2004). Virtual reflective centres are role-playing simulation exercises that are reported to enhance critical thinking and promote social presence online (Ronaldson, 2004).

Cubbon (2014) used virtual reflective centres in an online graduate course for advanced nursing practice students. Through random assignments of students to either a patient or a nurse practitioner role, the instructor gave each student the information needed to fulfil the roles during a real-time online "appointment." As a summation, the instructor distributed reflective questions related to the exercise and hosted an asynchronous group discussion. Participants in the virtual reflective centre exercise emphasized that it facilitated the development of a sense of community in this virtual classroom because it provided a safe, structured environment in which they could engage in an interactive learning exercise. Students commented that the dramatic element of the exercise helped to make the activity novel and engaging, which motivated socially meaningful interaction.

Conceptual quilting

Conceptual quilting was developed by the authors and has been used in online graduate courses as a summary activity. Students are asked to construct a virtual quilt that is comprised of ideas, metaphors, theories, and other details from the course that they found most meaningful. The "quilt" needs to be in a medium that can be shared electronically with the class. The construction of the conceptual quilt encourages learners to reflect as they interact again with course materials. Further interaction with the instructor and other students comes when students post their quilts to an asynchronous online discussion forum and respond to comments. This often results in a resurgence of dialogue around a course theme that was depicted in the quilt. Anecdotally, students comment that conceptual quilting helps them consolidate their learning and bring closure to the course. From a social interactive perspective, the sharing of the completed quilts is a way for students to acknowledge the impact that others (teachers and peers) have had on their learning.

HOW ARTISTIC PEDAGOGICAL TECHNOLOGIES WORK

We propose that the educational impact of arts-based teaching technologies arises initially because of the enhanced interactions they help create. The interpersonal interactions among students and between students and teachers, and the intrapersonal interaction between student and self, are most relevant to this discussion. These interactions may lead to the experience of social presence, as those in the virtual classroom reveal elements of their personal characteristics and become more "real" and known to one another and to themselves. Social presence cannot be established, indeed cannot exist, without interpersonal and intrapersonal interactions. These interactions do not necessarily take place spontaneously in virtual classrooms. Specific teaching technologies that have social interaction (leading to social presence) as a goal are needed to facilitate this outcome.

Not all forms of social presence are equivalent. For example, certain activities aimed at social presence are deemed more authentic, perhaps experienced as more "human" or "real" by participants. The quality of social presence generated through APTs has been described as palpably "human" by the students. Because APTs are founded in the arts, which are human-centred (created by, valued by, shared by, and appreciated by people), APTs help to facilitate interpersonal and intrapersonal social presence that is less artificial.

Not all interactions are alike in terms of effect on social presence and the eventual formation of community. Frequency of interaction alone is not an adequate assessment of interaction levels. While the number of times that students interact with peers, teachers, course materials, and themselves may be important, it is the quality of those interactions that may be most critical to positive outcomes such as a sense of social presence and community. For example, a brief e-mail exchange containing superficial greetings exposes little of the values, attitudes, or beliefs of participants. To be meaningful to the establishment of social presence and community, interactions must reveal something important and relevant about participants to others or to self.

Further, social presence in the online class needs to be part of a course from the beginning to the end. That is, participants need to establish their initial presence when the course begins, but they also need to demonstrate ongoing participation in the course (Kehrwald, 2008). Teaching technologies such as Photovoice that require student and teacher contributions throughout the course may help facilitate becoming known to each other at the beginning of a course and also can provide ongoing evidence of participation. Further, APTs such as Photovoice potentially allow participants to systematically reveal more of their personal values, beliefs, and priorities as the course proceeds. This may facilitate progressively more personal and perhaps more authentic and meaningful social interaction.

Essentially effective social presence in the online class is a dynamic experience. It evolves over the duration of the course with participants becoming more comfortable with one another through ongoing meaningful interactive experiences. Eventually this leads to the establishment of a culture of community.

The establishment and growth of social presence is related to three conditions: ability, opportunity, and motivation (Kehrwald, 2008). APTs help to meet each of these conditions. First, *ability* refers to students being able to reference their own experiences and bring these to the learning community in an appropriate way. Kehrwald emphasized that novice learners do not come to online classes with this skill; they may not have the ability to send and to read social presence cues. Students need learning activities that help them gain this ability. Photovoice invites learners to share something about themselves with the class. It becomes one vehicle for students to establish their social presence in the course, and because the same strategy is used often in the course, it teaches students how to share socially in the online milieu. Participants also model this skill for one another, and those students who may be unskilled at sending and reading social presence cues have the option of waiting, watching, and learning how to participate prior to making a contribution.

The second condition is *opportunity for interaction*. Opportunities need to be purposefully created in online courses to facilitate the frequent meaningful interactions that cultivate social presence. Because APTs are used regularly (in the case of Photovoice, weekly), there is a consistent, scheduled opportunity for participants to interact. While opportunities for interaction are easy to create, they need to be such that learners are not overwhelmed by the demands of interaction within large groups (Harrison & Thomas, 2009; Heejung, Sunghee, & Keol, 2009). Most APTs, such as virtual reflective centres, are suited to smaller class sizes, to allow for participation by all students. The Photovoice activity requires students to make one or two short responses. Long responses with references are discouraged in this activity. This keeps participants from being overwhelmed by a large number of long posts they feel obliged to respond to.

Technologies that require students and teachers to contribute in a visible way signal that they are available for interactions (Kehrwald, 2008). APTs all have a tangible element that provides these signals. In the case of Photovoice, the weekly photo posting provides evidence of the participation of the teacher. Student involvement is evidenced by responses to the Photovoice question. Likewise, the conceptual quilts posted by students are evidence that they are members of a specific educational community. The responses and questions raised in reaction to the quilts are evidence of "attendance" and the involvement of other class community members.

The third condition for the establishment and growth of social presence is *motivation*. Teaching tools need to motivate students to participate. Motivation often comes because students believe that participation has some benefit for them. If the activity creates interest, motivation may be enhanced. For example, the Photovoice activity has mysterious elements (one student commented that she never could guess what photo would be hidden under the "electronic paperclip"), arousing curiosity and motivating participation. We speculate that perhaps part of what makes Photovoice motivational is that students find it engaging. It catches their attention; one student described it as a "hook" that captured her interest. Once students are focused on the course theme, the Photovoice activity engages them in dialogue with themselves as they puzzle over the image and think about their response to it. Because there is no correct response to art, their reaction is necessarily personal. As the class members begin to share their personal responses to the image in the public forum, there is some social expectation (motivation) to reciprocate by doing the same, and a public dialogue results in meaningful social interaction.

Students may be demotivated if they believe excessive time and effort is required to participate. There is no requirement to participate in Photovoice or conceptual quilting, which allows students to lurk without participating. Without exception, in our experience, over the time of the courses, all students eventually regarded the Photovoice exercise as worthwhile, and contributed. Keeping class sizes reasonable helps to prevent participants from being overwhelmed by the number of postings related to each Photovoice activity. Students receive positive feedback from peers and instructors regarding their participation in these activities, fuelling motivation.

Vygotsky's (1978) Social Development theory (SDT) helps explain how APTs influence interaction, social presence, and the creation of a culture of community in the online class. Teaching and learning, whether occurring in a traditional or virtual classroom, are essentially social experiences. According to SDT, social interaction is fundamental to cognitive development. Consciousness and cognition result from socialization and social behaviour. Vygotsky focused on the connections between people and the sociocultural context in which they act, and interact, in shared experiences (Yasnitsky, 2011). SDT learning is characterized by mediation through language, the discovery of differing perspectives, and the achievement of shared meaning (Yasnitsky, 2011). Vygotsky's SDT promotes learning environments in which students play an active role in learning. Teachers, rather than being transmitters of knowledge, collaborate with students to facilitate the acquisition of new knowledge, skills, and attitudes. Learning becomes a reciprocal experience involving the self and others.

When educators apply SDT to online education, learners require effective teaching tools to facilitate interacting from a distance, particularly with teachers and other students. When effective teaching strategies are used, online learners can achieve social connections with other students and teachers that, according to SDT, facilitate learning.

We propose that APTs stimulate these authentic human interactions required to promote social engagement in the virtual class. For example, music, artistic images, and literary works are infused with the humanness of the composer, artist, or author. When APTs are part of, or the foundation for, a course activity, they introduce into the course some aspect of another human. While a traditional learning activity in an online course may appear rather barren and anonymous, a song, photograph, or poem is often infused with the values, preferences, and beliefs of the one who created it. We suggest that when another "real" person is introduced into the online course using an APT, the potential for human interaction is enhanced. From the students' perspective, now there is someone to interact with.

The stimulation provided by the inclusion of such a strategy seems to be a catalyst for interaction for several reasons. One respondent in a study involving the use of Photovoice wrote, "Seeing a new photographic image appear each week in my course forum was like seeing the artwork that might be displayed in my professor's home. It told me something about her, about how she saw the world. It made her more real somehow and made it comfortable for me to e-mail her and ask questions." Another student offered a comment that helps to further the explanation regarding how the inclusion of an APT in a course stimulated meaningful interaction: "I felt like I got to know my professor because of the type of photos that were included in the course. I could tell that she had an appreciation for nature . . . and probably had a kind heart. I participated more freely because I felt like I knew her from the photos."

To achieve genuine, appropriate, and authentic interaction that results in substantive discussion, debate, and reflection may require deliberate strategies on the part of the online teacher. We propose that the inclusion of APTs in online course design may precipitate engagement between students, and students and teachers, which—according to SDT—is necessary for learning.

APTs provide an opportunity for meaningful interpersonal and intrapersonal interaction. APTs require a contribution that provides class members evidence of the involvement of students and teachers in a course. Ongoing meaningful interactions facilitate authentic social presence, which lays the foundation for and facilitates the ongoing development of the culture of community. In a culture of community, participants embrace shared values, norms, and beliefs; a shared culture. A shared culture facilitates further meaningful interpersonal interactions, and the cycle is propelled (Figure 11.1).

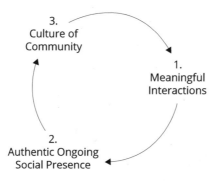

Figure 11.1 Development of a culture of community in the online classroom

Recently, to further the explanation of the relationship between APTs and community in online classes, Janzen, Perry, and Edwards (2012b) proposed that APTs help create quantum learning environments that connect learners, instructors, and technology. Quantum learning environments describe learning as multidimensional, having unlimited potential, holistic, and occurring on various planes simultaneously (Janzen, Perry, & Edwards, 2011). APTs, with their underpinnings of creativity, interaction, humanity, and layers of meaning, are compatible with the quantum view of learning. The potential for APTs to enhance community through creation of quantum learning environments is currently under further investigation.

FACTORS INFLUENCING APT DEVELOPMENT, ADOPTION, AND USE

Originally, Shea (2006) identified three foundational changes that have influenced online education: a philosophical shift from objectivism toward constructivism; a theoretical shift from behaviourism toward sociocognitive views of education; and a pedagogical shift from direct instruction to the facilitation of collaborative learning. More recently the shift from teacher-centered pedagogy to more personalized, social, and participatory pedagogies that emphasize community and aim for transformative learning has also been recognized (chapter 3; Sun, 2011; McLoughlin & Lee, 2010; Mayes et al., 2011).

Shea (2006) argued that these fundamental changes encourage teaching approaches that help to develop virtual learning communities. For example, student-centred, learner-directed, interactive, participative pedagogical methods are congruent with the establishment of community in the online class, with social interaction, and ultimately with learning. It follows that the development, adoption, and use of online teaching strategies, in this case APTs, is influenced by these learner-directed factors.

From objectivism to constructivism

Objectivists emphasize the accumulation of facts, and view learners as passive recipients of knowledge (Li, Clark, & Winchester, 2010). Differing views and individual experiences are often discouraged (Gulati, 2010). *Constructivists* embrace different worldviews and emphasize social relationships and cognitive interaction in learning environments (Bruner, 1966). Constructivists view knowledge as contextual and relative, and reject the notion that knowledge is an innate commodity that can be objectified or discovered (Bruner, 1966). In education, a constructivist approach assumes that teaching is not a process of transmitting intact knowledge to learners. Constructivists do not view learners as empty vessels awaiting filling or blank slates awaiting words. Rather, learners are viewed as builders who are continually creating mental representations of events and experiences. Key principles of constructivist thinking that guide teaching and course design include connecting all learning activities to a larger goal, encouraging learner responsibility, and ensuring that required tasks reflect the complexities of practice (Savery & Duffy, 1996). Teaching technologies that encourage learners to construct knowledge through activity and experience are favoured over lectures (Melrose, Park, & Perry, 2013).

Online learning environments are excellent venues for constructivist teaching technologies (Kehrwald, 2008). The potential for connectivity afforded by online communications facilitates opportunities for human-human interaction that, according to constructivists, precipitates learning. APTs such as Photovoice, conceptual quilting, and virtual reflective centres all purposefully create social interaction. In keeping with a constructivist philosophy, such interactive learning may involve the modification of attitudes, beliefs, and knowledge in all participants, including students and teachers.

From behaviourism to sociocognitivism

Behaviourism focuses on observable and measurable behaviours (Good & Brophy, 1990). For example, Bloom's (1956) taxonomy of learning is the basis for the development of behavioural learning objectives in which learning tasks are broken down into specific measurable tasks. For behaviourists, the achievement of objectives equates with learning success. *Cognitive theorists* view learning as involving internal processes, such as comparing new information to existing knowledge. This makes learning more active and complex. Learning strategies such as metaphors, chunking information, and the organization of instructional materials from simple to complex are used by cognitivists to facilitate learning.

Cognitivists view APTs favourably. Photovoice activities, for example, require students to engage in higher-order thinking, asking that they compare something they know to the theory of the course. For example, if the image presented is a photo of a tree with leaves changing colour, and the topic in the course is factors that influence organizational change, students are asked to recall what they know about weather, light, temperature, and seasonal influences on trees in the autumn, and to translate this into determining factors within an organization that might also create change. An internal thought process is needed, as changes in nature become a metaphor for changes in organizations. Likewise, in conceptual quilting students use internal mental processes to seek and find relationships between key themes in the course, and to find ways to weave these together in meaningful patterns that they can then display and explain.

From direct instruction to collaborative learning

The hallmarks of direct instruction are teacher control of one-way transmission of information, and measurable learning. Collaborative learning, on the other hand, involves joint intellectual efforts by students or students and teachers as they work together to seek understanding, meaning, or solutions. Students depend on and are accountable to one another as they participate in learning activities, and there is usually an end product to the collaborative learning activity. Collaborative learning online may result in the establishment of a community of learners. According to Jo Coaplen, Hollis, and Bailey (2013), collaborative pedagogical practices help build learning communities in the online classroom.

APTs can facilitate collaborative learning. For example, virtual reflective centres involve the active participation of all students, as each is assigned a role and invited to participate in a shared experience. Participants depend on one another to play their parts so the activity succeeds. Similarly, in a Photovoice activity, while students initially contribute their own interpretations of the photo, the resulting online discussion becomes a collaborative learning activity, as learners work together to formulate common understandings of the relationships between the photo and course topics.

APTs are congruent with constructivist learning's fundamental premise that knowledge is a human construction and that the learner is an active participant in the process of learning (Vygotsky, 1978). As online educators come to appreciate more diverse ways of knowing and understanding and focus more on social relationships in the class, educational technologies that have a human element, such as APTs, may become more common.

The shift from teacher-centered pedagogy to more personalized, social and participatory pedagogies that emphasize community (Sun, 2011; McLoughlin & Lee, 2010) is congruent with constructivist philosophy. Transformative learning is often the goal with a meaningful community experience the catalyst (Mayes, Ku, Akarasriworn, Luebeck, & Korkmaz, 2011).

CONCLUSION

This chapter provides a new understanding regarding emerging practices, specifically, APTs. Teaching strategies founded in the arts may assist online educators who aim to make online courses more meaningfully interactive. With meaningful interaction comes the potential for the experience of authentic ongoing social presence and the eventual establishment of a culture of community, which may bring with it many pedagogical benefits, including transformative learning.

As described in chapter 1, there is limited investigation of emerging practices in online education. The explanations presented in this chapter of why APTs are effective teaching strategies are only a start. Further research on the link between APTs and quantum learning theory might provide greater insight. The potential educational impact of such emerging technologies and practices (on students and teachers) has not yet been explored completely. This chapter contributes to these discussions and encourages educators, course designers, and researchers to experiment with including aspects of the arts in learning activities in online courses.

REFERENCES

Aldosemani, T., & Shepherd, C. (2014). Second Life to support multicultural literacy: Pre- and in-service teachers' perceptions and expectations. *TechTrends: Linking Research and Practice to Improve Learning, 58*(2), 46–58. doi:10.1007/s11528-014-0736-7

Andersen, R., & Ponti, M. (2014). Participatory pedagogy in an open educational course: challenges and opportunities. *Distance Education, 35*(2), 234–49. doi:10.1080/01587919.2014.917703

Ashbaugh, M. L. (2013). Expert instructional designer voices: Leadership competencies critical to global practice and quality online learning designs. *Quarterly Review of Distance Education, 14*(2), 97–118.

Baran, E., & Correia, A. (2014). A professional development framework for online teaching. *Techtrends: Linking Research and Practice to Improve Learning, 58*(5), 95–101. doi:10.1007/s11528-014-0791-0

Bertin, J. C., & Narcy-Combes, J. P. (2012). Tutoring at a distance. *Computer Assisted Language Learning, 25*, 105–9. doi:10.1080/09588221.2011.649087

Bloom, B. (1956). *Taxonomy of educational objectives.* New York: David McKay.

Brown, S. T., Kirkpatrick, M. K., Magnum, D., & Avery, J. (2008). A review of narrative strategies to transform traditional nursing education. *Journal of Nursing Education, 47*(6), 283–86.

Bruner, J. (1966). *Toward a theory of instruction.* Cambridge, MA: Harvard University Press.

Chang, Z. (2012). Student satisfaction, performance, and knowledge construction in online collaborative learning. *Journal of Educational Technology and Society, 15*(1), 127–36.

Cubbon, J. (2014). Use of online role play to enhance motivational interviewing skills of Advanced Nursing Practice graduate students. *Journal of Nursing Education.* Manuscript submitted for publication.

Edwards, M., Perry, B., Janzen, K., & Menzies, C. (2012). Using the artistic pedagogical technology of Photovoice to promote interaction in the online post-secondary classroom: The students' perspective. *Special Conference Issue of the Electronic Journal of e-Learning, 10*(1), 32–43.

Good, T., & Brophy, J. (1990). *Educational psychology: A realistic approach.* (4th ed.). White Plains, NY: Longman.

Gulati, S. (2008). Compulsory participation in online discussions: Is this constructivism or normalisation of learning? *Innovations in Education and Teaching International, 45*(2), 183–92.

Harrison, R., & Thomas, M. (2009). Identity in online communities: Social networking sites and language learning. *International Journal of Emerging Technologies and Society, 7*(2), 109–24.

Hawkins, A., Graham, C. R., Sudweeks, R. R., & Barbour, M. K. (2013). Academic performance, course completion rates, and student perception of the quality and frequency of interaction in a virtual high school. *Distance Education, 34*(1), 64–83.

Hawks, S. J. (2014). The flipped classroom: Now or never? *AANA Journal, 82*(4), 264–69.

Heejung, A., Sunghee, S., & Keol, L. (2009). The effects of different instructor facilitation approaches on students' interactions during asynchronous online discussion. *Computers and Education, 53*(3), 749–60.

Hendry, G., & Tomitsch, M. (2014). Implementing an exemplar-based approach in an interaction design subject: enhancing students' awareness of the need to be creative. *International Journal of Technology and Design Education, 24*(3), 337–48. doi:10.1007/s10798-013-9256-6

Holmes, B. (2013). School teachers' continuous professional development in an online learning community: Lessons from a case study of an e-twinning learning event. *European Journal of Education, 48*(1), 97–112. doi:10.1111/ejed.12015

Hou, H. (2012). Analyzing the learning process of an online role-playing discussion activity. *Journal of Educational Technology and Society, 15*(1), 211–22.

Huahui, Z., Sullivan, K. H., & Mellenius, I. (2014). Participation, interaction and social presence: An exploratory study of collaboration in online peer review groups. *British Journal of Educational Technology, 45*(5), 807–19. doi:10.1111/bjet.12094

Janzen, K., Perry, B., & Edwards, M. (2011). Aligning quantum learning with instructional design: Exploring the seven definitive questions. *International Review of Research in Open and Distance Learning, 20*(7). Retrieved from http://www.irrodl.org/index.php/irrodl/article/view/1038/2024

———. (2012a). The entangled web: The quantum perspective of learning, quantum learning environments and web technology. *Ubiquitous Learning: An International Journal, 4*(2), 1–16. Retrieved from http://ijq.cgpublisher. com/product/pub.186/prod.173

———. (2012b). Engaging students: Strategies for digital natives. *Academic Exchange Quarterly, 16*(3), 116–23.

Jo Coaplen, C., Hollis, E., & Bailey, R. (2013). Going beyond the content: Building community through collaboration in online teaching. *Researcher: An Interdisciplinary Journal, 26*(3), 1–19.

Kang, M. M., & Im, T. T. (2013). Factors of learner-instructor interaction which predict perceived learning outcomes in online learning environment. *Journal of Computer Assisted Learning, 29*(3), 292–301. doi:10.1111/jcal.12005

Kehrwald, B. (2008). Understanding social presence in text-based online learning environments. *Distance Education, 29*(1), 89–106.

Lee, S. (2014). The relationships between higher order thinking skills, cognitive density, and social presence in online learning. *Internet and Higher Education, 21*, 41–52. doi:10.1016/j.iheduc.2013.12.002

Li, N., Verma, H., Skevi, A., Zufferey, G., Blom, J., & Dillenbourg, P. (2014). Watching MOOCs together: Investigating co-located MOOC study groups. *Distance Education, 35*(2), 217–33. doi:10.1080/01587919.2014.917708

Li, Q., Clark, B., & Winchester, I. (2010). Instructional design and technology grounded in enactivism: A paradigm shift?. *British Journal of Educational Technology, 41*(3), 403–19.

Logsdon, L. F. (2013). Questioning the role of "21st-century skills" in arts education advocacy discourse. *Music Educators Journal, 100*(1), 51–56.

Lowenthal, P. R. (2009). Social presence. In P. Rogers, G. Berg, J. Boettcher, C. Howard, L. Justice, & K. Schenk (eds.), *Encyclopedia of distance and online learning* (2nd ed., pp. 1900-1906). Hershey, PA: IGI Global.

Maguire, C., Donovan, C., Mishook, J., Gaillande, G., & Garcia, I. (2012). Choosing a life one has reason to value: the role of the arts in fostering capability development in four small urban high schools. *Cambridge Journal of Education, 42*(3), 367–90.

Mayes, R., Ku, H., Akarasriworn, C., Luebeck, J., & Korkmaz, Ö. (2011). Themes and strategies for transformative online instruction: A review of literature and practice. *Quarterly Review of Distance Education, 12*(3), 151–66.

Mayne, L. A., & Qiang, W. (2011). Creating and measuring social presence in online graduate nursing courses. *Nursing Education Perspectives, 32*(2), 110–14. doi:10.5480/1536-5026-32.2.110

McLoughlin, C., & Lee, M. J. W. (2010). Personalised and self-regulated learning in the Web 2.0 era: International exemplars of innovative pedagogy using social software. *Australasian Journal of Educational Technology, 26,* 28–43. Retrieved from http://www.asci lite.org.au/ajet/submission/index.php/AJET/index

Melrose, S., Park, C., & Perry, B. (2013). *Teaching health professionals online: Frameworks and strategies.* Edmonton, AB: Athabasca University Press. Retrieved from http://www.aupress.ca/index.php/books/120234

Meyer, K. A. (2014). How community college faculty members may improve student learning productivity in their online courses. *Community College Journal of Research and Practice, 38*(6), 575–87.

Moisey, S., Neu, C., & Cleveland-Innes, M. (2008). Community building and computer-mediated conferencing. *Journal of Distance Education, 22*(2), 15–42.

Moore, M. (1989). Three types of interaction. *The American Journal of Distance Education, 3*(2), 1–6.

Ornelles, C. (2007). Providing classroom-based intervention to at-risk students to support their academic engagement and interactions with peers. *Preventing School Failure, 51*(4), 3–12.

Pamuk, S. (2012). The need for pedagogical change in online adult learning: A distance education case in a traditional university. *University Of Gaziantep Journal of Social Sciences, 11*(2), 389–405.

Paul, J., & Cochran, J. (2013). Key interactions for online programs between faculty, students, technologies, and educational institutions: A holistic framework. *Quarterly Review of Distance Education, 14*(1), 49–62.

Pecka, S. L., Kotcherlakota, S., & Berger, A. M. (2014). Community of inquiry model: Advancing distance learning in nurse anaesthesia education. *AANA Journal, 82*(3), 212–18

Perry, B. (2006). Using photographic images as an interactive online teaching strategy. *The Internet and Higher Education, 9*(3), 229–40.

Perry, B., Dalton, J., & Edwards, M. (2009). Photographic images as an interactive online teaching technology: Creating online communities. *International Journal of Teaching and Learning in Higher Education, 20*(2), 106–15.

Perry, B., & Edwards, M. (2005). Exemplary online educators: Creating a community of inquiry. *Turkish Online Journal of Distance Education, 6*(2), 46–54.

———. (2010). Interactive teaching technologies that facilitate the development of online learning communities in nursing and health studies. *Teacher Education Quarterly, Special Online Edition,* 147–72.

———. (2012). Creating an "invitational classroom" in the online educational milieu. *American Journal of Health Sciences, 3*(1), 7–16.

Perry, B., Janzen, K., & Edwards, M. (2012). Creating invitational online learning environments using learning interventions founded in the arts. *Opening Learning Horizons.* http://elearningpapers.eu/en/elearning_papers

Phelan, L. (2012). Interrogating students' perceptions of their online learning experiences with Brookfield's critical incident questionnaire. *Distance Education, 33*(1), 31–44.

Plante, K., & Asselin, M. E. (2014). Best practices for creating social presence and caring behaviours online. *Nursing Education Perspectives, 35*(4), 219–23.

Ronaldson, S. (2004). Untangling critical thinking in educational cyberspace [Unpublished doctoral dissertation]. University of British Columbia, Vancouver, BC, Canada.

Rourke, G., Garrison, D., Anderson, T., & Archer, W. (2000). Critical inquiry in a text-based environment: Computer conferencing in higher education. *The Internet and Higher Education, 2*(2–3), 87–105.

Savery, J., & Duffy, T. (1996). Problem-based learning: An instructional method and its constructivist framework. In B. Wilson (ed.), *Constructivist learning environments: Case studies in instructional design* (pp. 135–48). Englewood Cliffs, NJ: Educational Technology.

Shea, P. (2006). In online environments. *Journal of Asynchronous Learning Network, 10*(1). Retrieved from http://www.sloan-c.org/publications/jaln/v10n1/v10n1_4shea.asp

Skiba, D.J. (2006). Collaborative tools for the net generation. *Nursing Education Perspectives, 27*(3), 162–63.

Sun, Y. H. S. (2011). Online language teaching: The pedagogical challenges. *Knowledge Management and E-Learning: An International Journal, 3*, 428–47. Retrieved from http://www.kmel-journal.org/ojs/index.php/online-publication/index

Turketo, K., & Smith, J. (2014). Promoting achievement for Indigenous students in art education: A New Zealand perspective. *Canadian Review of Art Education: Research and Issues, 41*(1), 8–31.

Vygotsky, L. S. (1978). *Mind in society.* Cambridge, MA: Harvard University Press.

Wang, C., & Burris, M. (1997). Photovoice: Concept, methodology, and use for participatory needs assessment. *Health Education Behaviour, 24*, 369–87.

Wegerif, R. (2006). Dialogic education: What is it and why do we need it? *Education Review, 19*(2), 58–66.

Yasnitsky, A. (2011). Vygotsky circle as a personal network of scholars: Restoring connections between people and ideas. *Integrative Psychological and Behavioural Science, 45*(4), 422–57.

Yuan, J. J., & Kim, C. C. (2014). Guidelines for facilitating the development of learning communities in online courses. *Journal of Computer Assisted Learning, 30*(3), 220–32.

Ziegler, M. F., Paulus, T., & Woodside, M. (2014). Understanding informal group learning in online communities through discourse analysis. *Adult Education Quarterly, 64*(1), 60–78.

Concluding Thoughts

▶ *George Veletsianos*

Technological advances are rapid. The period between 2010 and 2016 has seen an increasing incidence of emerging practices promising to have a significant impact on education. The narrative surrounding these emerging technologies and practices has frequently focused on disruption and transformation. While past waves of educational technology innovations were also promising, their impact has often been disappointing. Yet today's digital learning environments look much different than the digital learning environments of five years ago, which, in turn, looked much different than the digital learning environments that preceded them.

The ways in which we practice and think about digital education are also changing. The field itself is in an emerging state, being shaped by cultural, social, political, and economic forces that are interacting with the technologies and practices of our time. It is significant in this context, however, to recognize that neither our technologies nor our practices are created in a vacuum. When technology is created, it is built with the developers' worldviews, values, beliefs, and assumptions embedded within it. For example, social networking sites structure relationships in specific ways (e.g., followers, friends) and perceive privacy in different ways. This is true for technologies repurposed for educational means (e.g., Twitter, YouTube, Ning, Elgg, Facebook, Flickr) as well as for technologies created specifically for educational purposes. Educational technologies espouse certain beliefs about the educational process and their default settings and suggestions may shape how they are used.

In this book, authors examined emerging technologies and practices in digital learning contexts, drawing attention to how the field is changing and may be changing in the future. Whether the result of technological advancements, changing mindsets, or cultural, social, political, and economic forces, educators, researchers, and practitioners are collectively refining digital learning. While the impact of emerging technologies and practices is neither as overwhelmingly positive as optimists expect, nor as poor as critics suggest, the ways that digital education is organized, enacted, and designed is undergoing significant change, in the same way that educational institutions have changed over time within the cultures that house them.

Two issues need to be highlighted to bring closure to this volume.

First, the field will benefit from longitudinal, interpretive, multidisciplinary, and mixed methods research to gain an in-depth understanding of digital learning. A number of emerging approaches influence the design, delivery, and assessment of digital learning. Important areas of inquiry and research include gaining a greater understanding of:

The symbiotic and reinforcing relationship between emerging technologies and emerging practices;

The changing role and nature of education and institutions of higher learning;

The state of learning in networked and non-institutional settings;

The ways that learning and teaching are enacted within emerging organizational models (e.g., learning in large online courses or in self-organizing groups via social media);

The changing roles of instructors.

To gain a greater understanding of these issues the field needs to explore emerging research methodologies to understand learning in context. As research into digital learning becomes more and more interdisciplinary, we need to foster and encourage more conversations among learning scientists, educational technology developers, learning designers, data scientists, content experts, and methodologists.

Second, researchers need to examine the purposes of digital learning and the roles of the various actors involved in its prominence. A similar exploration has occurred in the context of schooling, where a number of theorists have examined the purposes that schooling serves. On the one end of the spectrum, *functional* theorists have argued that schooling serves noble intellectual, political, economic, and social purposes. From a functional perspective, schooling assists in the development of children's intellectual capacity, cognitive ability, citizenry participation skills, labour skills, and social responsibility. Even though the purposes of schooling appear noble from a functional outlook, these estimations are overly optimistic. In response to this optimism and assumed moral capacity of schooling, *critical* theorists have noted that our society is imperfect. For example, societies appear to be beleaguered by corruption and inequality across race, gender, and class lines. From this perspective, schools preserve and extend the status quo and do little to change current social statuses. Thus, a critical approach to schooling aims to change schools and create more equitable organizations. In the context of digital learning, emerging approaches and emerging technologies are often viewed from a functional and instrumental perspective. A critical perspective on digital learning is desperately needed, and I hope that future scholarship will engage with this perspective, not simply to criticize online learning for being unlike face-to-face learning, but to drastically improve the design and functions of education overall. Scholarship should evoke change, and academics, particularly academics in schools of education, should strive to improve our societies in meaningful ways. By applying research to practice, we can make strides towards creating equitable, effective, and supportive online learning environments.

Contributors

Terry Anderson is professor emeritus and researcher in the Technology-Enhanced Knowledge Research Centre at Athabasca University. His research interests focus on interaction and social media in educational contexts. He is the editor of *The Theory and Practice of Online Learning*, 2nd ed., winner of the 2009 Charles E. Wedemeyer Award.

R. S. Baker is associate professor in the Teaching, Learning, and Leadership division at the University of Pennsylvania. He was the founding president of the International Educational Data Mining Society and is the associate editor of the *Journal of Educational Data Mining*. His research is at the intersection of educational data mining and human-computer interaction. He develops and uses methods for mining the data that comes out of the interactions between students and educational software in order to better understand how students respond to educational software and how these responses influence their learning.

Angela D. Benson is an associate professor of instructional technology at The University of Alabama, where she conducts research on various aspects of distance and online learning. Dr. Benson is the co-editor of *International Perspectives of Distance Education in Higher Education* (2012), *Cases on Educational Technology Planning, Design and Implementation: A Project Management Perspective* (2013) and *Research on Course Management Systems in Higher Education* (2014). Her professional experience includes thirteen years as a systems engineer in the telecommunications industry. She holds undergraduate degrees in math and industrial engineering, master's degrees in operations research and human resource development, and a doctorate in instructional technology.

Amy Collier is the associate provost for digital learning at Middlebury College. She provides strategic vision and leadership to Middlebury as a leading innovator in creating and sustaining a global learning community through the effective use of digital pedagogies and technologies. She also conducts research to inform digital learning practices, focusing on how critical and narrative methodologies play a role in a deeper understanding of learners' experiences. She blogs at http://redpincushion.me.

Alec Couros is a professor of educational technology and media and the coordinator of Information and Communications Technology at the Faculty of Education, University of Regina. Couros is a scholar and advocate of openness in distributed learning environments. He has given hundreds of workshops and presentations, nationally and internationally, on topics such as openness in education, social/networked learning, instructional design, digital citizenship, and critical media literacy. His graduate and undergraduate courses help current and future educators understand how to use and take advantage of the educational potential offered by the tools of connectivity.

Michael Dowdy has worked in corporate learning and development in financial services, healthcare, and manufacturing for the past eleven years. His primary interests are in informal learning in the workplace and online communities of practice. He earned a Master of Science degree from the University of Memphis in instructional Design and technology (IDT) and is currently working towards a doctoral degree in the same field.

Margaret Edwards RN, PhD is dean and professor in the Centre for Nursing and Health Studies, Faculty of Health Disciplines, Athabasca University. Margaret and Beth Perry have worked as a team on research related to online teaching strategies since 2005.

B. J. Eib is manager of teaching and learning support in the Centre for Teaching and Educational Technologies at Royal Roads University. She has a strong background in instructional design and professional development with an emphasis on effective use of educational technologies. B.J. began her career as an elementary school teacher and has worked with educators at Indiana University and University of Calgary.

Cassidy Hall is the interim director of the Doceo Center for Innovation and Learning at the University of Idaho where she is also a clinical assistant professor of learning technologies in the College of Education's Curriculum and Instruction Department. Prior to her work at UI, she dedicated fifteen years to working in public education in Pennsylvania. Cassidy earned a M.Ed. in School Library and Information Technologies from Mansfield University.

Katia Hildebrandt is a PhD candidate, research assistant, and sessional instructor in the Faculty of Education at the University of Regina. Her dissertation work explores the intersection of digital identity and anti-oppressive education. Katia has previous teaching experience in middle and high schools in Baltimore, Maryland.

P. S. Inventado earned his Bachelor degree in computer science in 2005 and his Masters in 2007 from De La Salle University, Philippines. He taught for five years at the College of Computer Studies at the same university. He completed his doctoral studies in 2014 at Osaka University, Japan under Masayuki Numao through the Monbukagakusho scholarship. He is currently working with Peter Scupelli as a post-doctoral researcher at the School of Design at Carnegie Mellon University. Their research involves analyzing learning data to create design patterns to improve an existing math tutoring system.

Royce Kimmons is an assistant professor of instructional psychology and technology at Brigham Young University. His research interests include technology integration in K–12 and higher education, emergent technologies, open education, and social networks. More information about his work may be found at http://roycekimmons.com.

Trey Martindale works with talented graduate students as associate professor of instructional design and technology at the University of Memphis. He is a researcher with the Institute for Intelligent Systems, where he creates tutoring and instructional systems of the future. Dr. Martindale's expertise is in the design of online learning environments. His research efforts have been funded by the U.S. Department of Education, the Institute of Education Sciences, the U.S. Department of Defense, IBM, the Tennessee Department of Health, and Microsoft. He has published thirty-five scholarly papers and given many national and invited presentations on online learning and learning in the workplace. Dr. Martindale frequently serves as a consultant for companies and organizations, helping them improve workplace learning and performance. Recent clients include the University of Mississippi, FedEx, Cummins Engine, the University of Memphis, and the Wolf River Conservancy. For more information please visit: http://treymartindale.com.

Rolin Moe is an assistant professor and the director of Educational Technology and Media at Seattle Pacific University. Rolin received his EdD in learning technologies from Pepperdine University, where his study focused on assembling interactive learning spaces that combined tactile and digital experience. Dr. Moe's research utilizes a sociocultural lens on educational technology and media, exploring how popular and media discourses shape our expectations, practices and policies about education. His practical work outside of formal education celebrates the "gap" between artifact design and learning assessment, at organizations such as the Museum of Modern Art, Thesys International, and the nonpartisan Annenberg Learning Center at the Ronald Reagan Presidential Library and Museum. He is an award-winning EdTech blogger and correspondent for several EdTech periodicals including KQED's *MindShift*.

Beth Perry RN, PhD is a professor in the Centre for Nursing and Health Studies, Faculty of Health Disciplines, Athabasca University. Beth's areas of research include innovative online teaching strategies and exemplary online teaching practices.

Jen Ross is co-director of the Centre for Research in Digital Education at the University of Edinburgh (http://www.de.ed.ac.uk), and deputy director of Research and Knowledge Exchange in the School of Education. She teaches, supervises, and researches in the field of online education, with particular interests in digital cultural heritage, online distance teaching and learning, Massive Open Online Courses (MOOCS), digital futures, identity and audience online, assessment, and openness (http://jenrossity.net).

George Veletsianos is a Canada Research Chair in Innovative Learning and Technology and an associate professor at Royal Roads University. His research aims to understand the practices and experiences of learners, educators, and scholars in emerging online settings such as online social networks and digital environments. Individually and collaboratively, he has published more than fifty peer-reviewed manuscripts and book chapters and given more than a hundred talks at conferences and events worldwide. His research has been funded by the Canada Research Chairs Program, the U.S. National Science Foundation, the European Union, National Geographic, and the Swedish Knowledge

Foundation. He shares his research at http://www.veletsianos.com and can be contacted by email at veletsianos@gmail.com.

Elizabeth Wellburn enjoyed a thirty-year career in education technology in both the government and the academic environment. Elizabeth is now semi-retired, working on educational consulting projects and exploring a new life as a glass artist. Connecting ideas is important to her and she believes that information literacy and critical thinking should be the main goals of education in this information–rich era, along with things like the arts—which make us human.

Andrew Whitworth is senior lecturer at the Manchester Institute of Education, University of Manchester, UK and programme director of the MA in Digital Technologies, Communication and Education, which in 2012 was awarded a Blackboard Catalyst award for its innovative communications strategies. He is the author of two books that apply critical theory to studies of digital and *information literacy, Information Obesity* (2009) and *Radical Information Literacy* (2014).

Index